Applying Theory
to Educational Research

Applying Theory to Educational Research

*An Introductory Approach
with Case Studies*

Edited by

Jeff Adams, Matt Cochrane
and Linda Dunne

A John Wiley & Sons, Ltd., Publication

This edition first published 2012
© 2012 John Wiley & Sons Ltd.

Wiley-Blackwell is an imprint of John Wiley & Sons, formed by the merger of Wiley's global
Scientific, Technical and Medical business with Blackwell Publishing.

Registered Office
John Wiley & Sons Ltd, The Atrium, Southern Gate, Chichester, West Sussex, PO19 8SQ, UK

Editorial Offices
The Atrium, Southern Gate, Chichester, West Sussex, PO19 8SQ, UK
350 Main Street, Malden, MA 02148-5020, USA
9600 Garsington Road, Oxford, OX4 2DQ, UK

For details of our global editorial offices, for customer services, and for information about how
to apply for permission to reuse the copyright material in this book please see our website at
www.wiley.com/wiley-blackwell.

The right of Jeff Adams, Matt Cochrane and Linda Dunne to be identified as the authors of the
editorial material in this work has been asserted in accordance with the UK Copyright, Designs
and Patents Act 1988.

Wiley also publishes its books in a variety of electronic formats. Some content that appears
in print may not be available in electronic books.

Designations used by companies to distinguish their products are often claimed as trademarks.
All brand names and product names used in this book are trade names, service marks, trademarks
or registered trademarks of their respective owners. The publisher is not associated with any product
or vendor mentioned in this book. This publication is designed to provide accurate and authoritative
information in regard to the subject matter covered. It is sold on the understanding that the
publisher is not engaged in rendering professional services. If professional advice or other expert
assistance is required, the services of a competent professional should be sought.

Library of Congress Cataloging-in-Publication Data

Applying theory to educational research : an introductory approach with case studies / edited by
Jeff Adams, Matt Cochrane and Linda Dunne.
  p. cm.
  Includes index.
  ISBN 978-0-470-97236-6 (cloth) – ISBN 978-0-470-97235-9 (pbk.)
1. Education–Research–Methodology–Case studies. I. Adams, Jeff. II. Cochrane, Matt.
III. Dunne, Linda.
  LB1028.A56 2012
  370.72–dc22

                                    2011015211

A catalogue record for this book is available from the British Library.

This book is published in the following electronic formats: ePDFs 9781119950851;
Wiley Online Library 9781119950844; ePub 9781119979999; eMobi 9781119999034

Set in 10.5/13pt Minion by SPi Publisher Services, Pondicherry, India
Printed in Malaysia by Ho Printing (M) Sdn Bhd

1 2012

Contents

Contributors

Jeff Adams is Professor of Education at the University of Chester, where he is leader of the Professional Doctorate in Education programme. He was formerly leader of the Artist-Teacher MA programme at Goldsmiths College. He has taught art, education and art history at Edge Hill University, Liverpool John Moores University and the Open University, as well as in comprehensive schools. Jeff is currently part of a funded inter-university project researching creativity in teacher education; his other research interests include the professional development of teachers, contemporary art education, and documentary graphic novels. His books include *Documentary Graphic Novels and Social Realism* (Peter Lang, 2008) and *Teaching Through Contemporary Art* (with Worwood, Atkinson, Dash, Herne and Page; Tate, 2008). He is Principal Editor of the *International Journal of Art and Design Education*.

Martin Ashley is Professor in Education and Head of Research in the Faculty of Education at Edge Hill University, near Liverpool, UK. His primary methodological expertise is in ethnography, grounded theory, phenomenology and naturalistic enquiry as a means of understanding the impact on individual lives of social context. His substantive expertise is in the study of boyhood with a particular focus on the participation of boys in singing. *How High Should Boys Sing? Gender, Authenticity and Credibility in the Young Male Voice* was published by Ashgate in 2009.

Paul Bartle currently works as a programme leader in Professional Development in the Faculty of Education at Edge Hill University. He spent a number of years teaching modern languages in secondary schools before moving to initial teacher training as a Post Graduate Certificate of Education

(PGCE) course leader. Paul has also tutored members of the children's workforce undertaking first degrees. Paul's research interests include education policy and practice, and language and discourse. He is a part-time doctoral student.

Paula Beer is a Lecturer in Information Communication Technology (ICT) Education at Edge Hill University. She has previously worked as an Information Technology (IT) project manager, taught secondary ICT and Adult Mathematics. Her research interests lie mainly with the use of play in education and she specializes in the work of the American psychologist and educational philosopher Jerome Bruner. She is currently undertaking a PhD concerning the use of play, discovery learning and collaboration in ICT education and strives to bring this ethos to her own lecturing of teacher trainees.

Karen Castle is Principal Lecturer in the Faculty of Education at Manchester Metropolitan University. She has previously worked as lead tutor for postgraduate studies in education as well as University outreach centre manager. Prior to working in higher education, she worked as a curriculum manager in further education settings. Her research interests lie mainly in professional development and work-based learning and development. She is currently undertaking an EdDoc at Keele University. Her thesis is an ethnographic study investigating teachers' approach to Continuing Professional Development(CPD). Her publications include: Retention and achievement: making a difference for NVQs, *The Research and Development Bulletin*, 2004, 2 (3), 17– 22; Managing change, in *Supporting Every Child* (eds G. Goddard and A. Walton) (Learning Matters, 2009) and *Study Skills for Your MTL* (Learning Matters, 2010).

Jill Cochrane has spent much of her career as a nurse in the specialism of paediatric intensive care, and has taken an active interest in the (often unac-knowledged) learning and teaching that takes place in clinical practice. Having gained an MA in Clinical Education, in 2008 she made the move from the NHS to higher education, and now lectures on this subject. Her doctorate focuses on informal inter-professional learning in the clinical setting.

Her first foray into publication was a case study, written while a nursing student in 1978. Her recent publications include: (with Heron and Lawler) Reflections on student nurse placements in the PICU, *Paediatric Nursing*,

2008, 20 (1), 26–28 and (with Crawford, Dixon and Murphy) Caring for a highly dependent child with fluid, electrolyte and nutritional requirements, in *Nursing the Highly Dependent Child or Infant*, (eds M. Dixon, D. Crawford, D. Teasdale and J. Murphy) (Wiley-Blackwell, 2009).

Matt Cochrane followed nearly 30 years as a Science and ICT teacher, by joining Edge Hill University as a Head of Department in the Faculty of Education in 2004. He teaches mainly on Postgraduate Initial Teacher Training programmes, but has also contributed to Postgraduate Professional Development. His current research is investigating the persistent inequities in the education system that led to an imbalance in the number of people from socially disadvantaged backgrounds attending university. He has co-written a textbook for trainee teachers of science, his contributions focusing on the planning and evaluation of lessons. Other research interests include impact studies on the effectiveness of courses that aim to improve the subject knowledge of both experienced teachers and trainee teachers.

Linda Dunne qualified as an English teacher in 1982. She has worked as a Lecturer at Edge Hill University since 2001, teaching on undergraduate and postgraduate professional development programmes in the areas of inclusive education, lifelong learning and research methods. Linda is interested in Foucauldian theory and poststructuralist ideas concerning subjectivity and the discursive formation of learner identities. Her concern is with applying theories empirically to critique the ways that children are represented in schools. She has published book chapters and journal articles and has presented at national and international conferences. Recent co-authored publications include 'From Boy to Man: a story of ADHD' in *Emotional and Behaviour Difficulties* and 'Does the camera ever lie? Interpretations of visual representations of disability' in *Studies in Higher Education*.

Rob Foster Prior to his retirement in 2010, Rob Foster was Head of Professional Development in the Faculty of Education at Edge Hill University. His responsibilities included the formulation and management of school-based models of teachers' professional development. He is currently an associate tutor and consultant on the new school-based Masters in Teaching and Learning (MTL). Rob was a secondary school teacher and manager for 25 years before moving into initial and continuing teacher training with Edge Hill. His principal research interests are employment-based professional learning, the impact of professional development in schools and Citizenship Education and Identity. He was until recently UK National Coordinator for the Children's Identity and Citizenship in Europe (CiCE) network. His publications include journal articles on innovative work-based approaches to training for Every Child Matters (ECM) and several CiCE international guideline booklets on professional development for Citizenship Education.

Mary McAteer qualified as a teacher in 1979, and has worked since then in a wide range of roles including secondary maths and physics teacher, primary maths, science and technology consultant, Lecturer in Educational Leadership, and leader of an MA in Education. Her current role is Director for a Primary Mathematics Specialist Teacher (MaST) programme. She has a particular interest in practitioner research methodologies, and has carried out and supervised research in a range of practice contexts using both quantitative and qualitative approaches, but with a particular emphasis on action research, narrative and (auto) biographical approaches. The focus of her teaching is research methodology, which she teaches to both MA and PhD students. She is currently writing a book on action research in education for the BERA/Sage Research in Education series. Her publications include: (with Wilkinson) Evaluating the efficacy of training staff in adult child interaction in a school for children with ASD, *Journal of Good Autism Practice*, 2009, 10 (2), 57–63; (with Dewhurst) 'Just thinking about stuff'. Reflective learning: Jane's story. *Journal of Reflective Practice*, 2010, 11 (1), 31–41 and (with Hallett, Murtagh and Turnbull) *Achieving your Masters in Teaching and Learning* (Learning Matters, 2010).

Graham Rogers Formerly Reader in Educational Development and Principal Lecturer in History at Edge Hill University, Graham Rogers has had a long career in teacher education. He has combined post-doctoral research in English agrarian history with a research interest in the teaching of the discipline and specifically in the context of the development of student teachers' critical thinking and their values in learning and teaching. From a pedagogic perspective he also has a keen, personal interest in the application of learning technologies.

Madeleine Sclater is currently a Senior Lecturer in Learning Innovation within the School of Textiles and Design at Heriot-Watt University. Madeleine holds an interdisciplinary PhD from Glasgow School of Art and University of Glasgow in the fields of Education, Art and Design and

Technology. She has over 12 years experience of researching and publishing at international level within the field of Technology Enhanced Learning (TEL). She was one of the first early adopters of TEL within the UK Art and Design Higher Education community. Madeleine is consultant to a successful new ESRC/EPSRC funded project called Interlife: Interoperability and transition (2009–2011). Her current research is focused on developing and fostering creativity and design thinking within virtual worlds. Madeleine is one of the co-editors of *IJADE* (*International Journal of Art and Design Education*). Her publications include: (with Lally) Inter-Life: Community, Identity and Transition through Creative Engagement. European Conference on Educational Research, Network 16: ICT in Education and Training, Session 16 SES 03 B, ICT in Adult Education (Paper) [25 08 2010], (with Lally) Bringing theory to life: towards three-dimensional learning communities with Inter-Life, in *Fostering Communities of Learners: 13th Biennial Conference for Research on Learning and Instruction (EARLI)* (ed. G. Rijlaarsdam) (University of Amsterdam, 2009) and (with Bolander) Factors influencing students' orientation to collaboration in networked learning, in *Advances in Research on Networked Learning, vol. 4* (eds P. Goodyear, S. Banks, V. Hodgson and D. McConnell) (Kluwer, 2004).

Clare Woolhouse worked in two secondary schools and a Post-Compulsory Education and Training (PCET) college before moving to Lancaster University where she taught at undergraduate level for five years. Her interests are on the intersecting of gender, equity, self-identity and professional development. She is currently working in the Faculty of Education at Edge Hill University and has responsibility for the evaluation and research elements of two Training and Development Agency for schools (TDA) funded projects relating to specialist dyslexia training for teachers and training for Special Educational Needs (SEN) co-ordinators. Her role includes all aspects of designing, conducting and disseminating research and she also supports colleagues in developing their research interests. Her most recent articles include: (with Ainslie, Foster, Groves, Grime and Straker) Making children count: an exploration of the implementation of the Every Child Matters agenda, *Education 3–13*, 2010, 38 (1), 23–38; (with Cochrane) Now I think of myself as a physics teacher: negotiating professional development and shifts in self-identity, *Reflective Practice*, 2010, 11 (5), 607–618 and (with Dunne and Collinson) Re-visioning disability and dyslexia down the camera lens: alternative interpretations of representations on UK university websites and in a UK government guidance paper, *Studies in Higher Education*, 2011, 37 (8), 42–52.

Preface

This is a book about social theory and its application to research in the field of education. Many books on theory are written by academics who are familiar with their selected theories from the outset, and confident in their application, a confidence that has been developed through familiarity and practice. This book, on the other hand, offers a picture of experience from another, much more common perspective: that of the researcher new to a theory, and unused to its application. This is the key purpose and rationale of this book: to guide the reader by example and case studies, which are often grounded in the fresh discovery of others' theories. We think that this standpoint is important because it is often at that moment of understanding, the epiphany of realization, that the excitement of academic work is generated. This exhilaration is often what motivates and inspires researchers, keeping them returning to texts and notebooks to discover more. There's nothing quite like the first successful engagement with 'difficult' theory to make one feel scholarly, and to make substantial our tentative thinking.

This book offers an in-depth analysis of the processes and procedures of assimilating and applying theories to educational research design, methods and data using actual case studies as examples, written by the authors of those studies. The book does not attempt to provide biographies of important theoreticians, nor replicate a canon of significant theories, nor does it offer a comprehensive summary of contemporary theories relevant to education. On the contrary, it captures the voices of researchers from the field and their experiences of applying theory, sometimes in an ad hoc or tentative manner. These accounts are more akin, we believe, to the reality in education research for the beginner or novice researcher who is attempting to navigate the vast and complex field of social theory application.

Many frequently used theorists can be found in these pages. For example: Bourdieu, Butler, Foucault and Stenhouse appear, as do many others, and aspects of their work are discussed in some detail as they arise in the design of the contributors' research, or as they encounter them. This method of witnessing 'theory in action' does, we believe, offer an insight that is relevant to those new to research or coming across these theories for the first time.

Acknowledgements

Our grateful thanks and appreciation go to: The Edge Hill University Doctoral Society, whose members supported and encouraged this book from its inception, and many of whom are contributors to these pages; our colleagues from Edge Hill University and the University of Chester for their advice and assistance; Hazel Lopatkin, for permission to discuss her work and reproduce stills from her film 'Kalinka' in Chapter 13; all those who have read, checked and commented on our text, especially Dr Wendy Hyde, and finally thanks to Karen Shield at Wiley-Blackwell for her advice and patience.

Introduction

Jeff Adams, Matt Cochrane and Linda Dunne

Theory has a multitude of meanings, not all of which can be easily reconciled, making it a concept open to wide appropriation. For example, theory can simply mean an idea about a social configuration, or it can mean an intellectual formula that enables one to structure experience (or data, in terms of research); sometimes it is used broadly and is synonymous with philosophy, or it is used specifically as an interpretative description of experience. Theorizing can be an expansive business, in that it can be thought of as an act that generates new ways of thinking about the way the world is configured, and may be generalized and transferred to a multitude of new concepts in the expectation that it will throw new light on them (Dressman, 2008). Context is arguably another determining characteristic of the application of theory, in that the test of its effectiveness is the production of a robust and replicable explanation of experience or social phenomena.

Alternatively, theory may be thought of negatively, as reductive and limiting, imposing representations and proscriptions upon our knowledge that lead us away from new ways of thinking (Thomas, 2007). Theory in education is haunted by a suspicion of it being a covert signifier, a Trojan horse drafted in from other disciplines with the fervour of late twentieth-century postmodernism, speciously designating intellectual credibility by means of obfuscation. Pring (2005, p. 4) comments on the latter, arguing that theory need not necessitate arcane language, and that: 'it is partly the failure to recognize this that has given theoretical studies in education a bad name'. Consequently many education researchers are understandably wary

Applying Theory to Educational Research: An Introductory Approach with Case Studies, First Edition. Edited by J. Adams, M. Cochrane and L. Dunne.
© 2012 John Wiley & Sons, Ltd. Published 2012 by John Wiley & Sons, Ltd.

of theory, and as a result their work is characterized by scepticism, equivocation or ambiguity.

For these reasons theory is often the most troublesome aspect of academic work, whether it is students struggling to apply others' ideas to their data, or experienced researchers defending their research questions in a funding bid proposal. Often those new to research or academia will shy away from theory on the pretext that it appears too difficult, obscure, or simply too much trouble. Yet such avoidance can lead to theory creeping in the back door in the form of dogma or prejudice, and as a consequence may diminish the integrity of the research. The value of the work is governed by the quality of the thinking that underpins it, and this can be (and often is) measured by how well it extends or fits with its theoretical frameworks.

Applying theory to research is an important process; it is the means by which an approach to educational research can be argued and developed. Ball (1995), for instance, believes that theory is a vehicle for 'thinking otherwise', and that it allows us to open up spaces for the invention of new experiences. Moore (2004) also stresses the importance of developing a theoretical rationale, since it can facilitate the political goals of the research, such as equality and social justice. In this respect, applying theory to our work becomes an ethical issue: theory, especially in these critical forms, urges us to think more carefully about our taken-for-granted values, our motivation and our place in the research process.

Theory in Education Research

There is no aspect of education that has not been theorized, although in practice it doesn't always appear to be that way. An emphasis on method can sometimes mask a reductive or negative theorizing. For instance, those familiar with gender and sexuality theorists like de Beauvoir (e.g., de Beauvoir, 1989) and Butler (e.g., Butler, 1993) will recognize the shortcomings of a research project that attempts to ask questions about, say, boys' or girls' education, but fails to take into account the social performance of gender, the extended range of sexuality and the inadequacies of a rigid binary taxonomy of sexuality. Similarly, the work of Bourdieu (e.g., Bourdieu and Passeron, 2003) on cultural and social capital and their replication in educational systems has had enormous influence right across the social sciences, and has made its mark on the theoretical design of numerous research projects in education, such that its absence might well be conspicuous if the researcher avoided it in enquiries into social class, for instance, no matter how assiduous their methods.

Perhaps because of the fraught reputation of the application of theory, education research is characterized by an extremely well-developed focus on research methods, evidenced by the large and growing number of texts upon the subject (e.g., Cohen, Manion and Morrison, 2011; Punch, 2009; Bridges and Smith, 2007), and the seemingly obligatory detailed methodological explication, ubiquitous in education academic journals. For education research, methodology has come to signify a rigour, bordering on obsession, for endeavour in research: the meticulous attention to care in data handling practice, and giving credence to the idea of educational research being a technical rather than an intellectual practice (Ball, 1995). The relationship between theory and methodology is often in a state of dynamic tension, and is has a complexity that is illustrated by the theorizing of methodology itself (cf. Sparkes, 1992; Clough and Nutbrown, 2009; Hammersley, 2007).

Much educational research is characterized by a particular kind of instrumentalism that, for instance, accentuates school improvement agendas and pupil attainment, with an emphasis on measurable outcomes. Pring (2005) provides a philosophical perspective on educational theory and practice, as a challenge to more instrumentalist or overtly method-driven research that can impoverish educational practice. Such theory-barren research may be quite detrimental, despite its benign façade, if it perpetuates existing conditions or unquestioningly reiterates and reinforces dominant ideologies. Applying theory to educational research can provide a welcome antidote to seemingly 'risk-averse' policy climates (Maclure, 2006, p. 223), where many underlying values are taken as given, reduced to a competency or standard, and driven by assumed certainties (Allan, 2004). Theory can enable a critique and deep questioning of ontology, of our social being, and open up ways of thinking that do not necessitate compartmentalization or essentialize. In its critical mode theory can initiate the creation of other possibilities and new understandings in the pursuit of more socially just practices.

Theorizing in Practice

The question that remains for many researchers is how to take theoretical ideas, concepts and frameworks, and apply them to their individual pieces of research about practice. In these pages many encounters with theory are played out, enabling us to realize something of the 'real' of the encounter. Our contributors are at times empowered by their use of theory, and they are able to prise open issues that had hitherto been thought closed to them. Discovering and applying theory is not something that is easily left behind with the close of the working day, however. We often ruminate in our leisure or family hours, contemplating those knotty intellectual problems that have been triggered by our reading:

> When I was a new researcher I well remember the feeling of excitement and trepidation when I first felt that I understood, and could possibly apply, some philosophical theory to my work. Then I was fortunate to have an office adjoining a colleague who was a prolific writer, with dozens of academic articles and books to his name, mostly on the politics and policies of school organization, and more recently on theories of intelligence. He told me he liked to theorize and simultaneously compose text for his writing while walking his dogs. He conjured lines in his head to the rhythm of his walking, like a latter-day Wordsworth, editing and then memorizing the words and phrases, and once home, he'd quickly write it all down. He said he wrote longhand, and claimed that his words needed no further editing – once committed to the page that was it. He reminded me of the novelist Laurie Lee, who liked to write with a 2B pencil to avoid the disturbance of a scratching pen or a typewriter. My former neighbour had perfected his own technique, his way of theorizing, over many years, and it had become his art. Occasionally, when I come across his papers or the editorials in his journals, I think of his methods: rehearsing his theories, crafting them into embryonic texts and gradually polishing them into the finished article – all in his head. When I'm out in the early morning with my spaniel, running or walking through the back streets of my town, I catch myself trying to emulate his process, theorizing to the rhythm of my feet, applying a new concept, wrestling with the plausibility of the outcome, rushing home with the idea still bright, noting it down before it dulls. (Jeff Adams)

The process of doing a doctoral research project (and many of our contributors in the opening sections are) is often likened to going on a 'journey'. The research journey metaphor is something of a cliché, however, and implies an existing linear route with a final destination. Engagement with ideas and theories is frequently neither linear nor finite, and the use of theory problematizes this metaphorical representation of research. Applying theory to a research project can have the most profound effects. It can, for example, disrupt a seemingly straightforward project, or create a 'Eureka' moment, that clarifies data and enables seemingly authentic interpretation:

My experience of using theory is that it is liberating and perplexing. Prior to encountering poststructuralist theories, I had a 'position' that locked me into particular understandings of my area of study, which at the time was inclusive education. I regarded inclusive education as a political project based upon rights and entitlement. Over time, and with wider reading, I felt an inexplicable sense of unease, both with this position and with my approach to research.

'Finding' a theory that suited me was like entering a different world. It made me question my existing ways of thinking and practice, and to look beyond what was in front of me. This was discomforting because I thought I had embarked on a research project in a relatively fixed and seemingly 'safe' direction, and finding theory disrupted that trajectory. At times I feared that the new path I was treading was possibly misguided, because I lacked a sufficiently strong philosophical knowledge background to engage with, or write within, a more theoretical frame of reference. As I read more, my fears subsided as I came to accept the limitations of my own understandings. I learned that having a position can be troublesome (Simons and Masschelein, 2006) and I came to embrace uncertainty, self-doubt and fears and, moreover, to see them as an integral part of the research process. (Linda Dunne)

Engagement with theory allows a creative crossing of boundaries between disciplines like education, sociology, philosophy and psychology. As the chapters in this book illustrate, we may draw on one particular theory or several cross-disciplinary theories, depending upon the nature of the study. Theories may contradict or compliment each other, but it is in the process of *engagement* with theory that we come to 'recognize' theories in action and feel confident enough to apply them in a framework for a research project. However, a question that has to be faced is one of transference: how easily do theories transfer from one context to another? A theoretical framework designed for a specific time and cultural context does not always readily transfer to another: Freire's (1970/1993) theories of socially emancipating pedagogic strategies were developed in the particular circumstances of poverty in South America, for instance, and this may have significant implications for its application elsewhere. As some of the chapters in the final section of this book demonstrate, however, contextual impropriety or distortion may be avoided, or at least managed, through the use of multiple theories that provide hybridity and flexibility. Sometimes it is this very unorthodoxy that creates the frisson from which creative imaginings, and hence new understandings, arise.

University education departments, and teacher-educators in particular, often find developing and sustaining research activity problematic. Education tutors in the UK march to the beat of two drums: research activity requirements on the one hand, and professional training on the other (Adams and Shortt, in preparation). Partly as a result of this pressure, schools or faculties of education, rather like schools of law, business or medicine, tend to conduct research that is rooted in practice; the application of research to practice is a dominant feature of this field (i.e. action research). This focus helps to unite the diverse disciplines in education, and helps cope with the ever-growing complexity of education in relation to the public and to the state (Goldring and Schuermann, 2009). We have, in these education research practices, what Schulman *et al.* (2006) would refer to as 'signature pedagogies': the means by which we inquire and learn about our field is specifically associated with our profession as educators, and we are recognizable because of this way of going about research.

As a consequence of this identification with practice and the strong tradition of methodological assiduousness, education researchers sometimes feel alienated or bewildered by theory, and the process of familiarization can be tortuous, albeit eventually rewarding:

> The first problem in applying theory to educational research is trying to make sense of a seemingly infinite supply of theories and theorists. The first people I encountered on my doctorate appeared to have a breath-taking depth of knowledge about the subject. We 'newbies' watched in awe as the experienced 'older' students presented their thesis proposals, effortlessly answering questions about their chosen topic. Put in the hot seat myself a year later, and faced with the task of justifying my choice of topic and methodology, I found that I had discovered that the fund of theories and theorists was actually finite – the same writers will crop up repeatedly – both because they have written more about the topic, and also because they have been cited more often than most. Coming to the data analysis after this long process, I found that, through the application of theory, I was able to discover things about the data that I did not expect – the story began to write itself. It is as if the theory chooses the researcher, and not the other way round. (Matt Cochrane)

Many of the applied theories that characterize qualitative educational research are, as this book attempts to demonstrate, useful and can enrich research and its meaning. However, we might consider the idea that theory and theorizing, in the sense of the development of the philosophical or critical idea (and in the context of its application in the cases in this book), might become less significant or even obsolete, perhaps due to the dominance of quantitative and 'evidence-based' governmental or funding body research imperatives. Giroux (2001, p. 3) describes how the whole rationale for education shifted during the twentieth century away from the classical Greek ideal of education for citizenship, towards one of social control, and 'attempts to construct a theoretical foundation to extend the notion of critique into relations and dimensions of schooling and school activity [are] often ignored by both traditional and radical educators'. Through this book we hope to resist this possibility, and encourage courageous 'experiment' in critical qualitative research, drawing on theoretical ideas from within and beyond the realm of education research.

Many of our contributors engage in critical, experimental forms of qualitative inquiry in the interests of social justice, deploying, through their theoretical thinking, radical critiques of social settings and institutions. There are formidable schools of thought generated by our contributors' engagement with social theory, which stretches their, and our, imagination.

Organization of the Book

This book is in many ways a celebration of theory. It is intended for those hoping to find a pathway through this seeming intellectual obstacle course; it hopes to provide fresh insights into some well-known theories, and offer ways of overcoming the trepidation of applying apparently difficult ideas to one's own work. The book takes the form of an edited volume of essays, with the chapters written by contributors who have applied theories to educational research. They are often writing from the standpoint of new researchers, and they articulate their experiences of the struggle to understand, assimilate and then utilize theories for the first time, of applying theoretical frameworks to their research projects, and finally sharing the revelations – or the errors – that ensued. The book is written in a case study format, with the authors recounting and narrating their 'lived' experience of theory. In so doing they attempt to make their chosen theories explicable, and account for the relevance of their choices to their work. Selecting and applying theories can be a daunting experience for any researcher, especially those new to the practice, and this procedure is fully discussed in this book. By sharing these moments, and demonstrating the reality of theoretical application, we hope to make many of the commonly used concepts and theories comprehensible.

We have organized our case studies into three Parts, according to the experience of our researchers and the completeness of the projects that they are discussing. In Part I we have case studies by researchers that are relatively new to research, often engaging in the field as part of their Masters or doctoral dissertation. Their experience is frequently one of trepidation as they employ unfamiliar theories, and try to make sense of the application, only too well aware of the pitfalls that can occur at each stage of the process: understanding, defining, justifying and transferring theory to their data, and then analysing the insights that it yields. Occasionally we find them troubled over the obscurity that appears to result.

In Part II we have a group of researchers who are more familiar with both research and the application of theory. Their projects are well established, which provides them with the opportunity to experiment with theory and to reflect on their progress. They share with us their successes, and sometimes the wisdom they derived from making the choices they did – or perhaps of being given a theoretical framework that did not necessarily yield the understandings they hoped for.

Part III comprises cases from experienced researchers who have reached a degree of equilibrium with their research and the application of theory in particular. All of their projects are complete or have considerable longevity, allowing them to reflect in some depth, and to discuss their theoretical applications with the benefit of hindsight. Their experience is nonetheless fresh, and bears the authenticity of practice in the field, although sometimes they too struggle with the perennial and thorny problems of applying theories established elsewhere, and with different imperatives, to the specificity of their own empirical data or set of practices.

Each chapter has a common format to emphasize and clarify the different aspects of the application of theory. Each opens with a *Key Theoretical Approaches* frame, which details the particular theories and theorists that are to be used in the chapter, with a list of key texts. Some of the authors advocate reading primary sources (i.e. the original text) to gain a fuller understanding of particular theories, while others recommend reading supported by secondary sources. Often this is dependent upon the complexity of the ideas presented within a particular theory; some theories are more accessible than others and therefore it makes sense to rely on primary sources. Next there is *Introduction to the Research Project,* which gives a description of the specific context within which theories were applied. This is followed by a section entitled *Theories Explained and their Use Justified in the Context of this Research Project,* which gives the author an opportunity to get to grips with their theories, and in the process provide an amplification and clarification of the key ideas and their relationship to the specificities of their project. This is pursued in the next section *The Application of Theory to the Research,* where the procedure of application, with all its complexity and attendant issues, is explored and discussed. *The Relevance and Effectiveness of Using Theory* section follows, and here the authors reflect on the appropriateness or otherwise of their chosen theoretical frameworks. The final section, entitled *Summary Conclusions and Recommendations,* covers a range of summary items:

- The discovery of the appropriate theories
- The ease or difficulties with understanding the theories
- The difficulties of application to data and texts
- What the application of the theories revealed
- How the absence of these theories might have impaired understanding
- The limitations of the theories
- Reflection and recommendations of the experience
- A small selection of recommended texts for further reading

Each of these topics provides an opportunity for the authors to reflect upon the research process through the lens of theory, and share their discoveries in some detail with the reader. As the chapters show, both new and more experienced researchers find that grappling with theory can be both rewarding and perplexing.

To settle the many dilemmas of using and applying theory is beyond the scope of this book, and it is not our intention; rather, we are concerned with the experience of new researchers encountering and wishing to use theory. It is the moment of application that is our focus, where the user engages with theory in the proximity of their research designs and data, and our contributors air many cases of such engagements.

References

Adams, J. and Shortt, D. (in preparation) Teacher educators and the value of research (submitted for publication).

Allan, J. (2004) Deterritorializations: putting postmodernism to work on teacher education and inclusion. *Educational Philosophy and Theory,* 36 (4), 417–432.

Ball, S. (1995) Intellectuals or technicians? The urgent role of theory in educational studies. *British Journal of Educational Studies,* 43 (3), 255–271.

Bourdieu, P. and Passeron, J.C. (2003) *Reproduction in Education, Society and Culture* (trans. R. Nice), Sage, London. (Originally published 1970.)

Bridges, D. and Smith, R. (eds) (2007) *Philosophy, Methodology and Educational Research*, Blackwell, Oxford.

Butler, J. (1993) *Bodies that Matter: On the Discursive Limits of Sex*, Routledge, London.

Clough, P. and Nutbrown, C. (2009) *A Students' Guide to Methodology: Justifying Enquiry*, Sage, London.

Cohen, L., Manion, L. and Morrison, K. (2011) *Research Methods in Education*, Routledge, London.

de Beauvoir, S. (1989) *The Second Sex* (trans. H. M. Parshley), Vintage Books, New York. (English translation of *Le deuxième sexe*, Gallimard, Paris, 1949.)

Dressman, M. (2008) *Using Social Theory in Educational Research: A Practical Guide*, Routledge, London.

Freire, P. (1970/1993) *Pedagogy of the Oppressed* (trans. M. Bergman Ramos), Penguin, London.

Giroux, H.A. (2001) *Theory and Resistance in Education: Towards a Pedagogy for the Opposition*, Praeger, Westport, CT.

Goldring, E. and Schuermann, P. (2009) The changing context of K-12 education administration: consequences for EdD program design. *Peabody Journal of Education*, 81 (1), 10–43.

Hammersley, M. (ed.) (2007) *Educational Research and Evidence-Based Practice*, Sage, London.

Maclure, M. (2006) 'A demented form of the familiar': Postmodernism and educational research. *Journal of Philosophy of Education*, 40 (2), 224–239.

Moore, R. (2004) *Education and Society: Issues and Explanations in the Sociology of Education*, Polity, Cambridge.

Pring, R. (2005) *Philosophy of Education: Aims, Theory, Common Sense and Research*, Continuum, London.

Punch, K.F. (2009) *Introduction to Research Methods in Education*, Sage, London.

Schulman, L.S., Goldie, C.M., Bueschel, A.C. and Garabedian, K.J. (2006) Reclaiming education's doctorates: a critique and a proposal. *Education Researcher*, 35 (3), 25–32.

Simons, M. and Masschelein, J. (2006) The learning society and governmentality: an introduction, in *The Learning Society from the Perspective of Governmentality* (eds J. Masschelein, M. Simons, U. Brockling and L. Pongratz), Blackwell, Oxford.

Sparkes, A. (1992) The paradigm debate: an extended review and celebration of difference, in *Research in Physical Education and Sport* (ed. A. Sparkes), Falmer, London.

Thomas, G. (2007) *Education and Theory: Strangers in Paradigms*, Open University Press, Maidenhead.

Part I

New Voices
Beginning Researchers Apply Theory

Introduction

The first section introduces researchers who are describing their first major research venture. All are highly experienced, reflexive practitioners in a variety of educational fields, and have a keen intuitive understanding of the issues around either educating the next generation of practitioners, or the continuing development of current practitioners. The management of the latter can be a demanding and difficult role, since often the educator is dealing with people who are experienced professionals themselves, and who consequently have much to say about the relevance and quality of their own experience. It is no coincidence, therefore, that three of these first chapters are concerned with different aspects of professional training and career development. By focusing on the outcomes of their teaching, they are seeking greater insight into, and understanding of, the learning that takes place in the fields from which they have recently emerged.

The authors' accounts of sifting through theories and selecting those most relevant to them show that starting a research project is a process of encounter and discovery, and it is instructive to see such a variety of approaches from such different angles. Each methodology is distinctive to the researcher, and while the fields themselves have similarities, the research projects are very different.

Some of these accounts portray the early stages of that research. Jill Cochrane, in her work on situated learning for health practitioners in Chapter 1, 'Learning and Maintaining Professional Expertise Within a Multi-Professional Critical Care Team', explores a range of theoretical perspectives in an attempt to analyse the often concealed processes that

Applying Theory to Educational Research: An Introductory Approach with Case Studies,
First Edition. Edited by J. Adams, M. Cochrane and L. Dunne.
© 2012 John Wiley & Sons, Ltd. Published 2012 by John Wiley & Sons, Ltd.

led to informal learning in the workplace. Cochrane asks how much of this kind of learning can be acknowledged, and whether it can be quantified. The question of acknowledgement is crucial since, theoretically, progress with informal situated learning may be dependent upon sustained and informed workplace support. The conclusion is that the use of Activity Theory is helpful here.

While Paul Bartle is also concerned with learning through practice in Chapter 2, the contrast in approaches could hardly be greater. In 'The "Q" Standards and Initial Teacher Training: Thoughts on the Discursive Formation of Teachers and their Trainers', Bartle illustrates ways of thinking about the power behind the language of the Professional Standards for Qualified Teacher Status and the relationships that the text can affect and shape for those involved in its mediation. Bartle alludes to post-structuralism, feminism and Critical Language Analysis (CLA) to consider how individuals may create meaning for themselves out of their discursive mediation. He also explores the implications of the dominant ideological underpinnings of policy texts.

Karen Castle, in Chapter 3, 'Power and Status Theories in Teachers' Professional Development', uses Foucault's theories of power and Gramsci's concepts of hegemony to describe the rationale used by teachers who attended Continuing Professional Development (CPD) courses and then either carried on or discontinued their studies. This theoretical approach reveals in this case that some of the teachers involved were aware of the extra status that a postgraduate award would give them, and this encouraged them to pursue an award-bearing course, while others felt intimidated by the motivations of the management structure that organized the CPD, which had a powerful and contrasting de-motivating effect.

Paula Beer's project, described in Chapter 4, is distinctive for her attempt to recreate Sylva, Bruner and Genova's 1976 experimental project to analyse the role of play in the problem solving of young children. Principally organized around Bruner's theories of play and discovery learning, Beer's re-enactment is staged within new computer technologies, yet maintains the theories of play despite the distinctly contrasting environment. The process of coming to terms with Bruner's vast body of work, understanding his theoretical perspectives on learning though discovery and play, was for Beer a sudden and deep immersion in the world of theory, but one which ultimately led to the illumination of ideas that might otherwise have remained concealed.

1

Learning and Maintaining Professional Expertise Within a Multi-Professional Critical Care Team

Jill Cochrane

Key Theoretical Approaches in this Chapter: Hean's Analysis of Learning Theories Relevant to Inter-Professional Learning Allied to Engeström's Activity Theory

This project concerns the learning that takes place during the day-to-day practice of a multi-professional clinical team within a Paediatric Intensive Care Unit (PICU). Because the learning that takes place is complex and varied, it is necessary to identify and take into account the relevant and applicable theories of learning as a framework for the critical analysis of the accounts of the team's learning experiences. This encompassing view is the foundation of the project. Some researchers have focused on particular professions, while others concentrate on a particular theory of learning. I have used theories and my experience to identify a set of theories that relate to the ways in which clinicians may learn in critical care environment settings such as this. Engeström uses Activity Theory as a way of taking into

Applying Theory to Educational Research: An Introductory Approach with Case Studies, First Edition. Edited by J. Adams, M. Cochrane and L. Dunne.

account the multiplicity of personnel and learning activities and enables a framework of learning theories to be built.

Key texts

Engeström, Y. (2010) Expansive learning at work: toward an activity theoretical reconceptualisation. *Journal of Education and Work*, 14 (1), 133–156.

Hean, S., Craddock, D. and O'Halloran, C. (2009) Learning theories and inter-professional education: a user's guide. *Learning in Health and Social Care*, 8 (4), 250–262.

Introduction to the Research Project

The research considered in this chapter is a case study which, by using an eclectic combination of survey and semi-structured interviews, focuses on how clinicians in a critical care environment gain and maintain professional expertise as part of their everyday practice, and thus outside of formal education. Its utility will be to use the perspective of clinicians to determine the processes of such learning, its value to the participants, and to the underlying structures and people who support it. It is important to point out that this study is a work in progress; nevertheless, the role of literature can inform and enhance all stages of the research process, and the following account will identify how I have used theory to identify and frame my epistemological approach to the research design.

I have long been interested in the learning which takes place in clinical practice – from the start of my nurse training back in 1975, to the roles I have had within clinical education, and finally to my move to a lecturing post within a postgraduate clinical education programme. This experience has given me opportunities to reflect further and investigate more deeply the theoretical underpinnings, practical applications and experiences of learning within the clinical workplace; to consider the influence it has had on my philosophy of learning; and to clarify the personal context relevant to this research study.

There are two key aspects that define this study. The first is not only to take account of the perspectives of all professions within a clinical team, but also the specific clinical setting, including the clinical challenges encountered when working and learning together in a PICU. The second is to evaluate critically the ways in which learning takes place in this setting, and identify theories that underpin this. Other studies have focused on specific professions, or a particular learning theory in their approach, such as Eraut (2000, 2004); Lave and Wenger (1991); Cope, Cuthbertson and Stoddart (2000); Collins, Brown and Holum (1991). These studies, which relate theory to practice, have been highly relevant and provided an invaluable background, but a particular challenge for me has been to find a way of bringing together these influences in an ordered manner. For this I have used the work of Engeström (2010) and his application of Activity Theory, and the research undertaken by Hean, Craddock and O'Halloran (2009) investigating inter-professional learning, and I expand upon these later.

The participating clinical staff are nurses, doctors, physiotherapists and pharmacists, who work with and alongside their colleagues as part of their everyday work routine, each making their unique contribution to effective patient care. Some will have a wealth of experience on which to draw, others will be at an early stage in their career. Some may be undertaking formal programmes of learning, but for the majority of their colleagues self-directed, life-long learning is the order of the day. This research, as mentioned earlier, focuses on their experience of the learning that takes place as part of their everyday clinical practice.

The concept of continuing lifelong learning is encouraged and expected by the Department of Health (2001), and individuals are required to demonstrate how they have maintained their professional knowledge. Indeed such is the rate of change in practice that clinicians cannot afford to assume they know all they need to know at *any* stage of their career. Thus the research topic has relevance at all levels, from the individual to the wider organization, professional and political.

Applicable to all professionals, the novice to expert trajectory is identified by Dreyfus and Dreyfus (1986) as a learning journey, but how is this expertise developed and maintained, given all the potential changes that can impact on care delivery? What drives individual learning? What are the valuable learning experiences as identified by these clinicians? Since such professionals spend a large part of their career outside of *formal* education,

I am keen to understand their experiences of the processes underpinning their *non-formal* learning.

The clinical learning environment is a rich one – no patient or situation is entirely identical, and knowledge, therapies and interventions continue to develop. The importance of the clinical setting as a learning environment is acknowledged by Cope, Cuthbertson and Stoddart (2000), for example, who investigated the learning that occurs when undergraduate nurses undertake practice placements, while the work of Eraut (2004) has focused on gaining professional expertise in early career experiences. Both have focused on nurses as a discrete group, whereas I am including all members of the multi-professional clinical team.

The clinicians in my study rarely work in isolation. Teamwork is identified as increasingly important to patient outcomes, the reduction of critical incidents and improved patient safety (Hamman, 2004; Musson and Helmreich, 2004). Teamwork is of particular importance in this critical care setting, as members of the team work closely together, with professional boundaries becoming increasingly blurred. So I feel it is important to recognize that this working environment also gives opportunities for learning alongside each other, and from each other.

There is a plethora of knowledge, skills and behaviours required in order to become a professional. As part of the planning stages of this research study I investigated the varied forms of knowledge that clinicians would need in order to undertake their professional roles. My justification for this is that the different types of knowledge can be gained in different ways, and may be explained by any number of theories of learning. In the complexity of reality, this isn't easy, as forms of knowledge can overlap, and be used in varying degrees and combinations. There is a need to consider and understand this acquisition of knowledge and skills, and also behaviour modifications, in the light of appropriate learning theories. The potential relevance of learning theories to learning opportunities, has aided the investigation design into discovering how this manifests itself in the working lives of individual practitioners.

Theories Explained and their Use Justified in the Context of this Research Project

If, as I have argued earlier, the learning undertaken by clinicians in practice can take many forms, and is affected by the working environment and clinical activity, then I need a way of including and framing this activity such that others can follow my rationale, which is of particular importance in a (qualitative) case study. This has led me to the work of Engeström (2010) and Activity Theory, as a way of achieving this aim.

There is an additional challenge in that having identified a number of key learning theories I felt they would also benefit from a framework, showing their inter-relationships. In the account of Hean, Craddock and O'Halloran (2009), who identified theories underpinning inter-professional learning, I found that my adaptation of their framework has also enabled me to clarify and organize my thoughts, and signpost this for readers. The relevance of these theories and frameworks will become apparent as I expand on the detail of the activity and learning that takes place within a clinical environment.

Clinicians of all levels, from novice to expert, will come to the workplace setting with at least some background knowledge of fact, and varying levels of experience. If they have been introduced to the concept of the role of reflection in learning, and how it can be used to build or construct their experiences into a cogent whole (or have taken up this intuitively), then they will use this experience to develop professional expertise (experiential learning theory: Kolb and Fry, 1975).

The influence of their colleagues can guide and support this learning implicitly, just by working together. However, if colleagues have a designated facilitator role, or it is one that they assume, then this support may be more explicit (social constructivism: Vygotsky, 1978; cognitive apprenticeship: Collins, Brown and Holum, 1991). The very nature of the clinical environment in the critical care setting, where practitioners work closely among and alongside each other, lends itself to the observation and scrutiny of each others' practice in a way in which other professionals (e.g., school teachers) may not experience as a matter of routine. This gives rise to the importance of situated learning in this setting (Lave and Wenger, 1991), and the opportunities to learn from such exposure.

The work undertaken by Engeström (2010) considers that change, development and thus learning can take place in the midst of complex activities and inter-relationships. I have used his Activity Theory to take into account the interconnectivity of:

- The rules and norms of the workplace (*working practices of the PICU*)
- The subjects (*individual clinicians*)
- The community (*the professional groups*)
- The division of labour (*multi-professional working practices*)

- The tools (*knowledge construction theories*)
- The object (*workplace learning*)
- The outcome (*knowledge construction*). (Engeström, 2010 – my emphasis)

Although at first glance this theory can seem complex, it is this very complexity that typifies clinical workplace learning in general and in the critical care setting in particular. I have looked for ways of both unpicking and drawing together these effects and explain my approach in the following section.

The Application of Theory to the Research

The clinical setting that forms the focus of my research is one where I spent over 25 years in practice as a nurse, undertaking a number of roles from staff nurse to senior sister, and latterly as a clinical educator. This experience, alongside my move to lecturing on a clinical education programme, has conferred a wealth of understanding of how clinicians work and learn together in practice, but can also run the risk of evaluating my own perspective as the norm. This calls for a reflexive approach to help guard against such assumptions. Brookfield (1995) has written of the need to be a critically reflective teacher, and identifies four lenses of enquiry (autobiographical, students' eyes, colleagues' experiences, theoretical literature) through which insights may be gained. This forms the foundation of my own evaluation of what is relevant to the investigation of learning in clinical practice. Since I am undertaking a case study, such transparency is crucial – thus my lenses of enquiry include:

- a critical analysis of my own experience;
- the experiences of other interested and informed clinicians; and
- a review of the theoretical perspectives propounded in the wider literature. (Adapted from Brookfield, 1995)

Reflecting on my own experiences, I can attest to the importance of learning as part of everyday practice. I have found it difficult, for example, to understand such concepts as the physiology of oxygen transport without a combination of studying a written text or listening to a formal lecture, having discussions with colleagues to verify my understanding, and linking this

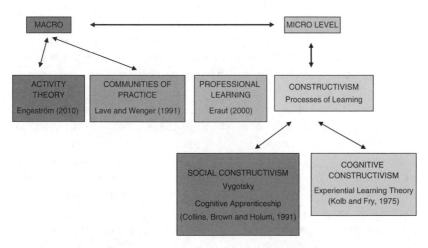

Figure 1.1 Figurative representation of theories and theorists relevant to my research. *Source*: Hean, S., Craddock, D. and O'Halloran, C. (2009) Learning theories and interprofessional education: a user's guide. Learning in Health and Social Care, 8 (4), 250–262.

to the observation and assessment of the impact of clinical interventions on individual children under our care. Teaching others further deepens my own understanding. Yet I have also worked alongside others who have valued learning in different ways – with a preference for less or more formal study, for example. These variations merely demonstrate that there is no universal mode of learning.

Moving on to the theoretical perspectives mentioned before, I show in Figure 1.1 how I have adapted the framework of Hean, Craddock and O'Halloran (2009) who identified learning theories relevant to inter-professional education and explained the evolution and inter-relationships between these theories in a way that I have found helpful. I have adapted a diagram they used (see Figure 1.1) in order to depict the relationships between the theories I have identified and justified as being central to my study.

The micro to macro continuum shows how learning can occur at the individual (micro) or societal (macro) level. Constructivist theories can take account of both of these forms. For the individual, constructivism theories explain how meaning and learning occurs within and in response to direct experience, that is, not divorced from practice. An early proponent of this is Kolb and Fry (1975).

Kolb's model is cyclical in nature and relates to the individual – whereby learning is best conceived as a process rather than merely an outcome.

This is significant for clinicians when considering the learning of excellence and expertise – at what point does one become an expert? Is it a finite journey, or one of continuing refinement? The importance of experience in the learning process is not to dismiss behavioural or cognitive processes, but to add to them. Put simply, we take part in an experience, observe and reflect upon it, think about and develop new concepts and connections, then move on to test these out in new situations. Knowledge is not a commodity 'out there' but within the person.

However, learning does not always take place in isolation. Vygotsky, a Russian psychologist who died in 1934, wrote among other things, of the ways in which children learn (Vygotsky, 1978), and further developed this work to explain aspects of adult learning as a communal activity. One of his contributions to theory was describing the 'Zone of Proximal Development' (ZPD). He considered that there was a gap between what a child can achieve alone, and that which can be gained from the support of an adult – the ZPD. He acknowledged the part that scaffolding (support) and fading (gradual withdrawal) provided by others can play in the learning process.

This is also relevant in the ways that adults learn, and relevant to the support given by more experienced staff to juniors, by understanding their 'comfort zone' and encouraging them to gain independence. From my own experiences, there have been times when I have encouraged a more junior staff member to move on from their comfort zone by asking them to imagine their 'worst case' scenario. I would then ask them what they would do, and who they would (and could) call on to assist them. This would usually enable them to see they had the skills and knowledge to take on the challenge, or more rarely, identify required learning. In either case, this is a valuable learning experience that needs capturing in my study.

Moving along the continuum, the inter-activity present in social constructivist theory broadens individual constructivist learning by, for example, including different views and concepts and different approaches to problem solving. An example of this form of learning would be that taking place during a multi-professional discussion. Members of the different clinical professions come together to analyse and evaluate the care and management of critically ill children: a rich learning environment giving opportunities to deepen understanding of individual cases and situations. The learning that takes place in this way is more of a communal activity, although further individual reflection may also occur.

Also part of the constructivist continuum is that of Cognitive Apprenticeship as outlined by Collins, Brown and Holum (1991). They describe the traditional apprenticeship in four phases. Initially, skills are modelled – by those more experienced and expert. However, there is a degree of 'watching each other' at work, novices and experts alike. Apprentices are then supported in their work by the 'scaffolding' role of others (with reference to the work of Vygotsky), whereby the inexperienced may be given easier tasks to undertake, or the simpler parts of a more complex procedure. This then leads to a 'fading' phase, such that the support is gradually withdrawn, and the learner is able to do the task independently. Finally, 'coaching' is a concept that occurs at every stage of this process – a guiding and encouraging role, moving towards independent practice.

This progressive independence is aspired to by the different professions contributing to the management of care. As an example, newly qualified staff nurses undertake an orientation programme, working closely with a more experienced nurse and taking part in formal activities in order to gain and demonstrate the skills and knowledge required to undertake this role with more limited support – to appreciate their level of expertise, and be able to prioritize who they might need to call on and when, should the need arise. But I am keen to understand the extent to which this aim occurs in practice. Understanding and applying this theory to the research design, and data analysis will add to its richness, and give greater opportunities for others to assess its applicability to their own setting.

The social context is also important, since it gives continued access to expertise; people with all levels of expertise can continue to develop and learn from each other. Another important concept is that when observing each others' practice it may be apparent that there are often many ways of undertaking the same task or procedure (provided key principles are adhered to), and that also there is seldom an 'all-knowing' worker. Part of socializing into the clinical setting will be to discover who to go to for particular expertise, which is yet another example of where learning can take place, and who may support it.

A greater emphasis on *where* the learning takes place is part of the focus of Lave and Wenger's Situated Learning Theory (Lave and Wenger, 1991). They describe how, by way of 'Legitimate Peripheral Participation' 'Communities of Practice' (COPs) are important in the development of situated learning. There is a potential for multiple COPs in critical care, due to the different professional groupings and roles staff undertake. Learning is situated in the professional's role as a member of a COP. This involves 'socializing' into the role of the clinician, wishing to become part of that particular community, therefore being an active participant. Community members benefit from the input of the new practitioners, by way of the questions they ask and the previous experiences they bring to bear, and this is also found in clinical practice.

In Lave and Wenger's (1991) original research, the COPs investigated comprised of single professional groups or craftsmen. In later work by Wenger, McDermott and Snyder (2002), there is recognition of being members of different COPs. This is similar to individuals in my study, who belong to different professional groupings, but who are also members of the COP that is the multi-professional healthcare team. I am keen to see whether their experiences of learning in practice involve the wider COP as well as their own profession.

To expand on the work of Engeström (2010) alluded to earlier, he has undertaken research, in a Finnish hospital, which has its focus on change and developments (and ultimately learning) within complex environments. This is comparable to the environment in my study. His questions are similar to those of Eraut (2004):

- Who are the subjects of learning, how are they defined and located?
- Why do they learn, what makes them make the effort?
- What do they learn, what are the contents and outcomes of learning?
- How do they learn, what are the key actions or processes of learning? (Engeström, 2010)

For my research, the subjects and their location are the qualified members of the clinical multi-professional team, working together as the critical care team of a PICU. The design and use of data collection tools enables me to capture not only the impetus and motivation to learn, but also the ways in which they learn, and the content and application of such learning. By using this theory to frame my questions for the survey and semi-structured interviews, and referring to it during the coding and thematic analysis, there is alignment throughout all processes. I can increase the reliability and authenticity of my research such that the questions relating to why, what and how participants learn capture the experiences of the individuals concerned.

The Relevance and Effectiveness of Using Theory

Arnseth (2008) has critiqued both Activity Theory and situated learning theory. I think both are still viable ways of shedding light on and analysing learning in practice although I am more amenable to Activity Theory as a way of accounting for interconnections related to learning in this arena. Arnseth (2008) concludes that Activity Theory gives external perspective and situated learning theory a more internal one: situated learning theory has a tendency to gloss over potential areas of conflict. This has implications for developments in practice – do the masters of such communities or experts always know best? Could there be the tendency to discourage less-experienced staff from developing new ways and ideas? The need to acknowledge and investigate the interactivity of learning, both vertical and horizontal, is important to the depth of my study.

Identifying relevant theories and how they interact and impact on everyday learning within critical care clinical settings gives structure to my study. Qualitative research in general and a case study method in particular depend on clarity of approach for their authenticity – a framework enables others to identify my thought processes and rationale.

At the start of my research journey, I knew that the focus would be on the learning that takes place as part of everyday practice within a PICU. I knew what I meant by this, but enabling others to follow my train of thought was not as straightforward. Also, the questions that critical friends asked were sometimes difficult to answer, as was committing my thoughts to paper. The use of theory to structure research design has been invaluable. During the planning stages I developed a mind map of all that impacted on working in clinical practice and its link to incidental/non-formal/everyday learning. Having worked in clinical practice for many years, and having an interest in supporting learning in the clinical setting, I felt I had identified and produced a comprehensive picture. That said, when I began to write, the analysis looked and read like a long list of unconnected learning theories – hardly groundbreaking.

Wider reading led me to the previously acknowledged paper by Hean, Craddock and O'Halloran (2009) that identified learning theories relevant to inter-professional learning. Whilst of interest per se, what really helped me was the way they depicted such theories as being developmentally related, and able to be considered as part of a macro–micro or societal–individual continuum. Thus I was able to adapt this to my own needs (as shown in Figure 1.1) in order to be able to indicate more clearly not only their relevance to my study, but position my rationale for the readers of my research.

Using theory has helped me to take a wider view during the planning phase of the research, and has helped order my thoughts and move from a long list of learning theories to a framework in which inter-connectivity is recognized and acknowledged. Moving forward, this framework will be used during the data collection and analysis phases of my study. Participants will have the opportunity to identify and elaborate on their learning experiences in practice; such a framework will aid thematic analysis.

Summary Conclusions and Recommendations

The discovery of the appropriate theories

These key theories were identified as a result of my wider reading and literature review. I first considered learning theories already known to me and searched for papers that had undertaken research of a similar nature.

The ease or difficulties with understanding the theories

Discovery of the work of Engeström and Activity Theory was very much a 'light bulb' moment, as it resonated firmly with my philosophy that learning in a complex setting needs to take into account those personnel and activities which define its complexity. Prior to this, I considered and included other theories (such as the work of Collins, Brown and Holum, 1991) as they provided a fit with my philosophy and could explain aspects of learning undertaken in this setting. Others seemed helpful on the surface, but on close examination were misaligned. On reflection, this alignment has enabled me to deepen my understanding of learning in practice, and how it may be researched.

The difficulties of application to data and texts

Data collection and analysis are yet to be attempted, although I plan on using these identified theories to aid in the identification of themes. Potential difficulties could arise if participants' examples of non-formal learning in practice fall outside of these inter-connected theories. Given that research is a dynamic activity, then the work I have already undertaken in this area provides a sound base should adaptations or additional theories need to be included.

What the application of the theories revealed

Applying theory enabled the possibility of taking a wider view of learning in practice. It provided a way of linking and framing discrete learning theories to depict their relationships and inter-connectivity.

How the absence of these theories might have impaired understanding

Before the identification of a possible framework, I had found that my thoughts and subsequent writing lacked a definable structure. I was also finding it difficult to explain to others the focus of my study. The framework on which my identified learning theories hang has enabled me to signpost my intentions in a way that is easier for others to follow. It has also helped me to identify areas for future development, such as categorizing my literature review.

The limitations of the theories

Although one of my key aims in this study has been to acknowledge and make reference to the complexity of working and learning in a multi-professional clinical setting, this may leave my study open to the criticism of a lack of depth due to the number of relevant theories I have identified. From my literature review I have been unable to find a study that has attempted to use such an amalgam of theories that could be both a strength (originality) and a weakness.

Reflection and recommendations of the experience

Discussing my plans, and listening to those of others at various stages of their doctoral journey has been immensely helpful by way of understanding their designs and answering their questions. Undertaking the writing of this chapter has given me the opportunity to justify my epistemological stance to a wider audience. Questions regarding clarification have both served to deepen my understanding and expose gaps in knowledge or argument that needed attention.

> *Recommended further reading*
>
> Engeström, Miettinen and Punamäki (1999) and Engeström and Middleton (1998) both provide a wealth of diverse examples of how Activity Theory may be used in research.

References

Arnseth, H.C. (2008) Activity theory and situated learning theory: contrasting views of educational practice. *Pedagogy, Culture and Society*, 16 (3), 289–302.

Brookfield, S. (1995) *Becoming a Critically Reflective Teacher*, Jossey-Bass, San Francisco.

Collins, A., Brown, J.S. and Holum, A. (1991) Cognitive apprenticeship: making thinking visible. *American Educator*, 6 (11), 38–46.

Cope, P., Cuthbertson, P. and Stoddart, B. (2000) Situated learning in the practice placement. *Journal of Advanced Nursing*, 31, 850–856.

Department of Health (2001) *Working Together – Learning Together: A Framework for Lifelong Learning for the NHS*, Department of Health, London.

Dreyfus, H.L. and Dreyfus, S.E. (1986) *Mind Over Machine; The Power of Human Intuition and Expertise in the Era of the Computer*, The Free Press, New York.

Engeström, Y. (2010) Expansive learning at work: toward an activity theoretical reconceptualisation. *Journal of Education and Work*, 14 (1), 133–156.

Engeström, Y. and Middleton, D. (1998) *Cognition and Communication at Work*, Cambridge University Press, Cambridge.

Engeström, Y., Miettinen, R. and Punamäki, R.-L. (1999) *Perspectives on Activity Theory (Learning in Doing: Social, Cognitive and Computational Perspectives)*, Cambridge University Press, Cambridge.

Eraut, M. (2000) Non-formal learning and tacit knowledge in professional work. *British Journal of Educational Psychology*, 70 (1), 113–136.

Eraut, M. (2004) Informal learning in the workplace. *Studies in Continuing Education*, 26 (2), 247–273.

Hamman, W.R. (2004) The complexity of team training: what we have learned from aviation and its applications to medicine. *Quality Safety in Health*, 13 (Suppl 1), 72–79.

Hean, S., Craddock, D. and O'Halloran, C. (2009) Learning theories and interprofessional education: a user's guide. *Learning in Health and Social Care*, 8 (4), 250–262.

Kolb, D.A. and Fry, R. (1975) Toward an applied theory of experiential learning, in *Theories of Group Process* (ed. C. Cooper), John Wiley and Sons, London, pp. 33–58.

Lave, J. and Wenger, E. (1991) *Situated Learning: Legitimate Peripheral Participation*, Cambridge University Press, Cambridge.

Musson, D.M. and Helmreich, R.L. (2004) Team training and resource management in health care: current issues and future directions. *Harvard Health Policy Review*, 5 (1), 25–35.

Vygotsky, L.S. (1978) *Mind in Society: The Development of Higher Psychological Processes*, Harvard University Press, Cambridge, MA.

Wenger, E., McDermott, R. and Snyder, W.M. (2002) *Cultivating Communities of Practice*, Harvard Business School Press, Boston.

2

The 'Q' Standards and Initial Teacher Training
The Discursive Formation of Teachers and their Trainers

Paul Bartle

> **Key Theoretical Approaches in this Chapter: Critical Discourse Analysis, Feminist Research**
>
> Poststructuralism offers the researcher a way of thinking about the power behind the language of a particular text and the relationships that the text can affect and shape. I draw on Derrida's (1978) notion of binary opposition and certain feminist writers (Smith, 1990; Weedon, 1997) for further exploration of text and power and consider implications for individuals who are involved in the discursive mediation of the 'powerful' policy text of the Professional Standards for Qualified Teacher Status. I allude to Fairclough's (2001) work on Critical Language Analysis (CLA). I consider how individuals may create meaning for themselves out of their discursive mediation. In the final section, I indicate how my subsequent research and study are leading me to consider the implications of the more general and currently dominant ideological underpinnings of policy texts.

Applying Theory to Educational Research: An Introductory Approach with Case Studies,
First Edition. Edited by J. Adams, M. Cochrane and L. Dunne.
© 2012 John Wiley & Sons, Ltd. Published 2012 by John Wiley & Sons, Ltd.

Key texts

Derrida, J. (1978) *Writing and Difference* (trans. A. Bass), Routledge and Kegan Paul, London.

Smith, D. (1990) *Texts, Facts and Femininity: Exploring the Relations of Ruling*, Routledge, London.

Weedon, C. (1997) *Feminist Practice and Poststructuralist Theory*, 2nd edn, Blackwell, Oxford.

Introduction to the Research Project

The research discussed here is an attempt at a critical and discursive engagement with an aspect of Initial Teacher Training (ITT) policy – the 'Q' (Qualified Teacher Status) Standards of the Professional Standards for Teachers (TDA, 2007). It started life as a thought-piece and assignment during the taught phase of my Doctorate in Education (EdD). This was at a time when I was beginning to engage with critical sociological theories, including policy-sociology. If it is any consolation to the reader, I still feel to be at the beginning of this engagement a number of years later.

The combination of my interest in language, the 'self' and 'intersubjectivity' (Crossley, 1996) resulted in my ideas for initial enquiries into 'policy' and its effects on the 'self' – or rather on the 'selves' of trainee teachers, school-based ITT mentors and university-based ITT tutors. Policy in this context can be viewed as a manifestation of language (Ball, 1990, 1994; Fairclough, 2001) that results in discursively (linguistically) mediated (inter)action in response to the policy. ITT policy presents, for example, desired goals and states of affairs through particular forms of language, including the ideological (Fairclough, 2001), and sets up mechanisms to support/promote and monitor the realization of that desired state of affairs – the achievement of Qualified Teacher Status (QTS). Policy can become the (all) powerful, 'authoritative' or 'hegemonic' voice or discourse (Ball, 1990, 1994; Fairclough, 2001; Usher and Edwards, 1994) and thus can shut down or marginalize other discourses (Foucault, 1974).

Theories Explained and their Use Justified
in the Context of this Research Project

Derrida (1978) advocates deconstruction as a means of understanding the world. His deconstruction involves binary opposition/duality – thus, for example, individuals/groups, power/powerlessness, knowledge/ignorance, and interaction/isolation. Derrida advances the view that one of the pair in binary opposition is weaker, less preferable or undesirable. He further maintains that the desirable cannot exist without reference to the undesirable. Indeed this would appear to be the case in most of the above, with the exception of the first pair. The 'individual' and 'individualism' have been central themes in traditional Western philosophy since the Enlightenment and yet we live our lives as members of groups whether they are constructed, for example, in terms of work relationships or in terms of friendships or family relationships. Immediately here, therefore, is the problematizing of the nature of individualism and group identity: how much leeway does an individual have within a group to be autonomous? Which is preferred and in what relational context – group or individual? Linked to this is the fourth binary pair: given that we live in groups, interaction is inevitable. The second pair raises questions such as: what is power?, where is it located?, who has it? what is it used for?, how is power maintained?, who is powerless?, why is s/he powerless? The same questions can be asked about knowledge/ignorance.

Already we are developing a framework for enquiring into the relationship between the individual and her/his social milieu. In the context of this writing my milieu was as an educator, primarily of beginning teachers but also as an employee in a publicly funded university. Therefore, my immediate social milieu was that of the workplace.

While Derrida (1978) is useful in helping us to open up a framework, Foucault (1974) significantly links power and knowledge together (power/knowledge) in contemporary society. The establishment of the Q Standards by the UK government took power and knowledge away from the professionals and the practitioners and placed them in a bureaucratic setting with ready access from and to politicians. Thus a basic shift in the power/knowledge structure occurred leading to disempowered professionals and practitioners and empowered politicians. This has had significant impact on the role of the teacher trainer in relation to the trainee and also on the trainer in referring to her/his wider professional milieu. All must constantly frame their discussions with reference to the Q Standards since all parties are 'measured' and judged in terms of their achievement and none has ready access to the bureaucracy to reformulate and redefine the Standards.

The prescriptive and polarizing language of the Standards that essentializes, universalizes and categorizes what it is to be(come) a teacher are features that poststructuralist and postmodernist writers (Foucault, 1974; Usher and Edwards, 1994) identify as aspects of 'modern' social organizations. These link to the rationalist tradition of Western thought that, for example, 'objectively' searches for 'truth' through scientific evidence and method. Feminist and pro-feminist writers critique and problematize this tradition and its allied social structures and context, opening it up to examination from a gender perspective.

A discussion of binary opposites also opens up ground where we can examine some possible insights into gendered aspects of the Q Standards and ITT training. We can link these to the ideas on self and subjectivity. In particular, I often use the terms 'hegemony' and 'normativity' here. Some feminist writers (e.g., Connell, 1995; Smith, 1990; Weedon, 1997; Whitehead, 2002) identify these as evidence of a 'masculinist' tradition discursively permeating and governing social organizations of which governments, schools and higher education institutions are examples. Likewise, other terms such as 'reason', 'rationality', 'positivist' and 'essentialist' are seen by feminists as further evidence of masculinist domination, both historically and currently.

Indeed, many of the same writers situate these notions along with hegemonic masculinity and patriarchy (Millett, 1977) as features of modernist, bureaucratized social organizations linked to processes where outcomes are apparently clear and claim to be operating in the interests of the wider organization. Here we can cite the aims of the Q Standards as training teachers to educate children for life in our society. Furthermore, a clear link is here discernable with the broad aims and purposes of the National Curriculum for England that use what may be regarded as masculinist language in relation to the purposes of education in society – namely, for example, to equip children to become entrepreneurial and autonomous individuals.

The particular resonances I have found for my work in this area come from Smith (1990) and other feminist and pro-feminist writers (e.g.,

Weedon, 1997) when they address the notions of text, subjectivity, objectivity and relations of power and agency. However, and in an attempt to achieve a perspective on poststructuralist and feminist approaches to these matters, I have found some of the stances of other writers useful – for example Giddens' (1991) approach to self-identity and modernity (see below), or Usher and Edwards' (1994) examination of postmodernism in relation to education.

Weedon (1997), arguing from a poststructuralist feminist perspective, maintains that we need a theory that enables us to examine the formation of and interplay between subjects and their relationship to state apparatuses of ruling. Smith (1990) gives critical insights into bureaucracy as an apparatus of ruling through 'textualization' – the textual objectification of the subject. Giddens (1991) in his turn sheds light on the personal implications of inter-subjectivity. In his discussions of the individual embarking on a project such as ITT he identifies areas of potential tension such as trust (1991, pp. 42–51), risk (1991, p. 40), creativity (1991, p. 41): the individual invests or experiences these in her/his pursuit of the project and its goal. The subject also brings prior experience with her/him to the project and thus, as a result, has expectations for the present and future and emotional memories of the past.

Confronted with the power of the normalizing and ideological aspects of the Q Standards, the individual experiences a constant assault on her/his subjectivity to reshape and realign it. This assault is common to all parties in the project. In Giddens' (1991) interpretation, the realignment of subjectivity to, for example, the demands of the Standards can be seen as causing disruptions to lifestyles in relation to experience grounded in tradition. This reshaping and realignment occurs in multiple contexts of action and experience affecting the public and private self, causing methodological uncertainty in terms of 'being' and also causing a reflexive development in terms of work and family or personal relationships. In short, it affects our own cognitive and emotional construction of our self.

We can link this to some of the ideas from feminist writers in their interpretation of masculinity, femininity, marginalization and understanding of the 'Other'. Giddens himself (1991, p. 109) is perhaps making a link to feminist notions of the 'Other' when he says that self-identity depends on an affirmative 'recognition of the other'. This can either be personally retrospective or personally future-postulative. Equally it can be inter-subjectively comparative in terms of real 'others' or the 'other' idealized and essentialized in the dominant discourse, that is, in the Q Standards.

The Application of Theory to the Research

My primary role in the workplace is the 'enabling' of trainee teachers to 'meet' the Q Standards (coupled with the assessment of their competence in 'meeting' them) through the dissemination of specialized knowledge. I am thus in an ambiguous relationship with the trainees – teacher and assessor (group, power, knowledge, interaction). This ambiguity is supposedly removed by the existence of the standards that are ostensibly 'neutral' and 'professional'. Informing this work with the trainees was my location in other groups within the university, for example, programme boards, partnership management committees, ITT boards and so on, as well as within national and regional bodies, where discussion and action centred on ensuring that ITT provision is compliant with the same standards and other governmental guidance and requirements (group, power, knowledge, interaction). Thus there exists a whole local and national apparatus that maintains, supports and advances a competence-based training model for ITT (group, power, knowledge, interaction). In other words, the knowledge that matters is contained within the standards and the power is found in the local and national structures that ensure the knowledge is disseminated. This system is all pervasive: this leads to further embeddedness and acceptance of the status quo (group, power, knowledge, interaction).

Against this background four aspects of this current situation merit examination and discussion:

- a wider understanding of the social origins and raison d'être of the system;
- the shifting locations of knowledge/ignorance and power/powerlessness;
- the ideological aspects of the system; and
- the entrapment of the individual and the consequences for her/him.

To return to the ideas of Smith (1990), Giddens (1991) and Usher and Edwards (1994), the model of ITT promoted through the Q Standards and their linked local and national apparatus can be seen as complicit in upholding and advancing the policy hegemony of a particular view of what becoming/being a teacher involves. Through bureaucratic means of textual communication and 'objective' measurement the individuals caught up in the system are subjected to/subordinated by the all-powerful and authoritative hegemonic view (see Gramsci, 1971) and by their actions and interactions become complicit in the promotion of the hegemony and its allied systems.

An examination of the language of the text of the Q standards presents us with an 'idealized' and 'essentialized' teacher. As well as the deictic[1] devices mentioned later we read statements phrased in the language of the 'obvious', for example:

> Those recommended for the award of QTS should: demonstrate the positive values, attitudes and behaviour they expect from children and young people. (TDA, 2007, p. 7)

The text of the standards also contains references for compliance to other policy hegemonies such as the National Curriculum, the Key Stage Three Strategy, the QTS tests for literacy, numeracy and Information Communication Technology (ICT).

However, the language of the 'obvious' is not so obvious in the context of a need to mediate the text via a three-sided discussion between higher education institution-based trainers, school-based trainers and trainee teachers. While the language of the text presents the actors with the outcomes of a normative process, it does not indicate how the normalizing itself should proceed. The text, therefore, occasions the growth of bureaucratic systems designed to mediate the text. Since the outcome of the process is stated and statutorily binding, it is the interpretation of process that leads to the growth of local policies and practices but set within the parameters of the legally binding framework. In turn local variations in policy and practice in mediating and normalizing the process led to the need for local and national monitoring mechanisms to ensure that normalized outcomes are met.

As tutors and mentors we mediate an interpretation of the text with the trainee teachers to enable them to 'meet the Standards' through, for example, regular individual tutorials, seminars, observation of teaching, formative and summative assessment, in-school mentor and tutor support. We also mediate the text for ourselves as tutors and mentors through various levels of management meetings, course boards, programme boards and national and local meetings of allied subject and management or monitoring specific areas.

---

1 Deictic devices and deixis – a use of language to establish a relationship between the writer and reader. Here the words 'those' and 'should' are used to establish distance between the text and the reader ('those' are not necessarily the people reading the text but the readers may want to be included in that group) and also a sense of conditionality and/or obligation (in effect 'If you want to be a teacher this is what you need to do').

Thus we objectify and bureaucratize our own selves and our trainees' selves in relation to the hegemonic core policy text through the production of other texts designed to be 'compliant' with the core text. Thereby there exists a process of textualization of the individual: our training process, with its linked monitoring and assessment procedures, becomes our discursive response to the hegemonic features of the text of the Q Standards. A state of decontextualized, intertextual, bureaucratized mediation therefore exists. Again through the work of Smith (1990, p. 224) we see that text establishes the parameters for discourse and that discourse occurs in power relations: 'The analysis of texts ... in their reading, are "active" in the actual organisation of relations. Textual analysis, as practiced [sic] here, explores the ubiquitous and generalizing organization of ruling relations.'

Smith's discussion of bureaucracy as an example of a 'relation of ruling' is enlightening here because she brings discourse and text into the frame: 'For bureaucracy is par excellence that mode of governing which separates the performance of ruling from particular individuals and makes organization independent of particular persons and local settings' (Smith, 1990, p. 213). The state bureaucracy in our context provides mechanisms for monitoring and enforcing the legally enshrined Q Standards through, for example, Ofsted. This is paralleled by the institutional bureaucracy charged with local monitoring and enforcement.

Smith (1990) further argues that texts support the maintenance not only of the bureaucratic system but also of the system governed by the bureaucracy. It is worthwhile discussing the text of the Standards for QTS in the light of Smith's thoughts on deixis. Deictic devices in the language of the Standards for QTS further exemplify and reinforce the distance and detachment of the trainee teacher from QTS by using formulae such as: 'Those recommended for the award QTS should ...' (TDA, 2007, p. 8) and '[They should] be aware of the professional duties of teachers and the statutory framework within which they work' (TDA, 2007, p. 7). Through these devices the Standards simultaneously offer a way into the assessment of trainees by tutors and mentors and self-assessment by the trainee teachers themselves. They appear to give trainees, mentors and tutors a goal: trainee teachers start off as outsiders aiming for the conferment of QTS and over time they can measure progress towards being worthy of the award.

It is perhaps in this context that we can see the importance of the location of power within this nexus. The exercise of power within the relationships shifts over time and according to local and individual contexts. For example, beginning trainees perceive that the tutor holds 'expertise' and 'knowledge'.

However, this expertise and knowledge come from continual engagement with the 'hegemonic' discourse. There is no opportunity here for a tutor to problematize the ideology underpinning the Q Standards in relation to the trainee's progress towards the award of QTS since the parameters of the discourse – statutory, normative, centrally and locally monitored – limit this. Similarly the trainee perceives that her/his knowledge and expertise are growing as a result of the process of training, but this is in itself limited by the hegemony of the Standards for QTS. Engagement between tutors, mentors and trainees serves to shape the subjectivity of all parties and to obfuscate the underpinning ideological nature of the outcome of the process. The process is authentic but its premise is ideological and prescriptive. Weedon (1997, p. 173) explains this against the background of 'common sense':

> Common sense suggests that we learn about the world through experience. Experience is by definition authentic, a source of true knowledge which is expressed in language. Language is a transparent tool for self-expression and the transparent relationship between the individual, experience and language allows little scope for theorizing contradictions either in our sense of ourselves or in meanings of our experience.

The Relevance and Effectiveness of Using Theory

For the purposes of my work, I interpret encounters with social and material objects as creating the self or the subject. Because these encounters with social and material objects are constant, so is the creation of subjective meaning and the self is, therefore, in a constant state of creation and 'becoming' (Weedon, 1997). Reading this chapter, for example, involves its subjective interpretation, a reflexive response to it, and an altered subjectivity on the part of the reader.

We are, therefore, part of a nexus of subjects and objects from which we literally cannot extricate ourselves and where the interaction between subjects can produce a social object and occasion a space where discourse and the mediation of meaning can occur. Bruner's (1990) thoughts on the self, subjectivity, meaning making and meaning sharing about social subjects are particularly relevant here where he sees the self as a culturally and historically conditioned construct (Bruner, 1990, pp. 107, 108). This resonates with my intention to demonstrate that we are not 'whole and coherent subjects with a unified sense of identity' (Weedon, 1997, p. 174).

At this point in the development of my discussion, however, I encounter a difficulty with many of the feminist writers as they can often appear to fall prey to the same essentializing habits of thought as the historically identified hegemonic masculinist system. While their work is illuminating when it discusses a historical, gender-based bias that disempowered and marginalized women, it is not possible to take this essentiaized view and apply it wholesale. The empowered and powerless actors in the system under discussion do not fall neatly into gender categories such as empowered males and powerless females by virtue of their sex.

Yet, following this train of thought, I would argue in favour of seeing the power/potency of the hegemony of the Standards and their allied managerial support structures as the essentialized and potent 'masculine' – the standard against which all else is measured and the goal towards which all strive, for example:

> In all these cases, performance management is the key process. Performance Management provides the context for regular discussions about teachers' career aspirations and their future development, within or beyond their current career stage. The framework of professional standards will provide a backdrop to discussions about how a teacher's performance should be viewed in relation to their current career stage and the career stage they are approaching. The relevant standards should be looked at as a whole in order to help teachers identify areas of strength and areas for further professional development. Newly qualified teachers (NQTs) will not be required to meet fully the core standards until the end of their induction period. The core standards underpin all the subsequent standards and, where there is no progression at subsequent career stages, are valid at all points of teachers' careers within both their immediate workplace and the wider professional context in which they work. Each set of standards builds on the previous set... (TDA, 2007, p. 3)

I would further argue that no actor within the system can therefore be truly 'masculine' or 'potent' since the nature of the discourse always marginalizes everybody to a greater or lesser extent through their attempts to mediate the discourse and through their constant subjective realignments to it. Connell (1995, p. 65) suggests: 'Patriarchal definitions of femininity (dependence, fearfulness) amount to a cultural disarmament that may be quite as effective as the physical kind'. Actors within the system are 'culturally disarmed' through the essentialized aspects of the standards and marginalized through the bureaucracy that, as we have seen, keeps them at a distance through objectifying and textualizing them.

I would further venture here that this 'cultural disarmament' and marginalization 'feminizes' the actors to extents that vary over time and in different locations. As I have attempted to demonstrate earlier, the codification and textualization of the policy makes it 'real' so that all actors, policy makers included, are drawn into an engagement that is subordinated to the text (the essential) itself. Modification and mediation can only occur in the context of the text (of the essential). Perhaps ironically then, even the authenticity of the experience is undermined since all experience is undertaken and occurs as a result of the hegemonic, essentializing text.

The mediating discourses are then normative, self-referential and self-perpetuating. We have examined, in part, the normative, deictic, masculinist text of the Q Standards and some features of how these affect the subjects caught up in the discourse through subjective interaction mediated by the text, inscription of the subject by the text, objectification of the subject through the text, conditioned agency imposed by the text, categorization according to the text and opportunities for subversion of the discourse.

Having postulated that the playing out of the discourse results to a large extent in disempowered professionals leads to some central questions relating not just to professional action and autonomy but also to wider issues concerned with the notions of equality and social justice. My demonstration that the self-perpetuating and self-referential discourse leads to the mediation of the actors' experiences and thoughts through the terms of the discourse itself puts them in a slave-like position of subordination. I find that we are here perhaps referring back to the work of emancipatory feminist writers. Smith (1990, p. 2) describes this 'consciousness-raising' phase of feminism:

> Speaking from experience was a method of speaking: it was not a particular kind of knowledge but a practice of telling wherein the particular speaker was authority in speaking of her everyday life and the world known to her as she was active in it.

It is perhaps time for education professionals to find a voice along such lines and to assert their right to be heard and to be 'present' in the discourse – not to be textualized and objectified. However, we can see how the current system itself militates against such an enterprise for the vast majority of trainees and their trainers.

Summary Conclusions and Recommendations

The discovery of the appropriate theories

As I stated at the beginning of this piece, my use of ideas from poststructuralism and pro-feminism gave me a way of thinking about power and relationships and how these related to my day-to-day work as an ITT tutor. This all came about as something of a reaction against my earlier 'education' in the 'grand narratives' of Marxism, Liberalism and Socialism that I had encountered in my undergraduate days. The process of discovery was gradual and seemed to be enabling a critical and reflexive exploration of a predominant aspect my working life.

The ease or difficulties with understanding the theories

I have quite an eclectic approach towards theory – a purely poststructuralist or pro-feminist approach can't answer all the questions. However, a good theory or good theories offer the researcher a way of asking questions and interpreting data and ways of making and sharing meaning together with frameworks for the deployment of the 'sociological imagination'.

The difficulties of application to data and texts

While my understanding of the theories at the time of writing seemed to meet my needs for beginning an apparently critical examination of the mediation of a policy text, I am further developing that understanding and application to critique the wider, dominant ideological and political discourses and allied power relationships that have an interest in shaping those policies.

What the application of the theories revealed

As a result of the application of the theories I have since gone on to questions about the dominant ideological and political interests at work in our society. This was because the examination of the policy discourse inevitably caused me to question the origins of the policy itself. I am thinking here principally in terms of the influence of neo-liberal ideology on educational policy and practice. I am interested to see how neo-liberalism will evolve following the recent financial crisis and how this will impact on education.

How the absence of these theories might have impaired understanding

The existence of these theories gave me a framework for developing my perception of what was happening in my working life. The theories gave me tools for asking questions and offering possible explanations. The 'logic' of the theories also encouraged me to be reflexive and developmental in taking the next step with my ideas – here perhaps going from examining the operation of a social system and actors to interrogating the system itself.

The limitations of the theories

I found the theories limiting from two points of view. First, poststructuralism is a useful tool for an initial deconstruction and examination of power and relationships. However, before deconstruction could occur, I needed to have an understanding of structures: I found Giddens' (1986) 'theory of structuration' invaluable here.

Second, I needed to keep in mind a policy context for this work and, while the theories are useful at a general level, they do not relate at the specific level of policy; Jenny Ozga's (2000) book is a good way into gaining an understanding of this aspect. Through her work I was able to relate my theme to issues of democracy and social justice for teachers and the children they teach. Ozga persuasively argues the place for critical theory as a means of enquiry into education policy where research can challenge dominant ideas that contribute to policy formulation. She further advances the view that policy research can highlight injustice and inequality through problematizing bureaucratic approaches to monitoring and evaluation.

Reflection and recommendations of the experience

My work would have been better informed if I had had a better understanding of the role of ideology in policy and how subjects can be seen as ideologically conditioned – perhaps I fell prey to the then current popular perception that ideology was dead whereas, in effect, the 'neutral' and 'objective' rationalities of education policy and practice can be argued to be masking the operation of a neo-liberal state and a neo-liberal interpretation of the 'professional'.

Recommended further reading

Giddens, A. (1986) explains the theory of structuration.
Ozga, J. (2000) provides a good background for discussion of policy.

References

Ball, S.J. (1990) *Politics and Policy Making in Education: Explorations in Policy Sociology*, Routledge, London.

Ball, S.J. (1994) *Education Reform: A Critical and Post-Structural Approach*, Open University Press, Buckingham.

Bruner, J. (1990) *Acts of Meaning*, Harvard University Press, Cambridge, MA.

Connell, R.W. (1995) *Masculinities*, Polity Press, Cambridge.

Crossley, N. (1996) *Intersubjectivity: The Fabric of Social Becoming*, Sage, London.

Derrida, J. (1978) *Writing and Difference* (trans. A. Bass), Routledge and Kegan Paul, London.

Fairclough, N. (2001) *Language and Power*, 2nd edn, Pearson Education, Harlow.

Foucault, M. (1974) *The Archaeology of Knowledge*, Tavistock, London.

Giddens, A. (1986) *The Constitution of Society: Outline of the Theory of Structuration*, Polity Press, Cambridge.

Giddens, A. (1991) *Modernity and Self-Identity: Self and Society in the Late Modern Age*, Polity Press, Cambridge.

Gramsci, A. (1971) *Selections from the Prison Notebooks* (trans. Q. Hoare and G. Nowell Smith), Lawrence and Wishart, London.

Millett, K. (1977) *Sexual Politics*, Virago, London.

Ozga, J. (2000) *Policy Research in Educational Settings: Contested Terrain?* Open University Press, Buckingham.

Smith, D. (1990) *Texts, Facts and Femininity: Exploring the Relations of Ruling*, Routledge, London.

Training and Development Agency for Schools (TDA) (2007) Professional Standards for Teachers, http://www.tda.gov.uk/teachers/professionalstandards/downloads.aspx (accessed 19 January 2010).

Usher, R. and Edwards, R. (1994) *Postmodernism and Education*, Routledge, London.

Weedon, C. (1997) *Feminist Practice and Poststructuralist Theory*, 2nd edn, Blackwell, Oxford.

Whitehead, S. (2002) *Men and Masculinities: Key Themes and New Directions*, Polity Press, Cambridge.

3

Power and Status Theories in Teachers' Professional Development

Karen Castle

> ### Key Theoretical Approach in this Chapter: Power and Hegemony
>
> I use Michael Apple's theoretical approach to power, which is concerned with building a critical and democratic education system. His view is that this involves a struggle against the dominance or hegemony of 'intellectual elites' who have been instrumental in deciding what counts as official knowledge. Apple argues that educational policy and practice are influenced greatly by struggles between powerful groups and social movements. These, he suggests, react to ensure that their knowledge becomes the legitimate knowledge and, therefore, ensures their power within the larger social context. I also applied Foucault's and Gramsci's theories of power and hegemony to my research, in particular Foucault's argument that knowledge and power are inextricably linked, and that power is not something tangible and set with one group, but rather is something that is fluid and can be adopted by different groups.
>
> *Key texts*
>
> Apple, M. (2000) *Official Knowledge: Democratic Education in a Conservative Age*, Routledge, London.

Applying Theory to Educational Research: An Introductory Approach with Case Studies, First Edition. Edited by J. Adams, M. Cochrane and L. Dunne.
© 2012 John Wiley & Sons, Ltd. Published 2012 by John Wiley & Sons, Ltd.

Foucault, M. (1980) *Power/Knowledge: Selected Interviews and other Writings. 1972–1977*, Pantheon, New York.
Gramsci, A. (1971) *Selections from the Prison Notebooks*, New Left Books, New York.

Introduction to the Research Project

Teachers in England have been able to access Masters degrees as part of their professional development (CPD, Continuing Professional Development) for some time. Local authorities and universities, as well as some private training providers, have collaborated on the provision of Masters degree accreditation CPD for teachers over the past few years. My investigation as a novice researcher stemmed from two areas of concern. First, many experienced teachers were dismissing CPD and not engaging in any developmental activities despite there being funding and resources to support their engagement, and second, it seemed that a high number of teachers who were participating in CPD were doing so under duress. As a university tutor responsible for engaging teachers in CPD, I was in the fortunate position of having the opportunity to try to identify in more detail the influences on teachers' approach to their professional development. Justification for the ethnographic methodological approach was essentially based on my continual access to, and involvement in, teachers' professional lives, as well as my access to key staff in the local government education authorities and universities.

Other research that has been carried out in this area (Draper, 2000) found that teachers' professional development is controlled by schools through their interpretation of national initiatives and other external priorities. In particular in situations where the school had a specific objective on the school improvement plan, most of the CPD activities were centred round the needs of this plan, which often conflicted with the plans of individual teachers. That head teachers' views on teachers' CPD are often in conflict with the views of the teachers themselves was highlighted by several of my teacher respondents. For example, one secondary school teacher informed the investigation that it didn't matter what CPD teachers wanted to do, or whether it was accredited or not – even a Masters degree; if the head teacher didn't want the teacher to do it they would not be able to.

The conclusion I drew from this was that teachers would only be able to do CPD if it fitted in with the agenda of the head teacher.

Discussions with some head teachers verified that this could be the case. The reason they gave was that they often need to prioritize the school improvement plan. They fully appreciate that this may conflict with the CPD wishes of individual teachers within the school, but felt that there was no area for negotiation. Gray and Denley (2005, p. 2) refer to two studies into teachers' CPD carried out at Cambridge University and the university of Bath, both of which discovered that CPD was felt to play 'little or no useful role in the lives of teachers, beyond delivering government policy'. These findings are supported by another study by Arthur *et al.* (2006), who found that 38 per cent of English teachers undertook award-bearing CPD for personal rather that professional reasons. However, the recommendations of Arthur's study was for much more research in the area of teachers' CPD.

In England local education authorities have a key role in teachers' CPD, both from a funding point of view and from the point of having their own agendas. However, this creates the opportunity for further tensions, in particular in cases where the local authority has a conflicting agenda with the school and/or the individual teachers. My research identified that tensions such as these exist and in many cases cause teachers to dispense with CPD. Several discussions with local authority school advisors and school improvement officers revealed that they had a prescribed programme of CPD activities for teachers. This programme was, in the main, developed round the key government priorities for teachers and any local initiatives. Blandford (2000) concurred with the view that local government education authorities need to meet their own needs in terms of teachers' CPD, but that these needs sometimes conflict with the teachers' preference and the schools' agenda.

Working as a university tutor responsible for teachers' CPD has enabled me to witness many conversations and debates with teachers concerning their CPD. I have also been able to work with local authority schools' advisers and CPD leaders. Head teachers and school CPD leaders have also participated in my research. A major part of my role was to register teachers on the university's accredited CPD programme. I began by assuming that teachers would want to take part in CPD. I believed that they would want to achieve accreditation, as I felt that this could lead to them obtaining more senior positions, and offer them more opportunity. My view was also that by taking part in CPD, they would be improving their practice, which could lead to overall school improvement. Why wouldn't teachers, therefore, want to achieve postgraduate credits for the work that they were doing for their CPD?

Many of the teachers acting as respondents in this study claimed to be participating in CPD in order to secure some means of professional status or identity for themselves. Many felt that by taking part in, and eventually achieving a Masters degree, they were achieving a certain professional identity and level. Professionalism and associated identity and status in general have been the focus of much research and debate. Couldron and Smith (1999) have identified that the way in which teachers acquire their professional identity has implications for their CPD. They argue that teachers' identity is not just about being seen as a teacher by themselves and colleagues, but being seen as a teacher by others in society. It is about being socially recognized as a qualified person. That qualification begins by being awarded Qualified Teacher Status (QTS), but then continues by achieving awards through CPD. However there is a contradiction in terms of how teachers view their professionalism. For example, some teachers engage in Masters level CPD, as they perceive that this will provide some professional security and offer them a good chance for promotion. These teachers feel that by achieving a Masters degree they are sending a message to colleagues, the head teacher, pupils and parents, that they are serious about teaching, and that they are legitimizing their professional identity as a teacher. Teachers also feel that if, in the future, teaching jobs were under threat, having a Masters degree may go some way to helping to secure their posts.

As a contrast to this view, many teachers feel that they no longer hold any real professional status to people outside of the profession. They compare teaching now to that of several years ago, when they feel that teachers were respected by the community and pupils. They use the analogy of teachers of the past having a status within society simply because they were teachers, whereas today this is not the case. They offer this as a reason not to engage in any CPD Masters programmes.

My study aimed to dig deeper into these views and other interpretations and in so doing, offer some explanation as to how teachers approach accredited CPD. However, I felt that there needed to be a theoretical framework around which the study could be woven, and this became a challenge for me. My relative newness to academic research of this nature led to the need to obtain a deeper understanding of the research process, in particular the use of theory. Why did I need to use any theory? All I wanted to do was find out what influences teachers' approach to CPD, but where did the theory come into that? The next section identifies the ways in which I began to use theory in the development of my research.

Theories Explained and their Use Justified in the Context of this Research Project

Once I had completed the data interpretation and analysis, there were two main themes that emerged. In the case of teachers dismissing CPD, the notion of power relations was a major contribution. Of those teachers who did engage in accredited CPD, professional identity and status were the main influences. Once I had made this discovery, it seemed that I needed to support or underpin this with something more substantive. A brief journey back to my memories of my school sociology reminded me of Foucault's work and his theories of power, and how they can be interpreted. This brief frisson led to me delving deeper into other theories of power. I was then able to identify that hegemony was at play in my study, which led me in turn to Gramsci, and to the realization that using theory is necessary in the framing and interpretation of my research.

Gramsci (1971) adopted the term hegemony to refer to the ideological rule of one social class over another (Slattery, 2003). Hegemony has been defined by Gramsci (1971) as an ideological rule – a means of controlling dominant ideas and the way in which people think and behave as workers. Gramsci was concerned with the way in which power was seized and sustained by the ruling factions using ideological leadership. The ideological rule or control of dominant ideas and people's way of thinking is what Gramsci (1971) referred to as the highest form of hegemony. Although Gramsci was concerned with the power of capitalism and the ways in which, in the Western world, people's thoughts and behaviour were controlled by the state, his theory of hegemony has been interpreted in a manner that allows it to be used to support educational research. This interpretation is demonstrated by Raymond Williams, whose work informs that of Michael Apple. Williams (1974) asserted that hegemonic practices are at work in our education systems today. He argued that educational institutions are the main agencies for the development of the dominant culture. This dominance can be identified by the way in which people's thoughts, practices and actions are influenced by what is passed off as 'the tradition', yet which has actually been selected by the dominant body within, and which creates inequality throughout the institution (Apple, 2004). Furthermore, Apple explains that the powerful are able to offer what may appear to be compromises, but what are in fact not compromises at all, rather further ideas to ensure their domination. These are not 'compromises among equals' as the dominant are always able to determine the level and detail of the compromise (Apple, 2000, p. 10).

Similarly, Foucault held the theory that power and knowledge are joined together and are indivisible (Foucault, 1980; Slattery, 2003, p. 208). On one hand, he determined that those who have power can subject others to their rule; on the other, Foucault identified that power can also be used by the people being ruled; for example, when a patient challenges the diagnosis that one doctor has made and obtains a second opinion from another. Foucault held the view that the power–knowledge relationship underpins the fabric of modern society, and the way in which this becomes evident is through discourse, where those who hold power and knowledge are able to control discourse, thereby maintaining their hold on ideological power.

Mahony and Hextall (2000, p. 102) affirm that 'there is currently much debate and an enormous amount of literature about both the reconstruction of professionalism within teaching and the reconstruction of teachers as individual professionals'. This is evident in several policy documents concerning teacher professionalism derived from the English central government (DfEE 2000, 2001; DfES, 2005; DCSF, 2008). Mahoney and Hextall's notion of a reconstruction is supported by Whitty (1997, p. 304) in that he refers to a 'de-professionalisation' of teaching, brought about by CPD for teachers which focuses on the craft of teaching skills, rather than on professional knowledge or understanding.

In relation to this and with respect to the individual professional identity of teachers, Couldron and Smith (1999) argue that the professional identity that a teacher assumes is in part given but is also partly achieved by the way in which teachers 'locate themselves within the social space that is the school'. The knowledge that teachers have accrued through experiences is what Goodson (2003) believes to be the key factor in determining the kinds of people teachers are and believe themselves to be. Teacher identity and the way in which teachers see themselves and each other seems to have some influence on the way in which they approach their professional development. The reforms and transformations to the teaching profession and school organizations can lead to some teachers feeling their identity is threatened (Goodson and Ball, 1985). Many teachers argue that there are constant changes and reforms affecting schools and teaching. This would seem to suggest that teacher identity is in flux.

The Application of Theory to the Research

It wasn't long before I realized that promoting CPD to teachers wasn't easy. Many teachers demonstrated with great clarity that they would not be engaging in any CPD. Others began CPD courses but withdrew at some point during the programme. A low number of teachers did engage with Masters level CPD. It became evident that there were tensions between government policy and the agenda of local authorities and that of the teachers themselves. Teachers were dismissing CPD at the outset and disengaging from it at other stages. However, the reasons for the disengagement and dismissal were more interesting. There were many teachers who felt that power relations between the head teacher and local authority created an air of coercion.

In the field of teachers' CPD, Gramsci's (1971) theory of hegemony can be seen in terms of how local authorities fund and promote CPD. The local authorities may have specific priorities or preferences for teachers' CPD. These may concur with the wishes of teachers; however, on many occasions they do not, and in several cases local authorities are able to control the only legitimate CPD available to teachers. This legitimacy is observed in the CPD programmes to which the local authorities grant accreditation. Accredited courses hold a value for teachers in terms of them being able to use the credits to accrue towards higher qualification. Similarly, head teachers demonstrate hegemony in terms of the type of CPD they allow teachers to access. The head teacher may need the staff of the school to engage in a certain type of CPD in order to fulfil the school improvement plan. However, in many circumstances, this conflicts with the needs or wishes of individual teachers, but given the head teacher's role within the establishment, they are able to control the legitimacy of the CPD within the school.

Applying Apple's theories of power (2000, 2004) to these situations, one can identify that the head teacher and local authority CPD agenda is not necessarily shared by the teachers, yet, in some cases, this agenda is promoted as the tradition. Similarly, in the case of the university, hegemonic practice can also be identified. A university may claim funding for each teacher who registers for CPD, and several teachers reported that significant amounts of money are transferred to a university for each of them who engage in accredited CPD. This practice has led many teachers to question the motivation for universities in registering teachers for accredited CPD programmes. For many, this questioning has led to them dismissing CPD.

Foucault's theory of power (Foucault, 1980) can be seen in evidence here in so far as the teachers are appropriating power by dismissing or disengaging from CPD. For example, many teachers adopt a controlling stance by dispensing with CPD, despite head teachers, local authorities and universities advising to them to the contrary. A practical example can be seen in the UK government initiative to introduce a new Masters degree in Teaching and Learning (MTL). In April 2010 the UK government offered funding for newly qualified teachers in the North West of England to complete the MTL, and this course was fully funded and developed by a consortium of universities to be delivered in the work place. Yet, despite the fees being paid, and the flexibility of the delivery, the majority of teachers chose not to engage in the MTL and declined to register. Teachers view CPD as an option, as opposed to being something that is mandatory and in so doing exercise their own choice.

For those that did pursue CPD, Foucault's assertion that knowledge and power are inextricably linked (1972) applies: the knowledge that teachers develop via both professional development and classroom practice serves to underpin decisions that they make. For example, in improving their knowledge by taking part in CPD programmes, and potentially gaining higher qualifications, teachers can gain access to positions within schools that enable them to be able to hold power, or status, make decisions and influence policy and practice. Several teachers who had engaged with accredited CPD did so as they felt it would have a positive impact on the way they were seen by colleagues and parents. One teacher in particular said that once he had completed a Masters degree, the head teacher, his colleagues and parents would take him more seriously as a professional. He felt that having a Masters degree signifies a higher level of professional identity and status. Goodson (2003, p. 18) has determined that 'the university provides a major legitimating base for professional status'. He further argues strongly for a greater collaboration between university faculties and teachers in schools in order that teachers have access to research and knowledge. The head teachers responding to my research would be concerned with the practicalities of this model, however; there would be an issue for many in respect of being able to provide cover for teachers to access university provision, for instance. Many head teachers are anxious that the time needed by teachers to carry out study for a Masters degree, as well as other professional development activities, is unrealistic given their teaching commitments and the extra curriculum activities that they are often involved in. Contrastingly, Mahony and Hextall (2000) advocate that a clear identity for teaching is reliant on teachers having a commitment to constant professional development. However, my research has revealed that the nature of the professional development remains a bone of contention in many instances.

The Relevance and Effectiveness of Using Theory

Using theory has provided an opportunity to support and underpin some of the issues identified by my research. By applying it to teachers' approach to their CPD, it has been possible to identify that power relations can have a significant impact on how teachers develop and how they are seen by others. By identifying the theory of hegemony and comparing this to the power relations both within schools and across local authorities, universities and schools, one can shed some light on competing agendas and tensions within the CPD arena. Similarly, Foucault's theory on the distribution of power can give some credence to the actions of those teachers who have had the confidence to dismiss CPD.

When using Goodson's theoretical approach to teachers' professional identity, I have been able to gain a clearer understanding that knowledge accrued over a period of time and from both inside and outside the classroom serves to indicate how teachers see themselves professionally. Furthermore, it is possible to use this theory to develop thinking around the type of professional development that seems to impact on, and influence, teachers' approach to their decisions to engage with developmental activities. This then seems to act as a basis for how teachers locate their identity. It may also offer some understanding to the conflict and tensions that arise between the different agendas for teachers' professional development.

In using a theory, it is important to acknowledge that there may be competing theories that are equally valid. Also, that the theory serves to offer suggestion and reason, that it is not something that needs to be followed by the letter. Instead, an understanding of theory might offer the opportunity to construct arguments for powerful organizations to work collaboratively for the benefit of teachers' professional development.

Summary Conclusions and Recommendations

The discovery of the appropriate theories

There are other theories that could be adopted in this situation. Weber's bureaucracy theory (Weber, 1968) for example, focuses on power being attached to the office rather than the person and is evident in hierarchical organizations, and there are correlations with my research in that the local authorities, schools and universities have clear hierarchies. However, I chose not to pursue Weber as his theory seemed best suited to looking at offices within a single organization, and my research needed me to consider several organizations working in collaboration where there was no parity across hierarchy design.

The ease or difficulties with understanding the theories

The main issue for me was to identify whether to start with the theory or to start with the data. As a new researcher I was unsure, and armed with much literature on different theories, it was difficult not to try to make my research 'fit' with one of the many theories. I had long conversations with colleagues, fellow students and managers, in the vain hope that they would be able to somehow clarify my uncertainties, but it was only I who could accomplish this, I knew what teachers were saying in terms of CPD, and therefore I needed to organize my thoughts. Once I had interpreted the data – that was the turning point for me – I began to understand the match with the theory and I began to understand how I needed to apply it. I also developed the confidence to be able to select appropriate theories and disregard others.

The difficulties of application to data and texts

Texts can vary enormously in terms of the emphasis and perspectives they apply to the same situation. The process of finding suitable texts is lengthy and often daunting, as there are so many texts available. I never did find an easy or quick way of doing this, and spent many hours reading papers, journals and excerpts from books in order to build my own library. I did, however, develop an electronic database of references, which I found invaluable. I also visited libraries with a digital audio recorder and recorded spoken book excerpts and references that I could download later to my electronic database. I am confident that this saved me valuable hours. The data were vast and disparate, which posed a problem of storage and organization and I'm still not sure whether I organized this effectively. Once I had written the transcripts and interpreted the data, my study started to get serious and I began to feel that the research would have some real meaning. I feel that I did not manage the data well in the early stages. I did not anticipate the large amount of paper that results from an ethnographic approach. With the benefit of hindsight, I would have developed a more organized process for managing the data.

What the application of the theories revealed

The concept of hegemony enabled me to offer reasons for the way in which teachers perceived the power relations that impacted on their CPD. It seems that hegemonic practices are at play in schools, local authorities and universities and, where this is apparent to teachers, it affects the way in which they engage in CPD.

Goodson's concept of what goes on in teachers' lives affects their professional life and their identity in school helped me to better understand the complex area of teacher identity. I believe that teachers' professional identity is influenced by their professional development and their status. For example, many teachers engage with accredited CPD as they feel that obtaining a Masters degree will have a positive impact on their status with colleagues, managers and parents.

How the absence of these theories might have impaired understanding

Without a theoretical framework to support this research, it would have been difficult to make connections, and comparisons between teachers' approach to CPD. It would also have been difficult to know that I needed to look into the motivations of the different organizations. Silverman (2000, p. 86) has clarified the issue of theory as 'arranging a set of concepts to define and explain some phenomenon'.

The limitations of the theories

Theories cannot be a 'one size fits all' overarching principle. Situations are likely to require the use of part of a theory or parts of different theories. Theories need to be able to be interpreted and these inter-pretations could vary.

Reflection and recommendations of the experience

I am a very different person for living through this research experience. The experience has enabled me to understand better the discourse of teachers' professional development and also, how organizations such as universities, local authorities and schools collaborate (or not, in some cases) for the purpose of providing professional development opportunities for teachers. I no longer take for granted values and assumptions, as there is usually something happening behind them. That 'something' is often the crux of the issue, and it is that which provides such rich opportunities for researchers to investigate.

Recommended further reading

The following texts are useful in providing an opportunity to gain a fuller understanding of the sociological theories addressed in this chapter. They also offer the opportunity to cross-reference the theories and to identify how the ideas of sociological theorists impact on and influence our society.

Layder, D. (2006) *Understanding Social Theory*, 2nd edn, Sage, London.
Marsh, I. (ed.) (2002) *Theory and Practice in Sociology*, Pearson, London.
Ritzer, G. and Goodman, D. (2004) *Modern Sociological Theory*, McGraw Hill, London.

References

Apple, M. (2000) *Official Knowledge: Democratic Education in a Conservative Age*, Routledge, London.
Apple, M. (2004) *Ideology and Curriculum*, 3rd edn, Routledge, London.

Arthur, L., Marland, M., Pill, A. and Rea, T. (2006) Postgraduate professional development for teachers: motivational and inhibiting factors affecting the completion of awards. *Journal of In-Service Education*, 32 (2), 201–219.

Blandford, S. (2000) *Managing Professional Development in Schools*, Routledge, London.

Couldron, J. and Smith, R. (1999) Active location in teachers' construction of their professional identities. *Journal of Curriculum Studies*, 1999 (31), 711–726.

DCSF (2008) *Being the Best for our Children: Realising Talent for Teaching and Learning*, DCSF, London.

DfEE (2000) *Professional Development: Support for Teaching and Learning* (Questionnaire and summary, 0009/2000), DfEE, London.

DfEE (2001) *Learning and Teaching: A Strategy for Professional Development* (Green Paper), DfEE, London.

DfES (2005) *Higher Standards, Better Schools for All* (White Paper), DfES, London.

Draper, I. (2000) Performance management: in from the cold. *Managing Schools Today*, November/December, 33–35.

Foucault, M. (1972) *The Archaeology of Knowledge*, Pantheon, New York.

Foucault, M. (1980) *Power/Knowledge: Selected Interviews and other Writings 1972–1977*, Pantheon, New York.

Goodson, I. (2003) *Professional Knowledge – Professional Lives*, Open University Press, Maidenhead.

Goodson, I. and Ball, S. (eds) (1985) *Teachers' Lives and Careers*, Open University Press, London.

Gramsci, A. (1971) *Selections from the Prison Notebooks*, New Left Books, New York.

Gray, S. and Denley, P. (2005) The new professionalism – rhetoric and reality? A view from the quagmire. Paper presented at the British Educational Research Association Annual conference 14–17 September, http://www.leeds.ac.uk/educol/documents/143808.htm (accessed 12 May 2011).

Layder, D. (2006) *Understanding Social Theory*, 2nd edn, Sage, London.

Mahony, P. and Hextall, I. (2000) *Reconstructing Teaching: Standards, Performance and Accountability*, Routledge, London.

Marsh, I. (ed.) (2002) *Theory and Practice in Sociology*, Pearson, London.

Ritzer, G. and Goodman, D. (2004) *Modern Sociological Theory*, McGraw Hill, London.

Silverman, D. (2000) *Doing Qualitative Research: A Practical Handbook*, Sage, Thousand Oaks, CA.

Slattery, M. (2003) *Key Ideas in Sociology*, Nelson Thornes, London.

Weber, M. (1968) *Economy and Society: An Outline of Intermediate Sociology*, Bedminister Press, New York.

Whitty, G. (1997) Marketisation, the State and the reformation of the teaching profession, in *Education: Culture, Economy, Society* (eds A. Halsey, H. Lauder, P. Brown and A. Wells), Oxford University Press, Oxford.

Williams, R. (1974) Television. New York. Schocken.

4

The Process of Technology Learning

Applying Bruner's Theory on Play, Discovery and Cultural Learning to the Acquisition of ICT Capability

Paula Beer

Key Theoretical Approach in this Chapter: Jerome Bruner's Theories on Play and Discovery Learning

This chapter examines Jerome Bruner's theories of play and discovery learning and how they can be applied to the acquisition of Information Communication Technology (ICT) capability in young children. It discusses the process of investigating Bruner's vast body of work and distils the areas relevant to an on-going research project that aimed to re-create Sylva, Bruner and Genova's 1974 experiment (reported in Sylva, Bruner and Genova, 1976) to analyse the role of play in the problem solving of 3–5-year-olds; a recreation that involved the replacement of a manual chalk retrieval task with a computer-based task. As well as updating the project from manual to digital tasks, I intended to recreate Bruner's own later extension of his discovery and play learning principles, to include discussion and negotiation between pupils.

Applying Theory to Educational Research: An Introductory Approach with Case Studies,
First Edition. Edited by J. Adams, M. Cochrane and L. Dunne.

Key texts

Bruner, J. (1960) *The Process of Education*, Harvard University Press, London.
Bruner, J. (1996) *The Culture of Education*, Harvard University Press, London.
Sylva, K., Bruner, J. and Genova, P. (1976) The role of play in the problem-solving of children 3–5 years old, in *Play: Its Role in Development and Evolution* (eds J. Bruner, A. Jolly, and K. Sylva), Basic Books, New York, pp. 244–257.

Introduction to the Research Project

I decided to conduct a research project that used Bruner's theories on discovery learning and play (Bruner, 1960, 1976) which are based on the premise that children become better learners when given the opportunity to discover principles for themselves to 'develop an attitude towards learning and inquiry, toward guessing and hunches' (Bruner, 1960, p. 20) and ideally to play with equipment prior to being given a task (Bruner, 1976). This freedom through play enables children to use their past and present experiences to construct their learning with less frustration and more focus. Bruner worked as Director on the Oxford Development Preschool Program with the researchers Paul Genova and Kathy Sylva, which over three years involved him in a number of experiments. Throughout his writings Bruner returns to one particular play experiment a number of times, and it seems that it came to exemplify his belief in the theories of discovery learning and play. Bruner's (1960, 1976) theories provided the theoretical framework that helped the design of my research project and not the analysis of data, as the project was on going at the time of writing.

In this chapter I argue, from my own experience as an ICT teacher, trainer and project manager, that ICT education is important and that children should be encouraged to discover ICT through playful negotiation with peers. The use of Bruner's (1960, 1976) theories enabled me to think more deeply about the subject. The origin of my research idea was my own teaching experience during which I observed very young pupils seeking out animation software on the network and becoming very adept at its use without any adult intervention or support. However, having read Bruner's (1960, 1976) theories, my thoughts on the matter expanded to incorporate discovery learning and play theory. I have also been inspired by the 'Hole in the Wall' experiment (Mitra *et al.*, 2005). In 1999 Sugata Mitra inserted an Internet-enabled computer in an outer wall of the National Indian Institute of Technology premises that was made available for the use of children from the adjoining impoverished area of Kalkaji, New Delhi. He found that with no adult guidance the children were able to teach themselves and their peers how to browse the Internet and use the basic functions of the interface. Mitra was particularly interested in technology being used to teach children who otherwise had little or no access to education. My interest, however, is sparked by his findings that the slum children progressed at a rate similar to those in Indian technology schools, and faster than those in mainstream Indian schools. It appears that the children progressed due to the conditions that enabled them to compare and discuss their findings, and to play in an non-pressurized environment (Mitra *et al.*, 2005).

At the time of writing, ICT and primary education in England are controversial areas in which to be involved. In 2009, Jim Rose released a report reviewing primary education, which states that the central aim of the review was to answer the questions 'what should the curriculum contain and how should the content and the teaching of it change to foster children's different and developing abilities during primary years?' (Rose, 2009, p. 2). Rose is very explicit about the importance of ICT to the curriculum and in the executive summary of the final report Rose states: 'In this day and age, the primary curriculum also needs to give serious attention to building children's capability with information technology' (Rose, 2009, p. 2). Also in 2009, a three-year wide-ranging independent enquiry (*The Cambridge Review*) into the condition and future of primary education in England was completed (Alexander, 2010). While both reports accept the need for ICT to be part of the curriculum, Rose (2009) places ICT as one of the key features of the curriculum, advocating strengthening the teaching and learning of ICT to enable children to be independent and confident users of technology by the end of their primary education. In contrast, the *Cambridge Review* considers that although ICT will reach across the entire curriculum it need not be taught as a discrete subject. Alexander's (2010) team regard ICT more as a tool to support the curriculum rather than an 'essential for learning and life' (Rose, 2009, p. 54). In both cases there is a lack of recognition of the role of play in ICT capability development, a problem that my study seeks to address.

The UK's government inspectorate of education, Ofsted's (The Office for Standards in Education, Children's Services and Skills) report into ICT (Ofsted, 2009) describes an environment in which transferable skills are not taught and teachers only involve children in aspects of ICT with which they are comfortable themselves. Of primary teaching, Ofsted says that the curriculum was not well balanced: 'Teachers tended to give more attention to those aspects of ICT where they themselves felt confident' and that 'At best, teachers integrated ICT carefully into the curriculum and it was helping to raise standards in other subjects'. (Ofsted, 2009, p. 4). Of secondary teaching, Ofsted says 'Teachers gave too much emphasis to teaching students to use particular software applications rather than helping them to acquire genuinely transferable skills' (Ofsted, 2009, p. 4).

So the policy stage is set. This evidence suggests that there is a need for the way we teach ICT to change, but how? Surely all educational research begins with a researcher having a suspicion that there is another way to do things? The specific inspiration for my project came from an experiment conducted in the 1970s by Kathy Sylva, Jerome Bruner and Paul Genova, who examined the role of play in the problem solving of very young children. Their experiment involved a team working with individual children aged from 3 to 5 who were challenged to retrieve a coloured piece of chalk from behind a transparent plastic screen using a combination of sticks and clamps. Prior to this challenge, each of the children was given training procedures. Each group was shown how a clamp worked, but only the first group was actually shown how to clamp sticks together to make a longer implement to retrieve the chalk. A second group was given free time to play with the equipment and a third group had no further opportunity. Unsurprisingly, this third group achieved the desired outcome the fewest times, but what interested the researchers was that the two other groups achieved the outcome with the same frequency of success. Further still, the researchers found that the 'play-group' were more incremental and tenacious in their approach. They persisted with the task even when their initial attempts were unsuccessful and they eventually solved the problem. The 'play-group' resisted frustration and did not give up because 'they were playing' (Sylva, Bruner and Genova, 1976, p. 16). In thinking about my research, I considered that perhaps the improved problem-solving capabilities demonstrated by the 'play-group' could be harnessed in some way to improve children's acquisition of transferable skills, and to address Ofsted's (2009) criticisms and concerns.

Theories Explained and their Use Justified in the Context of this Research Project

Bruner (1996, p. 89) helpfully pointed out that 'a theory that works is altogether a miracle: it idealizes our varying observations of the world in a form so stripped down as to be kept easily in mind, permitting us to see the grubby particulars as exemplars of a general case'. In this case the theories that I am attempting to use are Bruner's theories of play and discovery learning. In many of Bruner's works he makes reference to the importance of the role of play. In 1976 he contributed to a collection of essays on play in humans and animals, in which he (and colleagues) list a number of characteristics of play, which I shall paraphrase as follows (Sylva, Bruner and Genova, 1976, p. 244). Play is:

- the dominance of means over ends;
- practice in assembling bits of behaviour (or means) into unusual sequences;
- about lessening the risk of failure;
- about providing a moratorium on frustration;
- about providing the invitation to the possibilities inherent in things and events; and
- voluntary.

According to Bruner (1976), what distinguishes play from other activities is the transfer of focus from that which can be experienced to that which should be achieved. He acknowledges that play does have goals but that, when engaged in play, the 'means' activity which precedes the 'ends' is more important. Being released from the 'tyranny of the tightly held goal, the player can substitute, elaborate and invent' (Sylva, Bruner and Genova, 1976, p. 244).

I feel that this element of play is particularly significant as it manages to respect a requirement for an aim (the 'ends') while showing that the method of getting there (the 'means') is more important. For example, in a netball match, if the 'ends' is winning the match and affording league points, this can be achieved by the absence of the opposing team at a fixture. For a netball player there is no satisfaction in this as the 'means' (the playing of the game) is more important than the 'ends' (winning the game). In the context of my research project, the ICT task that I give to the children must be designed with this in mind. However, the means, which in Bruner's experiment had been the use of sticks and clamps, need to be laid out and accessible without reference to the ends (retrieval of chalk) in order for the play element to be realized. One only has to watch young children at play with the most basic of toys to understand this feature of play. In order to allow the children to 'assemble bits of the behaviour' the equipment must be laid out and various possibilities, not just the intended one, need to be available to them. In a computer-based task this translates to the child having free play access to the computer interface. In thinking carefully about my own research design, I reflected and drew upon the following aspects of Sylva, Bruner and Genova's, (1976) characteristics of play, as outlined above:

- *Play is lessening the risk of failure*: During the intended play phase of the activity it is necessary to ensure that the pupils understand that they are free to try things out and that success or failure is not an intended element of the activity.
- *Play provides a moratorium on frustration*: In this context a moratorium means a period of time in which an activity is not allowed. Therefore, although frustration is a part of life, during a period of play it is not allowed. Of course there is some frustration in playing but the majority of the time at play should be frustration free. In the context of my research, this would involve avoidance of the frustration of not achieving an externally set goal. Therefore, an external goal (such as 'reach the chalk') should be avoided during the period of play. In order to respect this feature of play, the activities should provide enough feedback and interactivity that their usage is absorbing and also appreciative, so that the end can happen spontaneously rather than in a forced way. In a computer-based task this would involve the child playing on the interface before being given a goal.
- *Play provides the invitation to the possibilities inherent in things and events*: This is similar to a man walking to work contrasted with a man walking for the sake of it; he is free to notice his surroundings. His surroundings become an open invitation to all that is possible. The activity should be flexible and open enough to provide children to play

alone or together and travel down paths with no particular end. It should be inviting!

- *Play is voluntary*: Possibly the biggest challenge of the project is putting children into an environment and imagining that their participation is voluntary. At this stage, to keep to this intention, I plan to allow children to play on the ICT interface but not to tell them that they have to do so. Interestingly, Bruner's way of illustrating when an activity is not play is to say 'The sulky child forced to "play" a maths games by his teacher is not really at play' (Sylva, Bruner and Genova, 1976, p. 244). During the original experiment, the researchers were given very stringent instructions on uniform responses to children who were not participating in the task. These were described as 'hints' and none of these involved coercing or forcing the children to participate in the task.

Primary teaching varies enormously from discovery, teacher led, collaboration to the didactic following of scripts. The type of learning that Bruner describes involves children discovering fundamental principles for themselves in order to develop an attitude to learning in which they try things out, make mistakes and persist, because ultimately the process itself is enjoyable. In his 1961 paper 'The act of discovery', Bruner describes the purpose and effect of discovery learning. His hypothesis is that it is only through actually attempting to solve a problem do we become good problem solvers (Bruner, 1961). This presented an interesting challenge for me, as I had believed that children should be free to prioritize the means over the end in order to be truly playing. However, what I am trying to achieve is a period of target-free play, combined with a problem solve, to develop discovery learning. In addition, Bruner states that this sort of pursuit not only develops great learners but also renders the learnt information more readily available when required (Bruner, 1961, p. 411). My hope is that by designing an activity that requires the children to investigate principles of the interface for themselves they will become capable learners able to problem solve.

The Application of Theory to the Research

In Bruner's original experiment the task was a retrieval of a piece of chalk from behind a screen using sticks and clamps. In order to transform the three-dimensional chalk task into a computer-based task I would need to choose an appropriate piece of software that was age appropriate and immediately accessible to seven-year-olds. Resnick *et al.* (2009, p. 63) describe their approach to designing an ICT program as an attempt to satisfy Papert's (1980) aim that programming languages should have a low floor, where it is easy to get started, and a high ceiling, with opportunities to create increasingly complex projects over time. I agreed with Resnick *et al.* (2009, p. 63), who considered that the floor needed to be made lower still, through using a programming language which was 'more tinkerable'. The software that I planned to use is built around the idea that play and discovery are the route to learning. It uses two-dimensional representations of blocks which, when logically placed, snap together to create executable programs. I was very aware of the move from a three-dimensional play activity to a two dimensional activity and wanted to keep some feeling of building to link the software activity with the chalk retrieval task. In addition the software is designed to be collaborative and has a very involved online community that share ideas and alter each other's creations to make new ones. Resnick *et al.* (2009, p. 65) explain that educational software needs to be linked to a community who share and support it to enable it to succeed. This again ties in with the idea of learning as a social activity.

Bruner (1966) believes that learning is an active process during which children construct their knowledge from past and present experiences. My research project is based on the idea of applying Bruner's theory of discovery learning but updating the research to take account of Bruner's later theories on the culture of education. In Bruner's 1986 publication *Actual Minds, Possible Worlds* he reflects on his own journey. He explains that he had previously written in depth about solo discovery learning but since wished to extend this idea as he had come to recognize that 'learning in most settings is a communal activity, a sharing of the culture' (Bruner, 1986, p. 127). More importantly, Bruner relates this progression from solo to community knowledge development through negotiating and sharing as a 'step en route to becoming a member of the adult society in which ones lives out one's life' (Bruner, 1986, p. 127). Gardner (2001, p. 94) explains how Bruner developed throughout his career coming to the conclusion (in *The Culture of Education*) that 'learning exists amidst the interactions and joint constructions of students attempting to construct knowledge'. It is this negotiation and joint constructions that I wish to reflect in my research.

The Relevance and Effectiveness of Using Theory

Interestingly, Bruner (2006, p. 37) himself felt that theory is often misunderstood: 'It is in effect a heuristic or guide that gets you from where you happen to find yourself to where it is you want to be'. He makes an interesting parallel between the design of a 'sloop' using theories of aerodynamics and hydrodynamics and the desire to educate. When selecting an educational theory, Bruner (2006, p. 37) stresses the importance of understanding 'what you want to use the knowledge for'. I wanted to use the knowledge to contribute to the field of ICT education and felt that having a historical perspective for my research would provide some direction.

To apply Bruner's theory of play and discovery learning (using his own gentle guidance), I needed to think about my own research and why I was beginning the enquiry. I wanted to find out if what I thought to be 'true' was true or verifiable: that is, if children are encouraged to play together with ICT applications they become better learners of ICT and capable of problem solving. In a sense this was my hypothesis. I needed to think about what it was that I was investigating and how I might test my hypothesis. In the same way that Sylva, Bruner and Genova did in 1974, I needed to design certain 'treatments'. In this case, a treatment is what happens to the child prior to being given the problem to solve. In the case of the Sylva, Bruner and Genova's experiment the three treatments were described (1976, p. 247) as play, observe principle and no treatment. An equivalent in the case of a problem solve involving software would be for the groups to be introduced briefly to the program interface then separated with the eventual aim of creating a 'dancing sprite', as shown in Table 4.1. (In this context a sprite is an animated figure that can be chosen or created by the user). In addition to see if there is a benefit of collaboration, the children will be playing with a partner in the play-group.

Knowledge of Bruner's theories enabled me to recreate and adapt the original experiment conducted by Sylva, Bruner and Genova (1976). Keeping Bruner's theories of play, discovery and collaboration in mind furnished me with the means to develop meaningful and connected treatments to enable me to plan to test out my hypothesis on learning, problem solving and the use of ICT.

Table 4.1   'Treatment' groups.

Name	Nature of experience prior to presentation of problem 1974	Nature of experience prior to presentation of problem Present Day	Free use of program interface/ sticks and clamps
Play	Adult demonstrates one clamp tightened onto middle of one long stick Child allowed free play with 10 blue sticks and 7 clamps	Adult demonstrates basics of ICT programme interface. Introduction to sprites stage, scripts, costumes, sounds. Child allowed free play *with a partner* and the program interface	Yes
Observe principle	Adult demonstrates one clamp tightened onto middle of one long stick Adult demonstrates construction of elated tool by rigidly joining two long sticks with clamps	Adult demonstrates basics of program interface. Introduction to sprites, stage, scripts, costumes, sounds. Adult demonstrates development of dancing sprite program	No
No treatment	Adult demonstrates one clamp tightened onto middle of one long stick	Adult demonstrates basics of program interface. Introduction to sprites, stage, scripts, costumes, sounds	No

Summary Conclusions and Recommendations

The discovery of the appropriate theories

I came across Bruner's theories when discussing research ideas with a colleague. I had heard a radio programme about the 'Hole in the Wall' project Mitra *et al.* (2005) in which it was clear that children had learned through pressure-free collaboration and play. My colleague suggested that I look at the work of Jerome Bruner, as it seemed to tie in well and give the possible research a more theoretical basis.

The ease or difficulties with understanding the theories

It has occurred to me while examining educational theories that one of the main problems in applying such theories is their complexity and sometimes nebulous descriptions. However, in the case of Bruner's theories, actually understanding the theories felt relatively straightforward. Nevertheless, grappling with the ideas and then staying true to the theories is a further challenge. In addition, there is the added dimension of Bruner having developed his theories during his lifetime to be considered. I wanted to understand how Bruner progressed throughout the span of his working life (Takaya, 2008).

The difficulties of application to data and texts

My original intention had been to create a straight computerized simulation of the stick, clamp and chalk experiment. However, I suspected that children who were of an age to be able to operate a computer might find such an activity too simplistic. Having decided to conduct the research with seven-year-old children I resolved to create a short activity in the ICT program which would be simple but interesting and motivational. Another challenge was overcoming the barrier of a program–computer interface. The original experiment did involve children in learning a new skill, followed by a problem solve. The new skill in the Bruner experiment was the manipulation of a clamp, and this is demonstrated to each of the three treatment groups. In my research the equivalent skill would be learning the interface. In order to stay true to Bruner's experiment, I resolved to aim to teach the interface through demonstration to all the children. This would enable a base line of interface knowledge from which the three 'treatments' could begin. The research will be with seven-year-old children who are (according to Piaget, 2001) in the Concrete Operational Stage, which begins around the age of seven and finishes before the child is twelve. During this time, according to this theory children begin to think logically about concrete events, but find it challenging to understand abstract or hypothetical concepts. Bruner sees development as more overlapping and explains it in terms of modes of representation. The first mode, enactive, is concerned with learning through movement and manipulation, the second is iconic learning, through pictures and the third and most challenging is symbolic learning through language and symbols (Bruner, 1966). So an ICT interface that requires some logical thinking, but a limited amount of symbolic representation, would seem ideally suited to the task.

What the application of the theories revealed

Applying the theory of play to my research provided a framework for the type of educational activity that can be called 'play'. The five features of play mentioned earlier enabled me to think more deeply about what can be called 'play' and what this gives the 'player'.

How the absence of these theories might have impaired understanding

If I had not been aware of Bruner's later development of theories to accommodate collaborative learning I may have stayed with the original model inspired by the Sylva, Bruner and Genova (1976) paper, in which children essentially worked alone. The revision of his theory to harness collaboration was very useful. In *Actual Minds Possible Worlds* (1986) Bruner describes how he linked his idea of children discovering on their own to the idea that a child must make his knowledge his own within a community.

The limitations of the theories

Bruner's educational theories are not located in any specific social context. One criticism of the original Sylva, Bruner and Genova experiment might be that while they do mention that the children are predominantly white and middle class there is no attempt to address this and seek out a wider community representation (Sylva, Bruner and Genova, 1976, p. 257). The school that I intend to use for my research is predominantly working class and white with a small number of children from ethnic backgrounds.

Reflection and recommendations of the experience

I would recommend wide reading from original texts on any chosen subject. A temptation can be to go to secondary texts and this is also important to see how others have applied the theorist's work. But finding the root of the theorist's beliefs is, I believe, essential. Why do theorists think what they think; what research were they involved in? Wider reading also raises some interesting links between theorists. For example I discovered that Howard Gardner was a student of Bruner (Gardner, 2001). In 1983 Gardner developed the theory of multiple intelligences (Gardner, 2006). He was one of the first people to reject the idea that intelligence was, as an entity, singular and measurable by an IQ test.

Recommended further reading

http://www.hole-in-the-wall.com/MIE.html. Sugata Mitra and team's website showing the breadth of their research into 'minimally invasive education'.

Palmer, J. (2001) *Fifty Modern Thinkers on Education: From Piaget to the Present*, Routledge, London. A useful summary of theorists.

References

Alexander, R. (2010) *Children, their World, their Education: Final Report and Recommendations of the Cambridge Primary Review*, Routledge, Abingdon.

Bruner, J. (1960) *The Process of Education*, Harvard University Press, London.

Bruner, J. (1961) The act of discovery. *Harvard Educational Review*, 31 (1), 21–32.

Bruner, J. (1966) *Toward a Theory of Instruction*, Belknap Press, Cambridge, MA.

Bruner, J. (1976) Introduction, in *Play: Its Role in Development and Evolution* (eds J. Bruner, A. Jolly, and K. Sylva), Basic Books, New York, 25–42.

Bruner, J. (1986) *Actual Minds, Possible Worlds*, Harvard University Press, London.

Bruner, J. (1996) *The Culture of Education*, Harvard University Press, London.

Bruner, J. (2006) The functions of teaching (an address delivered at Rhode Island College of Education, April 13, 1959), in *In Search of Pedagogy, vol. 1* (ed. J. Bruner), Routledge, Oxford, pp. 31–39.

Gardner, H. (2001) 'Jerome S. Bruner' in *Fifty Modern Thinkers on Education: From Piaget to the Present* (ed. J. Palmer), Routledge, London, 131–142.

Gardner, H. (2006) *Multiple Intelligences: New Horizons*, Basic Books, New York.

Mitra, S. 'Hole in the Wall', http://www.hole-in-the-wall.com (accessed 7 December 2010).

Mitra, S., Dangwal, R., Chatterjee, S., Jha, S., Bisht, R. and Kapur, P. (2005) Acquisition of computer literacy on shared public computers: children and the 'Hole in the wall'. *Australasian Journal of Educational Technology*, 21 (3), 407–426.

Office for Standards in Education (Ofsted) (2009) *The Importance of ICT: Information and Communication Technology in Primary and Secondary Schools 2005/2008*. HMI 70035, OFSTED Publications, London.

Palmer, J. (2001) *Fifty Modern Thinkers on Education: From Piaget to the Present*, Routledge, London.

Papert, S. (1980) *Mindstorms: Children, Computers, and Powerful Ideas*, Basic Books, New York.

Piaget, J. (2001) *The Psychology of Intelligence*, Routledge, New York.

Resnick, M., Maloney, J., Monroy-Hernandez, A.Y. *et al.* (2009) Scratch: programming for all. *Communications of the ACM*, 52 (11), 60–67.

Rose, J. (2009) *Independent Review of the Primary Curriculum*, DCFS No. 499, Department for Children, Schools and Families, Nottingham.

Sylva, K., Bruner, J. and Genova, P. (1976) The role of play in the problem-solving of children 3–5 years old, in *Play: Its Role in Development and Evolution* (eds J. Bruner, A. Jolly, and K. Sylva), Basic Books, New York, pp. 244–257.

Takaya, K. (2008) Jerome Bruner's theory of education: from early Bruner to later Bruner. *Interchange*, 39 (1), 1–19.

Part II

Emergent Voices

Accounts by Researchers Becoming Familiar with the Use of Theory

Introduction

Part I presented research undertaken by experienced educational practitioners who were relatively new to research. It was mainly concerned with different aspects of professional training or career development. The chapters in Part II are written by researcher-practitioners who have some experience of applying theoretical frameworks to their research and whose projects are established, on going or completed. Becoming more confident in engaging with and applying theory is part of the research process and, as these chapters indicate, theory can help researchers to take 'risks' in attempting to make sense of their data and overall research methodology and to push analysis further. The chapters presented here show how theory can consolidate and clarify, or unsettle and change a research project.

Rob Foster's chapter 'Teachers' Professional Identity: Theoretical Perspectives on Workplace Learning in the Teaching Context' focuses on the context of trainee teachers on a graduate teacher training programme and what motivated them to stay on the course. Foster looked at situations where learning took place in three contexts outside that of the traditional classroom. The chapter presents a somewhat similar question to that raised by Karen Castle's chapter in Part I about power and status theories in teachers' professional development, but it takes a wholly different approach. Foster's findings led him to recognize the significance to the learning process of the working context. This further led to theories about the nature of work-based learning and particularly to Lave and Wenger's (1991) situated learning theory to explain and clarify why the participants felt comfortable in what they were doing.

Applying Theory to Educational Research: An Introductory Approach with Case Studies, First Edition. Edited by J. Adams, M. Cochrane and L. Dunne.
© 2012 John Wiley & Sons, Ltd. Published 2012 by John Wiley & Sons, Ltd.

The process of theoretical engagement may be arduous but it opens up possibilities for understanding inequities between individuals and groups. In 'Children's University Aspirations and the Effects of Cultural and Social Capital', Matt Cochrane similarly shows how the use of theory can clarify data and led to a meaningful interpretation. In Cochrane's project, Bourdieu's theories of habitus and forms of capital were used to analyse the ideological constructs that give rise to the social experiences that contribute to identity formation. The concept of habitus enabled Cochrane to see how young peoples' statements about potential career paths and their experiences matched the concept. The conceptual framework enabled him to identify the connections between the various statements the participants made in their interviews. The research suggested that young people understood that there was a system of rules and practices they had to negotiate, and while they were willing to negotiate these, their actual choices were limited or constricted, and therefore inequitable.

There are many established and recognizable theories in the social sciences and no theory is likely to be a perfect 'fit' for a research project. In Chapter 7, 'Finding Theory through Collaborative Research', Clare Woolhouse explores how Michel Foucault's (1982) notion of power/knowledge was tentatively engaged with and subsequently applied in a study about teaching assistant identity carried out by three researchers from differing epistemological positionings. The researchers involved in the project reached agreement by trying different ways to coherently explain themselves to each other and to work through and address problems. It was in the process of exploring and discussing how to overcome problems that the researchers came to a deeper understanding of theory. Woolhouse shows how Foucault's theory gave the researchers alternative ways of thinking about the data and how, through collaboration, they were able to consolidate their understandings, approach and subsequent interpretation. The researchers found that discussing different interpretations in detail was extremely beneficial and they also came to recognize that there is no 'right' way to work with or apply theory.

As stated earlier, encountering theory, or new ideas, can lead to disruption and change in the research process. Linda Dunne shows how her work was influenced by systems of discourse and power, as theorized by Foucault, in her chapter: 'How Applying a Discourse-Based Approach to Investigate Inclusion Changed a Research Project and a Way of Thinking'. Dunne used discourse theories to explore the concealed interests and power relations that underpin seemingly liberal political policies, in this case the UK government's policy on inclusion. She traces the political trajectory of this particular concept and observes its transformation and distortion into policy. This moment was accompanied by a realignment of Dunne's thinking as a critical theorist, and she gives an account of the unsettling stages of that intellectual change and transformation.

References

Lave, J. and Wenger, E. (1991) *Situated Learning. Legitimate Peripheral Participation*, Cambridge University Press, Cambridge.

Foucault, M. (1982) The subject and the power, in *Michel Foucault: Beyond Structuralism and Hermeneutics* (eds H. Dreyfus and P. Rabinow), Harvester Press, Brighton, pp. 208–288.

5

Teachers' Professional Identity
Theoretical Perspectives on Workplace Learning in the Teaching Context

Rob Foster

Key Theoretical Approaches in this Chapter: Situated Learning, Non-Formal Learning and Tacit Knowledge in Professional Work

Jean Lave and Etienne Wenger's theory of situated learning argues a relational view of individuals and learning, that is, that learning is not so much the acquisition of knowledge by individuals as a process of social participation. The nature of the situation impacts significantly on the process. Michael Eraut analyses the concepts of non-formal learning and tacit knowledge and explores ways in which different kinds of tacit knowledge and modes of cognition are combined in professional work. Donald Schön develops the concepts of reflection-in-action and reflection-on-action. Reflection-in-action is essentially 'thinking on our feet', that is, drawing on our experiences to develop understanding and inform actions in the situation as it happens. Reflection-on-action, after the event, is the process of exploring why we acted as we did.

Applying Theory to Educational Research: An Introductory Approach with Case Studies, First Edition. Edited by J. Adams, M. Cochrane and L. Dunne.

Key texts

Eraut, M. (2000) Non-formal learning and tacit knowledge in professional work. *British Journal of Educational Psychology*, 70 (1), 113–136.
Lave, J. and Wenger, E. (1991) *Situated Learning. Legitimate Peripheral Participation*, Cambridge University Press, Cambridge.
Schön, D. (1983) *The Reflective Practitioner. How Professionals Think in Action*, Temple Smith, London.

Introduction to the Research Project

The research project explored the training and early employment experiences of teachers in England who trained through the employment-based Graduate Teacher Programme (GTP). In particular, the research sought to investigate and analyse the factors that contribute to the success of this training route in terms of entry to and retention in teaching. The research involved the collection of qualitative data in order to illuminate the findings from an initial, largely quantitative, survey. A purposive sample of respondents (65, some 10 per cent of respondents to the initial survey) was interviewed to enable some tentative analysis of possible trends and patterns in addition to illustrating and exemplifying the findings from the quantitative data.

Recruitment and retention data (e.g., CEER, 2004) have consistently indicated that a high proportion of trainees following employment-based routes in England enter teaching employment at the end of their training and are retained in teaching. The findings of this research are in line with the body of evidence (e.g., CEER, 2004, 2005; Ofsted, 2005; Stewart and Thornton, 2006) indicating that, compared to Higher Education-based postgraduate and undergraduate routes, the GTP has lower drop-out, higher recruitment into jobs and better retention rates in the early years of teaching. A total of 97 per cent of respondents to the initial survey had entered teaching either immediately upon or shortly after completion of their training. Most of the remaining 3 per cent were either seeking a teaching post or intended so to do in the future. The picture in terms of retention was similar, with 98 per cent still in post, most still in their first school which was also their training school.

The analysis looked initially at issues around the maturity and commitment to teaching of Graduate Teachers, for example, previous relevant experience and other factors influencing their decision to enter teaching. It then linked these starting points to the training experience itself, for example, quality of mentoring, professional status, balance between immersion in the practical realities of the job and opportunities for broader experience and reflection on learning. Further elements explored were: how well prepared to enter teaching did Graduate Teachers feel? To what extent was their decision to enter teaching and their retention in the profession influenced by their experience of work-based learning?

One striking feature to emerge from the research was the very high proportion of respondents with significant experience of schools and classrooms prior to commencing their training, for example as a classroom assistant, technician or unqualified teacher. The Ofsted inspection report (Ofsted, 2005) confirmed this finding. It can be argued that mature trainees, a very large percentage of whom have already had some experience of working in schools (not necessarily teaching in schools but technician and support roles) had made a carefully thought through and balanced decision to train as a teacher. They were aware of the reality of schools and still found it an attractive proposition. This echoed the findings of early research into the GTP (e.g., Foster, 2000; Griffiths, 2003) who came to the conclusion that relevant prior experience and learning was a crucial element in the success of many GTP trainees. For the great majority of respondents in this research, the training process had been a very positive experience, with the mentoring and support provided by the host school rated very highly. Graduate Teachers had a more positive view of themselves as professionals than trainees on other routes because they were regarded by colleagues and pupils as 'proper teachers' rather than as trainees. Some felt that their schools invested more time and effort to their support than was the case for, say, PGCE trainees (Post Graduate Certificate of Education students normally on a one year university training programme) on a six-week placement.

Theories Explained and their Use Justified in the Context of this Research Project

In terms of the research framework for analysing findings, my starting point was Schön's (1983) reflection-in-action and reflection-on-action. The former is sometimes described as 'thinking on our feet'. It involves looking at our experiences, connecting with our feelings and drawing on knowledge of theoretical models and frameworks. It requires us to develop new understandings that inform our actions in the situation as it unfolds:

> The practitioner allows himself to experience surprise, puzzlement, or confusion in a situation which he finds uncertain or unique. He reflects on the phenomenon before him, and on the prior understandings which have been implicit in his behaviour. He carries out an experiment which serves to generate both a new understanding of the phenomenon and a change in the situation. (Schön, 1983, p. 68)

Reflection-on-action takes place after the fact. We may record the incident in a write-up or discuss the situation with our supervisor. The process of reflecting-on-action allows time for us to analyse and explore how we acted or what was happening with other participants. This provides us with the opportunity to develop both questions and ideas about the practices and activities. It can clearly be argued that all teacher training programmes seek to develop reflective practitioners and it can further be argued that the university-based elements of such programmes, such as PGCE, ensure opportunities for the reflection-on-action dimension of Schön's model, so it was particularly important for me to investigate the extent to which the 'total immersion' model of the employment-based route enabled participants to undertake reflection-on-action (an issue to which I return in the next section).

Exploring the critiques of Schön's theories led me to the work of Eraut (2000). He makes a distinction between formal and non-formal learning but stresses that formal learning should not be seen as superior. Eraut points out that in many settings, learners experience a mix of formal and non-formal learning approaches. A key factor in learning is the extent to which there is an intention to learn. Eraut elaborates three categories of intentionality: deliberative learning (conscious, planned learning); reactive learning (near spontaneous – the level of intentionality will vary); and implicit learning (no intention to learn coupled with a lack of awareness at the time of learning). When considering the specific context of teacher education, Eraut makes the point that informal encounters and experiences serve as a vital, albeit under-assessed and under-theorized element of teacher learning. He argues that informal support in a time of need or emergency may be perceived as more important than the assistance that one might receive from assigned helpers or mentors. Many of the Graduate Teachers involved in this research indicated that they had received as much or more support from colleagues outside the formal training arrangements as from their mentors or heads of department.

It became apparent as the analysis progressed that Graduate Teachers saw themselves as members of 'communities of practice' and were experiencing situated learning, therefore the work of Lave and Wenger became central to the theoretical underpinning. The theory of situated learning argues that learning takes place through what is referred to as communities of practice. According to Wenger (1998), a community of practice defines itself in three dimensions: what it is about, how it functions, and what capability it has produced.

A community of practice involves much more than the technical knowledge or skill associated with undertaking some task. Members are involved in a set of relationships over time (Lave and Wenger, 1991, p. 98) and communities develop around things that matter to people (Wenger, 1998). Since the theory advocates learning through interaction, Lave and Wenger argue that the learning and interaction occur much more effectively through communities of practice by engaging learners in a situation where they actively interact and participate with one another to come up with solutions to the problems facing them. In this theory, knowledge is considered to be acquired through communication and collaboration with fellow learners in a situation that is moderated by the intention of the learners to acquire knowledge and develop solutions to the problem at hand. Communities of practice have a homogenous interest in their pursuit of knowledge and are governed or influenced by the environment in which they are situated. Therefore, participation in a community of practice is stated to be: 'Participation in an activity system about which participants share understanding concerning what they are doing and what that means in their lives and for their communities' (Lave and Wenger, 1991, p. 17).

The theory argues that members of the community are engaged in the realization of their interests and have to interact with other members and the environment of the interaction in order to learn. Wenger's later work (1998) further developed the notion that communities of practice are created over time by the sustained pursuit of shared interest.

The Application of Theory to the Research

Graduate Teachers are employees of their host schools (albeit on fixed-term training contracts) and therefore one of the key issues in the analysis of their training experiences is the extent to which the 'total immersion' model enables their training needs to be prioritized over the day-to-day management needs of the school. This is particularly relevant to consideration of

Schön's reflective practice and how far Graduate Teachers have opportunities for the kind of reflection envisaged in the Schön model. According to Eraut (2000), there exists a definitive problem in relation to time, that is, when time is particularly short, the decisions must be made in the immediate, which gives limited scope for reflection.

The evidence from this research is that much depends on whether Graduate Teachers are supernumerary rather than filling a teaching vacancy. In their comments about the quality of the training experience, respondents were very clear that it was hard for training to be successful in cases where trainees were used to fill teaching vacancies in the schools. These views are directly in line with the conclusions of Ofsted:

> It is expected that trainees in receipt of (salary) grants should be additional to school staffing and should not be filling a teaching vacancy. However, a few schools, especially those facing teacher shortages, ask trainees to teach classes for which there is no other teacher; this has a negative impact on the level of support and training they receive. (Ofsted, 2005, p. 19)

One of the tentative conclusions from my research is that the use of the GTP to fill teaching vacancies rather than to create supernumerary training places can put at risk the quality of the training experience, particularly in limiting opportunities for the reflection-in-action and reflection-on-action of the Schön model. Taking a comparison with PGCE, training providers seek not to place PGCE trainees in schools or departments unable to offer appropriate mentoring and support; yet these are the very departments that sometimes take on a Graduate Teacher into a vacant post, a situation that is to some extent exacerbated by the prioritization of shortage subjects. In such circumstances, striking a balance between meeting the training needs of the Graduate Teacher and securing the Graduate Teacher's contribution to the needs of the school is difficult. These Graduate Teachers tend to have substantial timetable commitments and other aspects of their training entitlement are either fitted around the teaching or do not happen at all. As one Graduate Teacher commented:

> I've read my Schön, so I know exactly what I'm supposed to be doing in terms of reflection. But all my time is taken on preparation and survival; when all your efforts are going into keeping the wheel turning, you don't have time to get off and look at which way it's going. (Graduate Trainee (GT) 4)

However, the Eraut model of learning provided a valuable means of analysing the learning experience, even for those Graduate Teachers who were filling vacancies. On the Eraut model, opportunities for 'deliberative learning' for these Graduate Teachers were often quite limited but they were able to identify ways in which 'reactive on-the-spot learning' was happening all the time. Some also indicated that, reflecting one or two years into their teaching career, they were able to identify how they had gained 'implicit or tacit learning' from the immersion process, even though they had not fully recognized this at the time. One commented:

> At the time, I felt as though I was flying by the seat of my pants, learning a bit as I went but essentially just trying to survive. I can now see that I was actually internalizing a lot more in terms of professional knowledge and understanding than I realized. (GT 11)

For the majority of respondents in this research, the training process had been a very positive experience. Many Graduate Teachers saw themselves as professionals rather than trainees; they felt they were regarded by colleagues and pupils as 'proper teachers', whereas PGCE trainees on placement in the school were seen very much as trainees. Most rated the mentoring and support provided by the host school very highly. However, they also emphasized the extent to which they had felt supported by and part of the whole community. In the words of one respondent:

> I got on really well with my mentor and she was always very helpful but I had as much help from other people who were not written into my training plan. For example, some of the Newly Qualified Teachers in other departments were a real source of support and shared experience. (GT 15)

Careful reading of the Lave and Wenger theory of situated learning confirmed my view that what was being described by many Graduate Teachers was a community of practice. In these communities, the fact that learners are organized around a task and knowledge makes them develop a sense of social interaction and identity: 'A "community of practice" involves much more than technical knowledge or skill associated with undertaking some task. Members are involved in a set of relationships over time' (Lave and Wenger, 1991, p. 17). Communities of practice need resources that in some way carry the knowledge of the community, that is, there must be practice on the means through which the tasks must be approached and carried out and that is shared among the members.

The experiences of many Graduate Teachers were also consistent with the Lave and Wenger notion of 'legitimate peripheral participation', that is, novices begin on the periphery of the organization and progressively move towards the centre as they acquire knowledge from those who already have the knowledge – the experts:

> Learners inevitably participate in communities of practitioners and … the mastery of knowledge and skill requires newcomers to move toward full participation in the socio-cultural practices of a community. 'Legitimate peripheral participation' provides a way to speak about the relations between newcomers and old-timers, and about activities, identities, artefacts, and communities of knowledge and practice. A person's intentions to learn are engaged and the meaning of learning is configured through the process of becoming a full participant in a socio-cultural practice. (Lave and Wenger, 1991, p. 29)

In communities of practice, the learners are allowed to think in a different way about taking on tasks in groups, associations and networks in which they are involved. Acting in the periphery, as explained by Lave and Wenger in the theory, still requires the participation of the community. In the words of one Graduate Teacher:

> I felt very inadequate at the beginning because I didn't feel I was contributing, but experienced colleagues were always encouraging me to add my two pennyworth and were very positive when I did chip in, so I began to feel I was adding something as well as learning. (GT 9)

The knowledge is deemed to be in the centre of the community and even if it is argued that the learner may legitimately acquire knowledge at the periphery, Lave and Wenger claim that communities of practice still form a vital part of the instruction. Interaction by the newcomer with the 'old-timers' who have knowledge in the community is central; legitimate peripheral participation is not about internalization of knowledge but interaction with the wider community of practice. The theory, therefore, puts learning in the context of the community at its core. The people are required to be full participants in the community as opposed to being engaged in their individual endeavours to acquire knowledge. The reference by Lave and Wenger to the 'person acting in the world' refers to acting in the community. As an integral part of the situated theory, learning should occur in a situation that will influence the behaviour of the learners.

The Relevance and Effectiveness of Using Theory

There is a significant amount of literature linked to issues such as peoples' reasons and motivation to become teachers and factors influencing the decision to leave teaching. There is also a substantial literature on models of teacher development, the content of training courses, the place of educational theory and the respective roles of university tutors and school-based mentors in supporting trainee teachers. However, there is to date relatively little research on the GTP, particularly in relation to the possible reasons – to do with the individuals and/or the training model – why recruitment and retention rates are so much higher, issues which have potentially far reaching consequences for Initial Teacher Training (ITT) recruitment, the nature of ITT programmes and, particularly, recruitment into teaching posts.

In developing this piece of research, I started with the theoretical perspectives on reflective practice offered by Schön, since virtually all ITT programmes express the aspiration to produce reflective practitioners. In exploring Schön's model, some of the critical commentaries led me to wider perspectives on the nature of work-based learning, especially Eraut, who I found very useful in helping to understand and interpret Graduate Teachers' learning 'on the job'. However, most relevant of all to my work was the 'situated learning' theory of Lave and Wenger. I did not begin with a thesis involving situated learning; this emerged from initial analyses of my findings. Situated learning helped me to understand, interpret and explain the professional learning and identity of Graduate Teachers.

Summary Conclusions and Recommendations

The discovery of the appropriate theories

Schön was a fairly obvious starting point, since the development of reflective practitioners is a key aspiration of virtually all ITT programmes. I was expecting that the analysis would lead me into issues of power and structure in school and that I would, therefore, be considering theories such as Foucault's on power and agency. I also expected that experiential learning would be an important theme and there is a lot of research and theorizing on this theme, from Dewey onwards. However, the emphasis from my research findings was very much on work-based learning, incorporating elements of experiential learning but also recognizing the significance to the learning process of the working context. This led me to Eraut's theories about the nature of work-based learning and particularly to Lave and Wenger's situated learning.

The ease or difficulties with understanding the theories

For me, the most important thing is to go straight to the original texts and read them thoroughly to gain your own understanding of what the authors were seeking to argue and the evidence base they were using. The work of researchers such as Schön and Lave and Wenger is extensively quoted in all manner of publications and it is tempting to believe that you 'know about' their theories on the basis of a few brief quotes and how other writers describe the theories in ways that support their own arguments.

I was fortunate in my choice of theoretical perspectives in the sense that I find the writings of Schön, Eraut and Lave and Wenger to be clear and accessible. As I read, I was able to make connections with some of my primary evidence and this, in turn, strengthened my understanding of the theories.

The difficulties of application to data and texts

The theoretical perspectives developed by Eraut and Lave and Wenger were based on situations and contexts with which they were familiar. Although there were features in common with the context of my research, there were also differences. It took a considerable amount of reflecting on and analysing my data before I was able to make use of their models to interrogate my research findings and to identify trends, patterns and connections within the evidence provided by my research participants.

What the application of the theories revealed

Eraut's theory of three types of work-based learning was particularly useful in analysing the descriptions by Graduate Teachers of their training process and their reflections two or three years into their teaching careers on the implicit learning that had been taking place without their being aware of it during their school-based training. Similarly, Lave and Wenger's situated learning through communities of practice provided a clear framework for analysing Graduate Teachers' comments about the importance of the working context to their professional learning.

How the absence of these theories might have impaired understanding

The theories, especially Eraut and Lave and Wenger, provided a conceptual and theoretical framework that enabled me to interrogate my research findings and to identify trends, patterns and connections within the evidence provided by my research participants.

The limitations of the theories

Once I was clear about the theories from reading the original works, I found it really useful to refer to the critiques and developments offered by other researchers. For example, Usher, Bryant and Johnston (1997) offer a most illuminating critique of Schön and the extent to which he 'neglects the situatedness of practitioner experience' (p. 168). Similarly, some subsequent work on Lave and Wenger's situated learning has sought to refine the principle of what constitutes a community of practice. For example, Hodkinson and Hodkinson (2004) studied the workplace learning of teachers in four subject departments of two English secondary schools and identified these departments as communities of practice, operating as close-knit groups to mediate school-level influences. This led me to look more closely of some of my research evidence and challenged my initial assumption that, for the Graduate Teachers, the community of practice was the whole school.

Reflection and recommendations of the experience

For much of the early part of my research project, my invariable response to the question 'how are you getting on?' was to say that I had a theme but not a thesis. I was generating a lot of interesting data about Graduate Teachers, their behaviour and perspectives, without having a clear idea of where it was leading in terms of an argument. The progressive use of the Eraut and Lave and Wenger models of work-based learning has been crucial to me in making sense of my data and helping me to develop a credible thesis around school-based professional learning for beginning teachers.

Recommended further reading

Eraut, M. (1994) *Developing Professional Knowledge and Competence*, Falmer, London.

Eraut, M. (2007) Learning from other people in the workplace. *Oxford Review of Education*, 33 (4), 403–422.

Schön, D. (1987) *Educating the Reflective Practitioner*, Jossey-Bass, San Francisco.

Smith, M.K. (2009) Donald Schön: Learning, Reflection and Change, http://www.infed.org/thinkers/et-schon.htm (accessed 3 May 2011).

Wenger, E. (1998) *Communities of Practice: Learning, Meaning and Identity*, Cambridge University Press, Cambridge.

Wenger, E., McDermott, R. and Snyder, W. (2002) *Cultivating Communities of Practice: A Guide to Managing Knowledge*, Harvard Business School Press, Cambridge, MA.

References

CEER (Centre for Education and Employment Research) (2004) *Teacher Turnover, Wastage and Destinations*, DfES, London.

CEER (Centre for Education and Employment Research) (2005) *Teacher Training Profiles*, CEER, Buckingham.

Eraut, M. (1994) *Developing Professional Knowledge and Competence*, Falmer, London.

Eraut, M. (2000) Non-formal learning and tacit knowledge in professional work. *British Journal of Educational Psychology*, 70 (1), 113–136.

Eraut, M. (2007) Learning from other people in the workplace. *Oxford Review of Education*, 33 (4), 403–422.

Foster, R. (2000) The Graduate Teacher Programme – just the job? *Professional Development in Education*, 26 (2), 297–309.

Griffiths, V. (2003) Access or exploitation? A case study of an employment-based route into teaching. Paper presented at 'Teachers as Leaders: Teacher

Education for a Global Profession', ICET/ATEA conference, Melbourne, Australia, 20–25 July.

Hodkinson, H. and Hodkinson, P. (2004) Rethinking the concept of community of practice in relation to schoolteachers' workplace learning. *International Journal of Training and Development*, 8 (1), 21–32.

Lave, J. and Wenger, E. (1991) *Situated Learning. Legitimate Peripheral Participation*, Cambridge University Press, Cambridge.

Ofsted (2005) *An Employment-Based Route into Teaching*, Ofsted, London.

Schön, D. (1983) *The Reflective Practitioner. How Professionals Think in Action*, Temple Smith, London.

Schön, D. (1987) *Educating the Reflective Practitioner*, Jossey-Bass, San Francisco.

Smith, M.K. (2009) Donald Schön: Learning, Reflection and Change, http:\\www.infed.org/thinkers/et-schon.htm (accessed 3 May 2011).

Stewart, W. and Thornton, K. (2006) The exodus from teaching slows. *Times Education Supplement*, 11 July, p. 4.

Usher, R., Bryant, I. and Johnston, R. (1997) *Adult Education and the Postmodern Challenge*, Routledge, London.

Wenger, E. (1998) *Communities of Practice. Learning, Meaning and Identity*, Cambridge University Press, Cambridge.

Wenger, E., McDermott, R. and Snyder, W. (2002) *Cultivating Communities of Practice: A Guide to Managing Knowledge*, Harvard Business School Press, Cambridge, MA.

6

Children's University Aspirations and the Effects of Cultural and Social Capital

Matt Cochrane

Key Theoretical Approaches in this Chapter: Pierre Bourdieu's Theories of Habitus and Cultural Capital

The ideas of Pierre Bourdieu most frequently applied to education research are in the realm of class and privilege, and are often used to investigate inequalities in the education system. His theories of 'habitus' and forms of capital are commonly cited, especially when researchers explore how social groups are able to maintain a privileged position through their accumulation of cultural and social capital, or when analysing the ideological constructs that give rise to the social experiences that contribute to identity formation. Bourdieu describes how capital is invested in the family so that subsequent generations may use capital to their advantage in maintaining a privileged position in society. For example, wealthy parents are able to send their children to the 'best' schools in order to accumulate cultural capital in the form of academic qualifications, which universities will accept as fulfilling their entry requirements; underprivileged members of society find it difficult to obtain such capital. The concept is particularly useful here, because Bourdieu always intended for his work to be of

Applying Theory to Educational Research: An Introductory Approach with Case Studies,
First Edition. Edited by J. Adams, M. Cochrane and L. Dunne.
© 2012 John Wiley & Sons, Ltd. Published 2012 by John Wiley & Sons, Ltd.

practical use – Grenfell and James (1998) describe how Bourdieu sought to emphasize the link between the theory and practice of education; indeed he saw them as inextricably connected. Their book gives a range of fields in which Bourdieu's ideas have been used.

Key texts

Bourdieu, P. and Passeron, J.C. (1990) *Reproduction in Education, Society and Culture*, 2nd edn (trans. R. Nice), Sage, London.

Grenfell, M. and James, D. (eds) (1998) *Bourdieu and Education: Acts of Practical Theory*, Falmer Press, London.

Robbins, D. (1997) *The Work of Pierre Bourdieu*, Open University Press, Buckingham.

Introduction to the Research Project

Research in the UK repeatedly shows that people from the higher social classes (I, II and IIIN) are significantly more likely to enter higher education than those from classes IIIM–V. These distinctions in social classifications were also used by Reay, David and Ball (2005, p. 13). They referred to social classes I and II along with IIIN (non-manual) as 'middle class', and classes IIIM (manual) IV and V as 'working class'. This is a useful distinction as it is also appears in a 2003 government White Paper, 'The Future of Higher Education' (DfES, 2003). Table 6.1 (DfES, 2003, p. 17) displays the proportion of 18-year-olds from these two social groups entering higher education, and shows how the gap in attainment has persisted and even widened over a period of 40 years. Although both sets of figures rise steadily over the years, that for groups I and II gains more ground over the whole period. Whatever initiatives are put in place to encourage wider participation, all groups appear to benefit but the middle class groups benefit at least as well or better, so the investment into these initiatives is not finding its way efficiently to the most disadvantaged.

Much research has been done in this area (Reay, David and Ball, 2005; Ball, Davies, David and Reay, 2002; Furlong and Cartmel, 1997; Hanafin and Lynch, 2002). Those in higher socio-economic classes, already in a position of advantage, seem better able to take further advantage.

Table 6.1   Higher education (HE) entrants by social class group, 1960–2000.

| | Percentage of 18-year-olds entering HE by the age of 20 | | |
Year	Groups I, II, IIIN	Groups IIIM, IV, V	Gap (percentage points)
1960	27	4	23
1970	32	5	27
1980	33	7	26
1985	35	8	27
1990	36	10	26
1995	47	17	30
2000	48	18	30

Source: DfES (2003, p. 17). © Crown Copyright.

In fact, the problem is not as simple as it may seem. Government initiatives that seek to widen participation at the level of higher education have had effects in England, and there is evidence that the gap between socio-economic classes has closed (Raffe *et al.*, 2006); nevertheless, the gap in attainment is robust and persistent.

As Strand (2007) explains, the problem happens early on. The final column in Table 6.1 shows the gap in attainment, and this gap has its roots in the achievement of pupils at school. It is poor achievement at A-level that is the biggest reason why young people from underprivileged backgrounds are unable to get into university. For those that emerge with good results at A-level, social background makes less difference. But of course, those without A-levels will not enter university, and far more young people from socially disadvantaged backgrounds have poor A-level results. This does not mean that schools or universities overtly discriminate against young people; rather that young people from disadvantaged backgrounds find it much more difficult to negotiate their way through the education system.

Bourdieu used the term 'habitus' to describe a set of dispositions displayed by an individual and was 'the product of internalization of the principles of a cultural arbitrary capable of perpetuating itself' (Bourdieu and Passeron, 1990, p. 31). In other words, society is organized according to a number of unspoken rules (the 'cultural arbitrary') that led people to behave in certain ways, always operating without an awareness of the explicit existence of the rules. Critics such as King (2000) suggest that Bourdieu's analysis is too deterministic in nature – that people would not be in a position to 'break' the rules and transform their habitus if they were unaware of their existence. Other critics reject the analysis on the grounds that it is unable to explain the distribution and shifting nature of the data (Goldthorpe and Jackson, 2008). In other words, it looks good as a theory, but is no use in explaining the large-scale picture.

Answering his earlier critics in a foreword to the second edition of *Reproduction*, Bourdieu described the 'extremely sophisticated mechanisms by which the school system *contributes* to reproducing the structure of the distribution of cultural capital and, through it, the social structure', pointing out that it was false to assume that 'society reproduces itself mechanically, identical to itself, without transformation or deformation, and by excluding all individual mobility' (Bourdieu and Passeron, 1990, p. viii). Researchers such as Mills (2008) continue to argue that there is a transformational quality to habitus, and I would add that we should not expect to use the concept of habitus to predict outcomes, but that it is a very useful tool when used to analyse social structures, and through a study of habitus we can help to orientate young people towards a transformation from their disadvantaged situation.

Working as a teacher in a comprehensive school in England it was possible to observe these mechanisms in action, and I could see parental influence at work when the exam syllabus for 16-year-olds changed to include a new vocational science course. This was aimed at the pupils who were targeted to achieve below grade D, since the new course offered a genuine opportunity, and indeed after three years, roughly 75 per cent of them were achieving grade C and above. The significance of that is that normally a grade C would be regarded as a 'pass', but some parents would not allow their children to take the new course. They regarded it as a second-rate option and insisted that they should be allowed to go for the more traditional version, believing it would provide their offspring better opportunities in subsequent years.

This developed into a research project which sought to find out from the pupils themselves how they viewed their options when confronted by choices like these – between courses which carried some measure of esteem, and those which might not be valued by prospective employers and admissions tutors. I interviewed groups of children in year nine (aged 13–14) as they approached their decision-making before entering certificate-bearing courses for the first time. I returned to talk to the children again two years later to find how much their ideas had developed.

Theories Explained and their Use Justified in the Context of this Research Project

Bourdieu's social and cultural capital

Bourdieu describes social, cultural and symbolic capital, comparing them to economic capital and suggesting that they are commodities that can be accumulated and bargained with. Skeggs (1997, p. 8) provides a clear and helpful summary of the forms of capital:

- *Economic capital*, that is, capital in its monetary form;
- *Cultural capital*, which shows itself in a number of ways. It can be formally represented by qualifications, but also by features such as competence with language or self-confidence in challenging situations;
- *Social capital*, which refers to a person's membership of privileged and influential social groups; and
- *Symbolic capital* – none of the forms of capital are any use if they are not accepted, or legitimated by particular groups who are able to exert power.

It's probably helpful to start at the bottom of the list: symbolic capital is capital that has status and value conferred on it by dominant members of society. These are the people for example who control access to employment, or to higher education by 'legitimating' certain forms of capital in preference to other, possibly intrinsically equal, forms. In describing the other three forms of capital, it is interesting to look at examples of how they gain (or lose) symbolic value.

In this context, cultural capital has two forms: the qualifications which people gain as they progress through life; and equally importantly the knowledge they gain which helps them to negotiate their way through society. According to Reay, David and Ball (2005, p. 20), cultural capital 'encompasses a broad array of linguistic competences, manners, preferences and orientations ... [which] can be glimpsed in the narratives of young people from established middle class families'. Some qualifications carry more status than others – not just in the obvious sense that a Masters degree is at a higher level than a Bachelor degree, but also in the sense that some courses and some universities hold a different value in the employment market. So for example, in the UK some universities will require candidates for entry to have A-levels in the 'traditional' subjects such as History, Physics, Mathematics and so on, and will shun subjects such as Media Studies and Sociology.

People with social and cultural capital that has value as symbolic capital are in a good position to help their children negotiate their way through society and gain easier access to its benefits. In the UK affluent parents are able to purchase a house in a 'good' neighbourhood that ensures a place for their child at a favoured school (Wood, 2002). If for some reason their child is not allocated a place at the school, they are able to lobby the local authority and present a case, and they are very often successful. They will constantly intervene throughout their child's education in order to ensure that they are taught by the best teachers, and are placed in the best classes. They will try to make sure their child takes a course that has academic status and therefore ensure what they see as the best opportunities. They can do this because they have high-level qualifications themselves and know the system well. So put simply, cultural capital is what you know, and social capital is who you know. Bourdieu argued that this was the mechanism by which the middle classes maintained their position in society and prevented the working classes from progressing (Robbins, 1997).

The Application of Theory to the Research

The analysis below relates the responses of some of the participants in the project to the influences from their family background, since central to Bourdieu's theory is the notion that forms of capital are invested through the family.

While the participants demonstrated considerable faith in the justice of the educational system to treat them purely according to merit, they nevertheless were able to recognize that those with 'supportive' parents (even when they felt that the support moved across to pressure, they recognized that it was well-intentioned) were more likely to succeed in their exams. And sure enough, at this stage the 13-year-olds who had parents with high-level qualifications were better able to articulate a view for their future. For example they had more confidence in the concept of attending university for its own sake,

Table 6.2 University aspirations linked to cultural capital in the family.

Becky	Mother: Teaching Assistant Father: Joiner	Wants to study medicine
Emma	*M: Careers Advisor* F: Marketing Manager	'I want to go far away'
Gemma	F: Financial Adviser M: Housewife*	'I actually want to go to [the nearest university]'
Jasmina'	*F: Technician* *M: Teacher*	'I want to get as far out of town as I can ... this town's just gonna kill me ... it's such a dead end.,
Mike	*M: Art Lecturer* *F: Art Teacher*	'I'd never be able to get there' [Oxford]
Natalie	M: Unemployed F: Unemployed	'I'd like to be a vet, but if I don't get the grades I'll be a hairdresser.,
Oliver	F: Own Business M: Hospital Bed Manager	'I'd never be able to get there' [Oxford]
Paul	M: Podiatrist F: Podiatrist	'You wouldn't know anyone there [distant university] ... I know you wouldn't know anyone at [the local university], but you could come back easily'
Tracy	M: Housewife* F: Joiner	'it's [Oxford] too posh!"

Notes: *term used by Tracy and Gemma. All names are pseudonyms; some details have been disguised.

and would be more likely to travel to a distant university for the best courses. Those with little cultural capital in their families were more likely to choose a university near at hand, without comparing the quality of similar courses elsewhere. (See Reay, Davies, David and Ball, 2001 for similar findings.)

It was noticeable however, that at this stage pupils had enthusiasm, ingenuity and optimism about their future. It is certainly not the case that pupils without well-qualified parents are not interested in seeking qualifications for themselves, though it was clear that often they had naïve or ill-informed ideas about what they would like to do or about which university they would like to attend. Table 6.2 shows the responses they made to the question of whether they saw themselves as future university students. Parental experience of university is used as a proxy for cultural capital – where parents are indicated in italic type they have attended university. What is interesting is the tendency for the youngsters without this measure of capital to lean towards local or lower-status institutions.

The tendency is not exclusive, and as we see, Becky is working hard to achieve her aim of a medical career, and she is doing this by attempting to transform her capital: 'I just think of a doctor and then I think of myself and try and be that and match that, and I'm constantly looking at myself and trying to prove it'.

To Bourdieu, there was a distinct system by which the privileged classes maintained their position and inhibited entry for the disadvantaged by placing obstacles in their way in the form of arcane language and practices. He described how people acted according to subconsciously generated responses to situations, referring to this collection of dispositions as 'habitus'. Habitus is transferred and developed chiefly through the family, and thus children from families with the disposition to act positively in their education will do the same themselves. And those whose families are not disposed to intervene will be passive in their education too. However, as we see from Becky's example above, and as described by Mills (2008), transformations are possible within the analysis.

Paul Willis rejected this notion when he carried out a noted piece of research on a group of Birmingham schoolboys in the 1970s (Willis, 1977). They referred to themselves as 'the lads', and opted to reject the education system presented to them and subverted it instead. They carried this on into the world of work, treating it as a means to earn wages but nothing more. They were able to articulate this conscious decision, and presumably recognized that they had the option to do the opposite.

The young people in my research also recognized that they had options, and were able to seek answers to some of the problems they encountered. For example they made significant use of role models in deciding on their future careers – where they had a relative or friend in a given occupation, they could visualize themselves in the same role and work towards that occupation as a goal (Cochrane, 2010). Very often they were influenced by those close to them (family and friends), an observation also made by Hodkinson (1998). Those without role models looked for them elsewhere – one sought advice and guidance from a trusted teacher, and others had more distant relatives who could provide them with useful information to help them. This suggests that habitus, while helpful in describing a social situation, is also helpful to the subjects of the research – while not aware of the concept of habitus, they were clearly aware that there were people around them who had certain qualifications or knowledge that would be of use to them.

The Relevance and Effectiveness of Using Theory

Using Bourdieu's theory provides a very tempting explanation for the persistent gap in attainment between different social classes. By applying it to the interview data, it is possible to identify where the subjects were accumulating (or not accumulating) social and cultural capital, and how they were using this to make progress through the education system. They clearly understood that there was a system of rules and practices they had to negotiate, and while they were willing to negotiate these, there was a limit. Virtually all of them regarded universities like Oxford and Cambridge as 'too snobby' (Diane, aged 16) and 'much easier for posh people to get into' (Hazel, aged 16). They all knew that something more than high grades would be necessary for entry to the more prestigious universities. Interestingly, some were prepared to go to considerable lengths to develop their qualifications and experience to improve their chances. It was as if they were aware that their level of cultural capital was insufficient as it stood, and that they needed to invest some more. They did this by identifying role models who could provide them with advice and guidance, and to a certain extent adopting their practices. Becky (aged 16) for example was undertaking medical work experience with a charity in order to improve her chances of getting into medical school. I would argue that these young people were able to articulate their social dispositions with some clarity. In our conversations, they demonstrated a refusal to 'legitimate' the social capital displayed by one of their peers (e.g., by criticizing the way she dressed).

However, when using a theory, even one as established as this, it is often possible to view it with a degree of scepticism, or from a new angle. It was developed by Bourdieu to describe a malign purpose – the perpetuation of privilege by the middle classes and to the exclusion of members of working class families. Instead, an understanding of habitus might provide us with a mechanism for helping youngsters to progress in their education.

Summary Conclusions and Recommendations

The discovery of the appropriate theories

There are other theories that can be used in this situation – Foucault for example discusses power and agency, and clearly there are links here. However, I chose to go with habitus on the grounds that I was dealing with what the children concerned felt was a highly structured environment – both from the point of view of the family and the school. Bourdieu's theories were developed against just such backgrounds. A poststructuralist approach would tend to emphasize the differences in the children's experiences rather than the similarities.

The ease or difficulties with understanding the theories

The key here is in finding the start point. This inevitably involves a great deal of time travelling down blind alleys, writing passages that may seem to make little sense. I studied other theories of social interaction, had long conversations with kind people who were prepared to listen, and often felt that the whole subject was too difficult. But the material learned on such journeys is invaluable in helping the researcher to recognize the kind of theory that 'fits'. After a while, the theory you are studying begins to make sense; the books and papers on the subject start to develop clarity they didn't possess before – and then it becomes possible to start applying the theory with some confidence.

The difficulties of application to data and texts

All texts are concerned with their own situation. Developing the above argument has taken a considerable amount of time and effort thinking about the subject and working with the data generated, trying, rejecting and rewording ideas. This was indeed a lengthy process, but it was time well spent.

What the application of the theories revealed

From my point of view, the concept of habitus enabled me to observe the responses of the young people in the survey and see how their experiences matched the concept. It turns out that they understand far more of the concept than we might expect. They can be seen acting out the process of legitimation of social capital when discussing a friend who 'puts on airs and graces' (Hazel, aged 16).

How the absence of these theories might have impaired understanding

Without a conceptual framework to base these ideas on, it would have been difficult to identify the connections between the various statements the participants made in their interviews. Much of what they said might otherwise be dismissed as pointless. As Fraser (2004) points out, it is necessary to investigate situations even where the common-sense answer seems too obvious.

The limitations of the theories

It should not be forgotten that the term 'capital' used to describe sociological situations is metaphoric. It can be possible to pursue the metaphor too far by comparing it too closely with economic capital. Metaphors also have a tendency to put boundaries around ideas and inhibit other directions of thought or explanation.

Reflection and recommendations of the experience

It took a long time living with the data, discussing it with other researchers and exploring other possibilities before the concept of habitus took hold. One significant advantage of this is that I became immersed in the research. The participants were astounded by the degree of my recall when I returned to talk to them again after a gap of two years. This was not really surprising to me, since I had delivered a number of presentations on the subject in that time, and had become familiar with the transcripts. I cannot understate the value of the discussions and comments I received in this time in helping me develop the good ideas and reject the bad ones.

Recommended further reading

Fraser *et al.* (2004) in a book that is concerned with conducting research with children nonetheless provide an excellent start point when developing a methodology.

Reay, David and Ball (2005) apply Bourdieu's concept of habitus in an extensive piece of research into the choices faced by students (sixth form and mature) entering higher education.

Skeggs (1997) gives a very clear description of Bourdieu's concept and how it applies.

References

Ball, S., Davies, J., David, M. and Reay, D. (2002) 'Classification' and 'judgement': social class and the 'cognitive structures' of choice of higher education. *British Journal of Sociology of Education*, 23 (1), 51–72.

Bourdieu, P. and Passeron, J.C. (1990) *Reproduction in Education, Society and Culture*, 2nd edn (trans. R. Nice), Sage, London.

Cochrane, M. (2010) Do role models help to widen participation? An investigation into the effect of social background on choice of role model. *Widening Participation and Lifelong Learning*, 12 (1), 51–72.

DfES (2003) *The Future of Higher Education; Government White Paper*, Stationery Office, Norwich.

Fraser, S. (2004) Situating empirical research, in *Doing Research with Children and Young People* (eds S. Fraser, V. Lewis, S. Ding, M. Kellett and C. Robinson), Sage, London, pp. 15–26.

Fraser, S., Lewis, V., Ding, S., Kellett, M. and Robinson, C. (2004) *Doing Research with Children and Young People*, Sage, London.

Furlong, A. and Cartmel, F. (1997) *Young People and Social Change: Individualization and Risk in Late Modernity*, Open University Press, Buckingham.

Goldthorpe, J. and Jackson, M. (2008) Education-based meritocracy: the barriers to its realisation, in *Social Class: How Does it Work?* (eds A. Lareau and D. Conley), Russell Sage Foundation, New York, pp. 93–117.

Grenfell, M. and James, D. (eds) (1998) *Bourdieu and Education: Acts of Practical Theory*, Falmer Press, London.

Hanafin, J. and Lynch, A. (2002) Peripheral voices: parental involvement, social class, and educational disadvantage. *British Journal of Sociology of Education*, 23 (1), 35–49.

Hodkinson, P. (1998) Career decision making and the transition from school to work, in *Bourdieu and Education: Acts of Practical Theory* (eds M. Grenfell and D. James), Falmer Press, London, pp. 89–103.

King, A. (2000) Thinking with Bourdieu against Bourdieu: a 'practical' critique of the habitus. *Sociological Theory*, 18 (3), 417–433.

Mills, C. (2008) Reproduction and transformation of inequalities in schooling: the transformative potential of the theoretical constructs of Bourdieu. *British Journal of Sociology of Education*, 29 (1), 79–89.

Raffe, D., Croxford, L., Iannelli, C., Shapira, M. and Howieson, C. (2006) Social-class inequalities in education in England and Scotland, Centre for Educational Sociology, University of Edinburgh (Special CES Briefing No. 40).

Reay, D., David, M. and Ball, S. (2005) *Degrees of Choice: Social Class, Race and Gender in Higher Education*, Trentham, Stoke on Trent.

Reay, D., Davies, J., David, M. and Ball, S. (2001) Choices of degree or degrees of choice? Class, 'race' and the higher education choice process. *Sociology*, 35 (4), 855–874.

Robbins, D. (1997) *The Work of Pierre Bourdieu*, Open University Press, Milton Keynes.

Skeggs, B. (1997) *Formations of Class and Gender*, Sage, London.

Strand, S. (2007) Minority ethnic pupils in the longitudinal study of young people in England (LSYPE), University of Warwick (Research Report DCSF-RR002).

Willis, P. (1977) *Learning to Labour: How Working-class Kids Get Working-class Jobs*, Saxon House, London.

Wood, P. (2002) Space for idealism? Politics and education in the United Kingdom. *Educational Policy*, 16 (1), 118–138.

7

Finding Theory Through Collaborative Research

Clare Woolhouse

> ### Key Theoretical Approaches in this Chapter: Michel Foucault's Theory of Power
>
> This chapter provides a discussion on how Michel Foucault's (1982) notion of power/knowledge was engaged with, developed and applied in a project that involved three researchers who were exploring the experiences of teaching assistants who support teaching and learning in a number of British schools. In this research, a Foucauldian lens was cast on the data collected to interrogate how the connectivity between knowledge and power create a 'regime of truth' (Foucault, 1995, p. 131) that informs an 'art of existence' (Foucault, 1990a, p. 238). This regime can be conceived as orientating teaching assistants in how they come to identify or know themselves as such and become 'subjects'. The key focus for this chapter will be on how theory was engaged with by the researchers to facilitate alternative ways of thinking about the data and how, through collaboration, they dealt with the problems encountered, and the limitations of particular ideas when engaging with theory.

Applying Theory to Educational Research: An Introductory Approach with Case Studies, First Edition. Edited by J. Adams, M. Cochrane and L. Dunne.
© 2012 John Wiley & Sons, Ltd. Published 2012 by John Wiley & Sons, Ltd.

Key texts

Foucault, M. (1990a) *The Care of the Self: The History of Sexuality, Vol. 3*, Penguin, London.
Foucault, M. (1995) Truth and power, reprinted in *Michel Foucault, Power/ Knowledge: Selected Interviews and Other Writings 1972–1977* (ed. G. Colin), Longman, London, pp. 109–133.
St Pierre, E.A. (2001) Coming to theory: finding Foucault and Deleuze, in *Feminist Engagements: Reading, Resisting and Revisioning Male Theorists in Education and Cultural Studies* (ed. K. Weiler), Routledge, New York, pp. 141–164.

Introduction to the Research Project

The research carried out involved one experienced researcher leading the project and working to develop two early career researchers, who in the third year took over responsibility for running the final phase. The project focused on exploring the experiences of two cohorts of teaching assistants who worked to support children in UK schools, who were also engaged in a three-year Foundation Degree in Supporting Teaching and Learning. Our aim was to track the career trajectories and the personal and professional changes experienced over a three-year period by collecting mainly qualitative data. We used questionnaires, focus groups and individual life history interviews that involved the teaching assistants producing a life history time line and narrating it with attention given to the events and experiences they identified as significant (Webster and Mertova, 2007, p. 73).

Initially the research was situated in relation to UK government policy regarding the professionalization of the Children's School Workforce (DfES, 2003). The research focused on the teaching assistants' perceptions of their role, positioning within schools, and experiences of 'earning and learning' under the UK lifelong learning agenda (Department for Education and Employment [DfEE], 2000). However, during the course of the study, and particularly in the third and final year, the analytical framework that was employed altered and we began to explicitly engage with the work of Michel Foucault.

Theories Explained and their Use Justified in the Context of this Research Project

The research ran over an extended period, which gave the researchers the luxury of revisiting and developing the theoretical framework over time. As the two early career researchers took more responsibility for directing the research we increasingly explored points of engagement between the data we were collecting and ideas from our respective doctoral theses, which fortuitously were both framed by the Foucauldian notion of power/knowledge.

In *The Archaeology of Knowledge* (2002, p. 98), Foucault argues that research can identify and study the function, conditions and governing rules of knowledge production within the social world. He studies modes of thinking and the implicit rules about given topics that restrict 'conditions of possibility for thought in a given period' and direct people's understandings of the world in which they live (Foucault, 1970: xxii). Foucault argues that these understandings and their shaping of people's lives are materialized via the intersecting of power and knowledge; that the production of knowledge is integral to the exercising of power. As he claims: 'There is no power relation without the correlative constitution of a field of knowledge, nor any knowledge that does not presuppose and constitute at the same time power relations' (Foucault, 1991, p. 27).

The key concern for Foucault is this dialogic relationship between knowledge and power. He seeks to interrogate how power/knowledge work together to invest bodies in order to 'create a history of the different modes by which, in our culture, human beings are made into subjects' (Foucault, 1982, p. 208). Foucault explores how the intersecting of knowledge and power defines the ways in which individuals 'know' themselves; how they manage themselves, how they relate to other individuals and how they mediate their place in society. He frames this coming to know oneself as a process of change by which individuals engage with and rework power/knowledge. As Foucault (1990b, p. 138) notes, the effects of power will be historically specific and will 'regulate the most intimate and minute elements of the construction of space, time, desire and embodiment'. However, while this 'knowing' is informed by power relations he does not conceive it as a form of docile capitulation since 'power is not a commodity, a position, a prize or a plot' (Foucault, 1990a, p. 82). Rather it is the effects of power that can be studied by exploring how power acts as a productive force that operates through individuals, technologies and institutions to structure knowledge of individual self-mastery.

Instrumental to our exploration of the effects of power/knowledge was an analysis of how the connections between forms of knowledge and relations of power influence individuals' beliefs, ideas and practices. Such connectivity produces subjects by creating 'regimes of truth' (Foucault, 1995, p. 131), which influence how individuals come to know themselves, and how they come to develop a particular 'art of existence that revolves around the question of the self, of its dependence and independence, of its universal form and of the connection it can and should establish with others, and of the procedures by which it exerts control over itself' (Foucault, 1990a, p. 238).

Although the two early career researchers involved in the research were familiar with Foucault's work, the decision to introduce a Foucauldian informed analysis was not taken lightly. There were lengthy discussions as we explored the possibilities for theoretical engagement with his work and as we attempted to explain our understandings of it to one another. While most research projects might not involve this process of continually rethinking theory, I feel it was particularly useful because at each stage of the analysis the theoretical framework was dialogically revisited. Also, as a research team we were only prepared to commit to our ideas once we all shared an understanding regarding how concepts (such as 'power' or 'knowing oneself') were to be interpreted and applied to the reported experiences of the teaching assistants who participated in the study.

As well as ensuring that we rigorously developed our theoretical engagements, this dialogic process also encouraged collaborative thinking and working to such an extent that the analysis, reports, conference papers and journal articles which were produced, were jointly written. This usually involved the three of us setting aside time to spend together in a computer suite working through transcripts of the focus groups or interviews, drafting and redrafting our shared writing line by line. This may sound laborious but we found it an innovative, collegial and enjoyable experience that introduced us to the different, creative ways in which we each thought and wrote. This process also meant that everything that was written had been reviewed by three individuals before being disseminated more widely (Dunne, Goddard and Woolhouse, 2008a, 2008b, 2009).

The Application of Theory to the Research

To apply Foucault's notion of power/knowledge to the situations and experiences of teaching assistants, we explored how their everyday practices in schools were influenced by and implicated in networks of power relations.

To do so we located and interrogated the discursive 'regimes of truth' that circulated among teaching assistants, to deconstruct the constitutive and regulatory effects of these regimes. A study was undertaken to explore how truths about what a teaching assistant is and what they do were produced via the discourse, experiences and practices of two cohorts of teaching assistants who were studying for a Foundation Degree. For example the teaching assistants repeatedly engaged with what we identified as a 'discourse of care' to voice the opinion that the teaching assistant role in primary schools is viewed as a caring (almost mothering) role rather than an educational one. In using Foucauldian theory to illuminate this discursive regime we traced how it was deployed to explain the location of female teaching assistants within the school hierarchy and their lack of formal professional recognition (95 per cent of the 300 teaching assistants who participated in the research were women).

In particular we concentrated on how the teaching assistants contested and resisted their positioning. To do so we analysed statements made in the interviews and focus groups to investigate shifts in how they 'knew' or perceived themselves as individuals and professionals. For example, we considered changes over the three-year period of study regarding how they talked about teaching and learning, their thoughts about the aims of professional development, and how they scripted their roles in school. One theme that repeatedly emerged was the difficulty many of them experienced in school and the impact this had for their self-understanding, confidence and motivation:

I thought 'what's expected of me?' I wasn't a failure at school, but I now know I could have done so much more had someone given me the choice.

It had taken me so long to get to here, I mean I was a mature student, I was 40 when I graduated and you just think, I never … you know, you've been a mum, you've run a house, you've been all that and never think you're actually capable, well maybe if you are capable your brain cogs have gone a little bit rusty and you're not going to get there.

So, if we look at it from my (negative) experience of school, that has directed what I'm doing now in a way, and I've gained in my confidence through doing all this learning (on the Foundation Degree).

My confidence and self-esteem has really moved up.

I quite like the role that I've got now because I suppose it can be a bit subversive in some way, I don't have to tow the party line all of the time. My role is more flexible and that's quite nice.

We explored such comments to identify how they drew on certain discursive regimes to explain how they acted. In particular we identified a discourse of disquiet and guilt relating to the different demands on them and the amount of time they were taking to study:

> Should I be doing this when I have got a family?

> I feel really guilty. I am literally locked in my room for days and days and weekends and that makes me feel guilty because I've got a young family.

> At some points throughout the course my personal life suffered under the pressure of managing full time work, family and the course.

> My young children missed out a lot over the three years.

> You see I feel guilty about doing anything else at the weekend, because you've got to fit everything else around it.

This discourse was intersected by issues relating to the structures and policies they were subject to; the power dynamics and relationships they were engaged in within school settings. As the teaching assistants noted:

> I have more responsibility and respect for the work that I do but not more pay.

> I was given the responsibility to teach whole classes but no extra pay.

> Teachers talk to you as if you know what you are doing now.

> I've gone (from primary) to a secondary school and there isn't a 'them and us' attitude with the main staff now, the teaching staff.

By exploring the different pressures and experiences the teaching assistants were subject to we traced how higher education study stimulated shifts in how the teaching assistants came to understand their roles in school:

> I will ultimately have a satisfying job and I felt really useful, I was actually having an impact on some of these little lives.

> I have greater recognition as a person as well as recognition for the qualification now.

I have learned not to take someone at face value; to question ... not to be so judgemental and it (the Foundation degree) made me stop and think about what I'm doing and why I'm doing it.

I've started observing the children differently and this course has really opened that out.

During the course of the study we drew out an analysis related to three recurring key themes, namely, the competing discourses of utilitarianism, care and disquiet that revolved around the teaching assistant role; issues regarding (the lack of) rewards and recognition; and the forms of struggle, resistance and negotiation that the teaching assistants engaged in to manage the competing demands of their professional, educational and personal lives. We felt that each of these influenced how the teaching assistants came to know themselves as particular types of individuals or 'subjects' and we identified this 'becoming' as an 'on-going story about the self' (Giddens, 1991, p. 54). In applying theory to the collected data I feel that we gained a deeper understanding of the teaching assistants' experiences and that the theory illuminated our understanding of the everyday negotiations in which these individuals were involved.

The Relevance and Effectiveness of Using Theory

Engagement with theory gave us alternative ways of thinking about the data we were gathering. By ensuring that we had a clear understanding of how we were going to deploy a theoretical framework, we found that using it analytically was not too difficult. For example, as we encountered problems in the processes of researching and writing we talked about them, we found that reaching agreement by trying different ways to explain ourselves coherently to each other was a way to work through and resolve problems. This process of negotiation was furthered in the second and third years of the project as we conducted follow-up focus groups and interviews with the teaching assistants, since this provided opportunities to discuss our findings with them in order to revisit our interpretations and develop our thinking further.

Discovering the 'right' theory for us was not a matter of choosing one and applying it. We spent a considerable amount of time thinking about how a number of theories might, or might not, work for us. This included a brief engagement with the work of Pierre Bourdieu (Bourdieu and Passeron, 1977) on economic, social and cultural capital (see Woolhouse, Dunne and Goddard, 2009). Understanding theory can be difficult and we found that discussing different interpretations in minute detail was extremely beneficial since, as St Pierre argues, there is no 'right' way to work with theory: 'Notwithstanding our close and responsible readings of their work, "your" Foucault or Deleuze cannot be "my" Foucault or Deleuze, for they have inevitably entered into our very different assemblages, (St Pierre, 2001, p. 150).

In making a choice about which theory to take as a departure point for the research project, it was necessary to consider the limitations of Foucault's work and find ways to deal with them while acknowledging that no theory is likely to be a perfect 'fit'. For our study, there were specific issues we needed to work through. In particular, we felt a need to address criticisms made of Foucault regarding his conceptualization of the subject as 'docile' and 'produced'. We found ways to negotiate these difficulties by talking through them together and by drawing on other academics who had addressed similar problems (e.g., Bartky, 1988; Diprose, 1994; Hartsock, 1990; McNay, 2000).

Hartsock (1990) argues that although Foucault aims to expose the workings of power and, therefore, provide scope for resistance, he also posits power as disciplining the subject and as all pervading. Hartsock (1990, p. 167) claims that while Foucault pushes for resistance he does not offer a way for relations of power between subjects to be transformed. Diprose (1994, pp. 34–35) agrees with this view and contends that there is no 'reality' to embodiment for Foucault and there is 'little chance for women to step outside institutions and social structures' and actively resist dominant knowledge or truths. However, we did not feel this meant that Foucault's work could not account for agency. His core focus is on subjectification (how individuals come to know themselves as subjects) not subjugation (how individuals are controlled via external forces). Foucault's innovative analysis of power focuses on practices that depend on free subjects, and so encompasses possibilities for resistance because for him, individuals are creative and freedom is a condition of power. As he states:

> Power is exercised only over free subjects and only insofar as they are free. By this we mean individual or collective subjects who are faced with a field of

possibilities in which several ways of behaving, several reactions and diverse comportments may be realised. (Foucault, 1982, p. 221)

The perspective taken by Foucault implies that there exists a multiplicity of sometimes contradictory elements, and subjects exercise power in a range of different ways. Indeed, he argues that individuals' practices can interrupt and shift modes of thinking and it is his stated aim to explore 'changes, analogies and differences' in the knowledge produced (Foucault, 2002, p. 193). In doing so, his view provides room to think through how subjects can be identified as produced through disciplinary practices but not determined by them, as guided on how to know and individually materialize themselves as particular types of subjects. Indeed, Smith (1990, p. 160) points out: 'Reason, knowledge, concepts, are more than merely attributes of individual consciousness they are embedded in, organise and are integral to social relations in which subjects act but which are not reducible to the acts of subjects'.

Therefore, our departure point for our analysis of Foucault's work was questioning the production of regimes of truth and the effects of these truths on individuals. We were able to interrogate the formulation of these regimes that identify teaching assistants as certain types of subjects. For example, in primary school settings, the 'caring nature' of teaching assistants was repeatedly invoked. We were also able to investigate how individuals engage with and negotiate circulating regimes of truth to produce themselves, or 'become', active subjects. We found engagement with Foucault's work useful because his characterization of power as productive and his theories on the interplay between power and knowledge informed our thinking about how 'being a teaching assistant' structures, and is structured by, gendered, social and economic power relations.

The process of theoretical engagement opened up possibilities for refiguring how inequities between individuals (e.g. between teachers and teaching assistants) are constituted, naturalized and legitimized through the intersecting of discourse, power and knowledge. This enabled us to politicize the production and exchange of meaning, and to consider how socially endorsed practices shape peoples' lives. Foucault's work also offered an explanation of how the organization of power relations is mobilized, without assuming teaching assistants are passive individuals who are 'acted upon'.

Summary Conclusions and Recommendations

The discovery of appropriate theories

Different researchers will decide upon using a particular theory for their research for a variety of reasons. Initially we focused on theories of social policy, but we felt that we wanted to push our analysis further. We tried engaging with the work of Bourdieu, but shifted our theoretical focus to the work of Foucault because his work was a suitable alternative since two of the researchers were familiar with it.

The ease or difficulties with understanding the theories

Some of the texts written by Foucault, such as *The Archaeology of Knowledge* (2002), cover complex ideas and despite multiple readings can be difficult to grasp. Some of his other texts take the reader through how his thinking about power/ knowledge can be applied to particular institutions (i.e. the development of the penal system in *Discipline and Punish*, 1991) or regimes of truth (i.e. the *History of Sexuality* series, 1990a, 1990b, 1992) and they are possibly more accessible. His ideas have also been engaged with by numerous other researchers and their work, such as that by Kingfisher (1996) and Rabinow (1991), can be extremely helpful in guiding interpretations of the theory.

The difficulty of application to data and texts

Applying any theory to research is likely to present a range of problems that need to be tackled, but I found that engaging in collaborative research enabled resolutions. It was in the process of exploring and discussing how to overcome problems that the researchers came to a deeper understanding of the theory.

What the application of the theories revealed

In the case of this research, the use of theory added a level of complexity to the analysis and provided the researchers with a more detailed and enlightening understanding of the experiences and difficulties faced by the teaching assistants who participated. It revealed, and enabled us to explore, the power dynamics that exist in schools.

How the absence of these theories might have impaired understanding

In the initial stages of the study the absence of a theoretical framework, or a clear understanding of the framework being applied, meant that our writing risked being descriptive rather than having rigorous analytical depth.

The limitations of the theories

All theories will have limitations, but working through these can enhance a researcher's understanding of the theory and the topic of research. In the case of Foucault, he has been particularly criticized for framing individuals as docile subjects. Addressing these concerns was, for us, a matter of collaborative discussion in which we explored how other academics tackled such problems (e.g., St Pierre, 2001; Diprose, 1994; Hartsock, 1990).

Reflections and recommendations

Working on this research was an enjoyable, rewarding experience that helped me to develop as an early career researcher and gain the confidence to present at conferences and go on to single author papers. It was worth the hard work and I am convinced that central to my enjoyment of the project was its collaborative nature, which gave us all new insight into the ways we came from quite different perspectives. We shared every aspect of the research and everything suggested was reviewed, discussed and reworked until it was clear in all our minds. The support, trust and camaraderie we established meant that I felt safe to take risks and able to try things that were outside my 'comfort zone' and which might not work.

Recommended further reading

Barkham (2008) provides conceptual guidance on the changing role of the teaching assistant, which informed our thinking with regard to investigating shifts in identity.

Foucault (1982) provides a nuanced, but somewhat complex, theoretical account of how subjects are materialized in relation to the intersecting of power and knowledge.

Foucault (1991) offers a relatively accessible introduction to the ways in which he theorizes how power and knowledge inform the production of subjects by investigating the history of the penal system and its management of prisoners.

Kingfisher (1996) draws on the work of Foucault to explore how a specific group of women (re)construct their identities through the discourse they use.

References

Barkham, J. (2008) Suitable work for women? Roles, relationships and changing identities of 'other adults' in the early years classroom. *British Educational Research Journal*, 34 (6), 839–853.

Bartky, S. (1988) Foucault, feminism and the modernisation of patriarchal power, in *Feminism and Foucault: Reflections on Resistance* (eds I. Diamond and L. Quimby), North Eastern Press, Boston, pp. 61–86.

Bourdieu, P. and Passeron, J. (1977) *Reproduction in Education, Society and Culture*, Sage, London.

Department for Education and Employment (DfEE) (2000) Higher Education. Speech presented by David Blunkett at Maritime Greenwich University in London, 15 February.

Department for Education and Skills (DfES) (2003) *Remodelling the Workforce*, HMSO, London.

Diprose, R. (1994) *The Bodies of Women*, Routledge, London.

Dunne, L., Goddard, G. and Woolhouse, C. (2008a) Mapping the changes: a critical exploration into the career trajectories of teaching assistants who undertake a foundation degree. *The Journal of Vocational Education and Training*, 60 (1), 49–59.

Dunne, L., Goddard, G. and Woolhouse, C. (2008b) Teaching assistants' perceptions of their professional role and their experiences of doing a foundation degree. *Improving Schools Journal*, 11 (3), 239–249.

Dunne, L., Goddard, G. and Woolhouse, C. (2009) Teachers use you: knowledge, discourse, and the role of the teaching assistant (Paper ID 527), ECER Annual Conference, University of Vienna, September.

Foucault, M. (1970) *The Order of Things*, Vintage, New York.

Foucault, M. (1982) The subject and the power, in *Michel Foucault: Beyond Structuralism and Hermeneutics* (eds H. Dreyfus and P. Rabinow), Harvester Press, Brighton, pp. 208–288.

Foucault, M. (1990a) *The Care of the Self: The History of Sexuality, Vol. 3*, Penguin, London.

Foucault, M. (1990b) *The Will to Knowledge: The History of Sexuality, Vol. 1*, Penguin, London.

Foucault, M. (1991) *Discipline and Punish, The Birth of the Prison*, Penguin, London.

Foucault, M. (1992) *The Use of Pleasure: The History of Sexuality, Vol. 2*, Penguin, London.

Foucault, M. (1995) Truth and power, reprinted in *Michel Foucault, Power/Knowledge: Selected Interviews and Other Writings 1972–1977* (ed. G. Colin), Longman, London, pp. 109–133.

Foucault, M. (2002) *The Archaeology of Knowledge*, Routledge, London.

Giddens, M. (1991) *Modernity and Self-Identity: Self and Society in the Late Modern Age*, Polity Press, Cambridge.

Hartsock, N. (1990) Foucault on power: a theory for women, in *Feminism/Postmodernism* (ed. L. Nicholson), Routledge, London, pp. 157–175.

Kingfisher, C. (1996) Women on welfare: conversational sites of acquiescence and dissent. *Discourse and Society*, 7 (4), 531–557.

McNay, L. (2000) *Gender and Agency: Reconfiguring the Subject in Feminist and Social Theory*, Polity Press, Cambridge.

Rabinow, P. (1991) *The Foucault Reader: An Introduction to Foucault's Thought*, Penguin, London.

Smith, D. (1990) *Texts, Facts and Femininity. Exploring the Relations of Ruling*, Routledge, London.

St Pierre, E.A. (2001) Coming to theory: finding Foucault and Deleuze, in *Feminist Engagements: Reading, Resisting and Revisioning Male Theorists in Education and Cultural Studies* (ed. K. Weiler), Routledge, New York, pp. 141–164.

Webster, L. and Mertova, P. (2007) *Using Narrative Enquiry: An Introduction to Using Critical Event Narrative Analysis in Research on Learning and Teaching*, Routledge, London.

Woolhouse, C., Dunne, L. and Goddard, G. (2009) Teaching assistants' experiences of economic, social and cultural change following completion of a foundation degree. *International Journal of Lifelong Education*, 28 (6), 763–776.

8

How Applying a Discourse-Based Approach to Investigate Inclusion Changed a Research Project and a Way of Thinking

Linda Dunne

Key Theoretical Approaches in this Chapter: Poststructuralist Discourse-Based Research

The key theoretical approaches used in this chapter are post-structuralism and discourse-based research. Poststructuralism may be regarded as more like a way of thinking than a tightly drawn theory (Peters and Burbules, 2004). It is, among other things, concerned with language, power and discourse. It is often associated with attempts to decentre and deconstruct discourses and practices that are taken as natural or as 'given'. In this respect, it lends itself very well to an analysis of taken for granted or common sense practices of schooling, such as the practice of inclusion.

For Foucault, discourses are powerful and are systems of thought composed of ideas, attitudes, beliefs and practices that 'systematically form the objects of which they speak' (Foucault, 1972, p. 49). They have the power to shape practices, ways of being and identities. The research presented in this chapter drew lightly on this notion of

---

Applying Theory to Educational Research: An Introductory Approach with Case Studies,
First Edition. Edited by J. Adams, M. Cochrane and L. Dunne.
© 2012 John Wiley & Sons, Ltd. Published 2012 by John Wiley & Sons, Ltd.

discourse to interrogate 'inclusion', as a discourse and practice. The chapter highlights the changes that occurred on encountering poststructuralist theories, in terms of thinking or understanding, and in refiguring the research process.

Key texts

MacLure, M. (2003) *Discourse in Educational and Social Research*, Open University Press, Buckingham.

Peters, M.A. and Burbules, N.C. (2004) *Postsructuralism and Educational Research*, Rowman and Littlefield, New York.

Introduction to the Research Project

The Salamanca Statement (UNESCO, 1994) encouraged international moves towards inclusion and inclusive schooling based on rights and entitlement for all children. Throughout its years in office, the UK Labour government periodically unleashed a series of policies and reforms related to inclusive schooling (e.g., DfEE, 1997; DfES, 2001a, 2001b, 2007). Social and educational inclusion agendas identify groups with diverse needs within the UK school population and inclusion is associated with issues of race, ethnicity, disability and gender. It also retains a strong association with 'special educational needs' (DfES, 2007) and the integration or 'main-streaming' of pupils who may previously have attended a special school.

Throughout the last decade or so, inclusion has become part of normative practices of schooling, despite it remaining a generalized, disputable concept that is wide open to interpretation. It has become a kind of recognizable 'truth' in the present context. In the early stage of my doctorate, around eight years ago at a time when inclusion was highly prioritized, I proposed to take a narrative research approach to critically consider meanings, experiences and interpretations of it from the viewpoint of educators. I aimed to explore the 'truths' behind inclusion and how understandings of it translated into practice. At that time I had what may be considered a humanist or pragmatic approach to research and tended towards critical and political 'realist' theorizing. I understood inclusion as a political and emancipatory project based on rights, and as a fundamental good. Yet I felt a sense of unease with my proposed research, thinking and practice as a lecturer on inclusive education professional development programmes. My approach and thinking seemed overly simplistic, literal and binary-driven. I struggled with the notion of 'emancipation' and emancipatory research, but could not locate the source of this struggle.

It transpired that what was needed were tools for understanding and changing practice and for helping to move beyond the literal in my own thinking. Poststructuralism provided plausible theoretical tools to challenge and change my ways of thinking and to reframe my subsequent research investigation and analysis. This chapter provides a personal account of how encountering poststructuralist theorizing around the notion of discourse affected my thinking and view of the world and how it changed my research study.

Theories Explained and their Use Justified in the Context of this Research Project

Poststructuralism and discourse-based research

Poststructuralism and poststructuralist theorizing, sometimes associated with postmodernism, avoids any attempt at a straightforward definition. It is commonly associated with the philosophical works of figures such as Derrida, Deleuze, Foucault and Lyotard, but as Peters and Burbules (2004) indicate, it cannot be reduced to a set of shared assumptions, a method, a theory or a school and may be regarded as a movement of thought that embodies different forms of critical practice. Educational research and practice has to some extent been characterized by what Lyotard (1984) called grand narratives, or stories about progress and scientific development that describe what will count as individual and institutional development. A poststructuralist approach might critique and question the notion and culture of the Enlightenment and essentialist ideas and assumptions (such as that of the centred, rational individual; science as 'truth' and a belief in linear social progress and mastery). I found the following helpful in grasping the nature of poststructuralism:

> Politically speaking, poststructuralism aims to expose structures of domination by diagnosing 'power/knowledge' relations and their manifestations in classifications, typologies and institutions. It aims to produce an 'incredulity towards meta-narratives', to unhook and disassemble the structures, the 'moves' and manipulations of official discourse. (Peters and Humes, 2003, p. 112)

Poststructuralism appealed to me in a number of ways. It offers a means of critiquing ontology and epistemology found in more scientific approaches to education. The area of special needs and inclusive education has a dubious history of heavily scientific, medicalized and seemingly authoritative approaches to research that have, arguably, created essentialized and pathologized ways of thinking about children and their particular needs. In the past, there has been much research 'on' children in 'the hunt for disability' (Baker, 2002). As Allan (2004) signifies, poststructuralist thinking can provide a powerful alternative to such approaches, as well as a critique of them.

Poststructuralism also appealed because it acknowledges the centrality and power of language and discourse to shape reality. Instead of language being seen as a transparent medium for transporting meaning, from a poststructuralist approach language itself has to be illuminated and deconstructed. From this perspective, what is regarded as truth is not certain or absolute, because it is caught in the depths of language, discourse and interpretation.

The notion of discourse, as understood here, extends beyond technical descriptions of linguistics, textual analysis and language in use. Discourses may be seen as systems of thought or 'as bodies of ideas that produce and regulate the world in their own terms, rendering some things common sense and other things nonsensical' (Youdell, 2006, p. 36). According to St Pierre (2000, p. 485), once a discourse becomes normal or natural, 'it is difficult to think and act outside of it'. Discourses can be seen as practices for producing meaning, forming subjects (or people) and regulating conduct within particular societies and institutions. MacLure (2003, p. 9) suggests that a discourse-based educational research project sets itself the task of taking that which offers itself as common sense, obvious, natural, given or unquestionable and tries to 'unravel it a bit – to open it up'. Doing discourse analysis involves interrogating our own assumptions and the ways in which we habitually make sense of things (Gee, 2005). From a poststructuralist perspective, discourses are very powerful and can be seen as practices for 'regulating conduct within particular societies and institutions' (MacLure, 2003, p. 175).

This is quite a leap from understanding discourse as benign or as pure meaning-making. In his archaeological work, Foucault (1972), who denied the label 'poststructuralist', claimed that all is discourse. Here, discourses are systems of thought composed of ideas, attitudes, beliefs and practices that 'systematically form the objects of which they speak' (Foucault, 1972, p. 49), meaning that they have the power to shape practices, ways of being and identities. In his later genealogies, Foucault focused on an analysis of power relations and was concerned with the way that certain forms of discourse become invested with power. For Foucault, discourse is inextricably linked to power and to knowledge; 'it is in discourse that power and knowledge are joined together' (Foucault, 1978, p. 100), and is a kind of vehicle for power -knowledge:

> In a society ... there are manifold relations of power which permeate, characterise and constitute the social body, and these relations of power cannot themselves be established, consolidated nor implemented without the production, accumulation, circulation and functioning of a discourse. (Foucault, 1980, p. 93)

From within this framework, the world is constructed by human discourses, giving us not so much hard and fast truths but rather 'truth-effects'. Socially constructed ideas and practices in society, conveyed through discourse, are given the status of truth. These truths construct norms around which people are incited to shape or constitute themselves and their lives (Todd, 2005). Reading the works of Foucault (1972, 1978, 1980) on discourse, power and knowledge enabled me to consider how the meanings and practices in which we come to be are highly regulated by systems of norms, as discourses, 'which precedes social subjects and whose intelligibility they permit' (De Lissovoy, 2008, p. 92).

Within a poststructuralist understanding of power, models of disability that relate to inclusion and inclusive education, such as the social/medical models (Oliver, 1996) are questioned and de-stabilized (Tremain, 2005). Studies that have taken a Foucauldian or discourse-based poststructuralist approach to critique the notion or facets of either special education or inclusion, (e.g., Allan, 1999, 2004; Graham and Slee, 2008; Youdell, 2006) were particularly influential in assisting my understanding of poststructuralist thinking and in signifying that, despite it being embraced as a social 'good' within a progressive narrative, 'inclusion' may create and construct social injustices.

The Application of Theory to the Research

On encountering poststructuralism and subsequently taking a different path in my research, I struggled with my own view of the world and with my embedded realist ontology. Self-doubt was etched into the realist discourses I had for so long inhabited and perpetuated. Self-doubt was partly characterized by a perceived self-lack; for example, I feared that I did not have a sufficiently strong philosophical knowledge base to engage with, or write within, a more theoretical or critical frame of reference. I felt that I lacked the requisite degree in philosophy to write with any credibility. Although I found poststructuralist ideas around discourse fascinating, I was not a discourse analyst or a Foucault 'expert' and I had read scathing critiques about researchers' potentially 'using and abusing' Foucault in their work (see Scheurich and Bell McKenzie, 2005).

Fears and doubts surrounding my engagement with newly found ideas persisted and at times I was tempted to abandon a discourse-based approach and 'play safe' by returning to my original research aim of exploring 'real' meanings and lived experiences of inclusion. At this stage, I remained caught in realist or humanist thinking because, among other things, such a research aim would be taking inclusion as 'given'. St Pierre (2000, p. 479) suggests that humanism produces its own failure, but that once they become intelligible, boundaries, limits and 'grids of regularity' can 'be disrupted and transgressed'. My realist thinking had me captured in a grid of regularity, a 'safety zone', from which I was struggling to escape. MacLure (2003, p. 71) suggests there is a need to abandon the purported clarity and assurance of 'plain view' that underpins realist ontology, for what it obscures; that is, 'the ambivalence, irony, simulation and trickery that are part of self-hood and social life'. The political point behind this is that 'the transparent virtues of clarity, righteousness, visibility and simplicity are not necessarily in the interests of those on the margins of power and prestige' (Maclure, 2003, p. 17). Seemingly simple and virtuous values, such as those often found in inclusive-oriented policies that talk self-evidently, yet vaguely, of 'rights', 'participation' and 'access', can sustain the subordination of marginalized groups and people in insidious ways.

Tremain (2002, p. 32) describes realist ontology as 'where real objects exist in nature apart from any contingent signifying practice'. Signifying practices, or representations within culture, along with similar concepts within poststructuralist theories around language and discourse, enlivened me and began to form the focus and developing theoretical framework of my study. Alongside wider reading in the area of sociology and philosophy, it became a matter of putting postmodernism to work on myself (Allan, 2004) by abandoning attempts to know 'exactly what is going on' through a willingness to embrace uncertainty, self-doubt, conflicts and fears and by accepting the limitations of my own understandings.

As I became absorbed by poststructuralist ideas around discourse, the focus and methodology of my research subsequently changed considerably from initially intending to investigate meanings and narratives of experience to a more theoretical consideration of representations, language and discourse. Atkinson (2000) shows how ontology can change and how these changes affect research and the writing process. My original (realist) research questions had been something like: what is inclusion? How can schools become more inclusive? What are people's experiences of inclusion? With my changing understandings they became quite different questions, with a shift from the 'what' to the 'how', and to a focus on discourse. I subsequently asked questions such as: how is the discourse of inclusion constituted and configured and what do its configurations evoke? How are the 'truth effects' of inclusion created and whose interests are served by the way it operates (as a discourse and practice)?

Instead of researching what inclusion might mean to people (taking it as a 'given'), I aimed to investigate the (discursive) object of inclusion itself, to question and critique it as a potentially hegemonic and normalizing discourse and practice. The underpinning theoretical framework was infused with the notion of 'discourse as practice' (Foucault, 1972, p. 46) and with an understanding that discourse is inextricably linked and bound together with productive power and knowledge (Foucault, 1978). I aimed to identify the particular knowledge(s) and 'truths' that circulated around inclusion and to consider their truth effects. Instead of collecting data from interviews and teacher/teaching assistant narrative accounts (as originally intended), data were gathered in a way that seemed more fitting for my research questions and paradigm. The data were inter-textual and comprised of drawings, talk and online discussions. The montage of data helped to trace and 'mark out' the discursive domain of the object of study.

Davies (2004) suggests that when poststructuralists talk about the way that sense is made they are not attempting to reveal something about the sense-maker (the subject), about his or her motives or intentions. In analysing the data, I was not looking for 'the person' or at the 'meaning' behind statements made about inclusion. I was looking for emergent discourses and working from an understanding that people's talk may be an effect of the discourses they are drawn to, or operate within, rather than an expression of their subjectivity. In this sense, discourse and discursive formations are already there. There are limits to what we say and what can be said and our social interactions are to some extent scripted. We 'recognize' discursive situations and draw upon a range of discursive repertoires open to us that seem appropriate for that situation. That which cannot be captured in words remains unintelligible.

In discourse-based approaches to research, there are no set formats, rules or guiding principles for analysis. Analysis is guided by the research topic, research questions and point of focus (Taylor, 2001). Graham (2005) offers original and very helpful suggestions on how to approach Foucauldian discourse analysis and I drew upon these to some extent, in addition to other sources (e.g., Gee, 2005). In analysing the data, I considered the words, language patterns and phrases deployed and located sections of texts, reiterations and statements that I came to see as regularities within a discursive field. I located what I came to regard as taken-for-granted words and signifiers, statements and families of statements. During analysis and subsequent critical readings of the data, I asked questions, for example: how are these statements framed or constructed and what are the ideological assumptions behind them? What do they evoke, enable or discredit and what might be the potential effects of them? The discursive field that emerged could possibly be traced or linked to a constituting field of power/knowledge or to a discipline, such as Psychology, as well as to practice, so I also asked: what knowledge base is privileged and excluded from these representations?

My critical reading or interpretation of the data was inevitably partial and subjective. In summary, it suggested that inclusion as a discourse and (dividing) practice was characterized by sub-discourses, or discourses within, that are constructed within a powerful othering and objectifying framework. A prevailing or dominant discourse that was threaded throughout the data descriptions was one associated with alterity or othering of perceived and frequently marked out or named difference. Autism, 'special needs' and 'problem behaviour' were specified as determinants of inclusion. Pupils and their 'needs' were objectified in that they appeared to become detached from the pupil (Youdell, 2006): 'Where there is a Statemented child there will also be some School Action and School Action Plus children as well so that others get support off the back of the Statemented child'.

School practices related to inclusion, such as the Code of Practice (DfES, 2001a), both divide and individualize children such that they appear to become de-contextualized objects of assessment. The grids of specification or categories within the discourse were related to reiterations of special needs, deficit and medicalizations of human differences that suggested that inclusion remains a 'perfecting technology' (Baker, 2002, p. 675). Paradoxically, certain 'types' of children, who are marked out (from a 'norm'), targeted and under surveillance, are seen as 'the included'. Inclusion was also characterized by a discourse relating to the self, self-government and to psychology derived self-oriented constructs such as self-esteem. Building a child's self-esteem (in a linear fashion) was a clear policy message (DfES, 2007) at the time of writing and was also a recurrent and dominant theme within my analysis. Inclusion appeared to operate within, and be aligned with the neo-liberal practice of creating self-actualized, enterprising individuals and entrepreneurial identities (see Ecclestone, 2007; Masschelein and Simons, 2002), or of individuals who work upon themselves so that the state does not need to.

The Relevance and Effectiveness of Using Theory

I began this chapter by suggesting that my research approach had, in the past, tended towards critical and emancipatory paradigms, and that my views of the world and of research had changed as a result of encountering poststructuralism. Prior to this change, I intended to research meanings of inclusion but had felt an inexplicable dissatisfaction with this approach. I had a keen interest in language and the way that children were spoken about, positioned and represented in schools but had been unsure how to investigate this. I had read Jenny Corbett's (1996) book *Bad Mouthing* that presents persuasive arguments about the power of language and the potentially damaging effects of language associated with special education. Gillian Fulcher (1989), one of the first writers to apply a theory of discourse to the language of special needs, was also influential in fuelling my early interest in language and discourse. So to some extent, delving into poststructuralist theories around language and discourse was inevitably 'the next step'.

Engaging with poststructuralist ideas revealed that there are hidden power dynamics in research paradigms that have an emancipatory intent. They can, for example, contain a desire to be right, a will to power and therefore to a particular truth. Emancipatory research begins from existing political and social standpoints and knowledge and, by doing so, can reinforce and recreate inequalities (Tremain, 2005). An emancipatory discourse, as it becomes established in mainstream, can itself become a totalizing one. However, poststructuralist is not a rejection of critical theory. According to Youdell (2006), it is an additional set of conceptual, analytical and political tools that may be used to pursue avenues for change. It retains but resituates what may be termed rights-based, emancipatory work.

Encountering poststructuralist ideas and theories awoke me from an ideological sleep (MacLure, 2003), or a kind of passivity, and was both exciting and unsettling. It taught me, among other things, to be critically aware of how meanings become institutionalized and reified and of the hidden discursive disciplinary power mechanisms that are all around but tend to go unnoticed. Viewing the world from a poststructuralist perspective enabled a certain inexplicable release or liberation and greater recognition of my own polarized, linear and essentialist ways of thinking and practice that carried its own dangers. In doing ethical work on myself (Allan, 2005), I became more aware of my own thinking, preconceptions and assumptions that normalize, and more able to question. Ball (1995, p. 267) claims that the point about theory is not that it is simply critical; theory in educational research ought 'to engage in struggle, to reveal and undermine what is most invisible and insidious in prevailing practices'. A poststructuralist approach to research enabled me to see that what is taken as natural, given or as true is capable of being seen otherwise. A research approach that abandons notions of fixed particular truths 'urges us to think, to opt for questions rather than answers, and to critique and seek possibilities rather than crave control' (McWhorter, 2005, p. xvi).

Summary Conclusions and Recommendations

The discovery of the appropriate theories

The application of a particular theory or theoretical approach to research perhaps depends to some extent upon the researcher's interests, way of thinking and view or understanding of the world (ontology and epistemology). Theory was not necessarily 'discovered', it was a gradual process. I had felt dissatisfaction with my initial research approach but did not know why. There were critical points or epiphany moments that occurred in minor events that fractured my humanist or realist perspective, challenged my set ways of thinking and offered exciting alternatives. For example, following a lecture at the start of my studies, a tutor advised me to read what seemed like quite a complex article that challenged the notion of participation as a fundamental good (Masschelein and Quaghebeur, 2005). Prior to this encounter and my subsequent engagement with similar readings, my research could well have been a 'celebratory' piece of work; possibly 'evidenced' by narratives of experience of success. With a different eye and critical, theoretical understanding, I attempted to grapple with, and tentatively unravel, some of the power mechanisms that surround simplistic notions of 'participation'.

The ease or difficulties with understanding the theories

Once a decision was made to adopt a poststructuralist approach I became absorbed in reading within and around it. Ideas within philosophy can be complex, obscure and challenging, but they are also exciting. Introductory or 'primer' books were helpful as 'a starter' to get an overview or flavour of poststructuralist approaches. MacLure's (2003) lively book on discourse and education was directly relevant and revelatory, as was Peters and Burbules (2004) text on poststructuralist theory and its application to educational research.

The difficulties of application to data and texts

Taking a discourse-based poststructuralist research approach was liberating and enabled a degree of creativity in data collection and interpretation. It enabled me to see how language, discourse and practice are inter-woven and how the way that children are spoken about and positioned in schools is not benign but has effects.

What the application of the theories revealed

The application of the theories revealed the power mechanisms at work in taken for granted practices of schooling and showed how children are positioned and subsequently objectified. The focus on discourse and its entanglement with power/knowledge enabled me to consider hidden disciplinary mechanisms and exclusions that operate under the guise of inclusion. Taking a discourse approach also provided recognition of the sheer power of language and how discourses create subject positions that speak things and people into existence, such as the 'special educational needs child' or 'the included child' (see Youdell, 2006).

How the absence of these theories might have impaired understanding

Without a theoretical or conceptual framework my research project would have been somewhat literal, mechanistic and dry. The theoretical framework allowed for experiment of ideas, or as a poststructuralist might put it, 'play'. Without theory, my study might have reinforced existing taken-for-granted 'already there' understandings and 'celebrations' of inclusion: the theory allowed for much greater critique and questioning.

The limitations of the theories

Poststructuralist research is tentative and wary of assumptions. It does not make claims to truth and may be seen to be incomplete, nihilistic and speculative. It can potentially diffuse the stark political struggle behind disability rights and inclusion. A scientific-oriented researcher in education might say that a poststructuralist informed research study is overly subjective and doesn't offer generalizations, correlations or wider application.

Reflection and recommendations of the experience

Before encountering poststructuralist ideas I had researched and taught within what I now recognize as a more traditionalist and rights-based narrative. To some extent I enforced the notion of inclusion as a simplistic and fundamental good and encountering Poststructuralism enabled me to question and to problematize it. This involved a questioning of my self and my values, which was discomforting. At times, I felt that perhaps it would be better to 'play safe', to abandon this newly found philosophy of ideas around discourse and continue with my original research proposal with what seemed to be a more 'grounded' approach. However, the force of my changing positioning and perspective, and the excitement of engaging with and pursuing new ways of thinking and seeing, meant that I was following a different route. Although I felt that I was floundering in uncharted territory, I could not go back!

Recommended further reading

Allan, J. (2010) *Rethinking Inclusive Education: The Philosophers of Difference in Practice*, Springer, London. This is a timely book that connects the politics and ideologies of inclusion to philosophers who explore notions of difference and alterity.

References

Allan, J. (1999) *Actively Seeking Inclusion: Pupils with Special Needs in Mainstream Schools*, Falmer Press, London.

Allan, J. (2004) Deterritorializations: putting postmodernism to work on teacher education and inclusion. *Educational Philosophy and Theory*, 36 (4), 417–432.

Allan, J. (2005) Inclusion as an ethical project, in *Foucault and the Government of Disability* (ed. S. Tremain), University of Michigan Press, Ann Arbor.

Allan, J. (2010) *Rethinking Inclusive Education: The Philosophers of Difference in Practice*, Springer, London.

Atkinson, E. (2000) Behind the inquiring mind: exploring the transition from external to internal inquiry. *Reflective Practice*, 1 (2), 149–164.

Baker, B. (2002) The hunt for disability: the new eugenics and the normalization of school children. *Teacher's College Record*, 104 (4), 663–703.

Ball, S.J. (1995) Intellectuals or technicians? The urgent role of theory in educational studies. *British Journal of Educational Studies*, 43 (3), 255–271.

Corbett, J. (1996) *Bad-Mouthing: The Language of Special Needs*, Falmer Press, London.

Davies, B. (2004) Introduction: poststructuralist lines of flight in Australia. *International Journal of Qualitative Studies in Education*, 17 (1), 1–10.

De Lissovoy, N. (2008) Conceptualising oppression in educational theory: toward a compound standpoint. *Cultural Studies ⇔ Critical Methodologies*, 8 (1), 82–105.

DfEE (1997) *Excellence for All Children: Meeting Special Educational Needs*, DfEE, London.

DfES (2001a) *Revised Code of Practice on the Identification and Assessment of Special Educational Needs*, DfES, London.

DfES (2001b) *Inclusive Schooling*, DfES, London.

DfES (2007) *Inclusion Development Programme*, DfES, London.

Ecclestone, K. (2007) Resisting images of the 'diminished self': the implications of emotional wellbeing and emotional engagement in education policy. *Journal of Education Policy*, 22 (4), 455–470.

Foucault, M. (1972) *The Archaeology of Knowledge*, Tavistock, London.

Foucault, M. (1978) *The History of Sexuality: An Introduction*, Penguin, Harmondsworth.

Foucault, M. (1980) *Power/Knowledge: Selected Interviews and Other Writings, 1972–1977* (ed. C. Gordon, trans. L. Marshall, J. Mepham and K. Soper), Pantheon, New York.

Fulcher, G. (1989) *Disabling Policies; A Comparative Approach to Education Policy and Disability*, Falmer Press, London.

Gee, J.P. (2005) *An Introduction to Discourse Analysis: Theory and Method*, Routledge Falmer, London.

Graham, L. (2005) Discourse analysis and the critical use of Foucault. Paper presented at Australian Association for Research in Education, Annual Conference, Sydney, 27 November–1 December 2005. Available online at http://www.eprints.qut.edu.au/archive (accessed 29 November 2007).

Graham, L.J. and Slee, R. (2008) An illusory interiority: interrogating the discourse/s of inclusion. *Educational Philosophy and Theory*, 40 (2), 277–292.

Lyotard, J.F. (1984) *The Postmodern Condition: A Report on Knowledge* (trans. G. Bennington and B. Massumi), University of Minnesota Press, Minneapolis.

MacLure, M. (2003) *Discourse in Educational and Social Research*, Open University Press, Buckingham.

Masschelein, J. and Quaghebeur, K. (2005) Participation for better or for worse? *Journal of Philosophy of Education*, 39 (1), 52–65.

Masschelein, J. and Simons, M. (2002) An adequate education in a globalised world? A note on immunisation against being together. *Journal of Philosophy of Education*, 36 (4), 589–608.

McWhorter, L. (2005) Forward, in *Foucault and the Government of Disability* (ed. S. Tremain), University of Michigan Press, Ann Arbor.

Oliver, M. (1996) *Understanding Disability: From Theory to Practice*, Macmillan, London.

Peters, M. and Humes, W. (2003) Editorial: The reception of poststructuralism in educational research and policy. *Journal of Education Policy*, 18 (2), 109–113.

Peters, M.A. and Burbules, N.C. (2004) *Poststructuralism and Educational Research*, Rowman and Littlefield, New York.

Scheurich, J. and Bell McKenzie, K. (2005) Foucault's methodologies: archaeology and genealogy, in *The Sage Handbook of Qualitative Research*, 3rd edn (eds N. Denzin and Y. Lincoln), Sage, London, pp. 841–869.

St Pierre, E.A. (2000) Poststructural feminism in education: an overview. *Qualitative Studies in Education*, 13 (5), 477–515.

Taylor, S. (2001) Locating and conducting discourse analytic research, in *Discourse as Data: A Guide for Analysis* (eds M. Wetherell, S. Taylor and S. Yates), Sage, London, 142–155.

Todd, L. (2005) Enabling practices for professionals: the need for practical poststructuralist theory, in *Disability and Psychology: Critical Introductions and Reflections* (eds D. Goodley and R. Lawthom), Macmillan, Basingstoke, p. 148.

Tremain, S. (2002) On the subject of impairment, in *Disability/Postmodernity: Embodying Political Theory* (eds M. Corker and T. Shakespeare), Continuum, London, pp. 32–48.

Tremain, S. (2005) Foucault, governmentality, and critical disability theory: an introduction, in *Foucault and the Government of Disability* (ed. S. Tremain), University of Michigan Press, Ann Arbor, pp. 1–27.

UNESCO (1994) The Salamanca Statement and Framework for Action on Special Needs Education. World Conference on Special Needs Education, Access and Quality, http://www.unesco.org/education/educpro/sne/salamanc/index. htm (accessed 12 May 2005).

Youdell, D. (2006) *Impossible Bodies, Impossible Selves: Exclusions and Student Subjectivities*, Springer, Dordrecht.

Part III

Voices of Experience

*Accounts by Researchers Versed
in the Use of Theory*

Introduction

These final chapters show how practice can change as a result of research, or how new forms of practice can develop. They are written by researchers who have experience of the research process, and the application of theory in particular. They have all participated in several research projects, and the research project that they refer to in these chapters has either been completed or collected enough data to enable significant analysis on the use and application of their theoretical frameworks. Their experience has enabled them to reflect and consider the importance of theory, and what it has come to mean for their understanding of the research procedures. They are able to offer their perceptions of those aspects of theory that concern us most: the promise of an explanation of social phenomena, as a revelation of new insights, and the means of revisiting questions formerly thought of as settled.

Each of these five cases is characterized by the combined use of theories, rather than the dominance of any one particular theory. This may be the result of a mistrust of the rigidity of some theoretical frameworks, or perhaps a recognition of the problem of transference of theory, where the change in context from where the theory originated is sufficient to distort its significance. By means of hybridity, the eye of the experienced researcher demonstrates awareness of these shortcomings and the need for flexibility; it may also be that their hopes for the explanations and understandings that theory is capable of yielding are more modest.

Also characteristic of these final chapters is the integration of theory with methodology and the recognition of the artifice of the divide between

Applying Theory to Educational Research: An Introductory Approach with Case Studies, First Edition. Edited by J. Adams, M. Cochrane and L. Dunne.
© 2012 John Wiley & Sons, Ltd. Published 2012 by John Wiley & Sons, Ltd.

them. In some cases, such as Mary McAteer's and Jeff Adams' Chapters (12 and 13), this takes the form of the direct theorizing of methodologies, with concern for the recognition of the empowerment potentially embodied in the critical reassessment of hitherto orthodox or traditional practices that have suppressed particular voices. This is literally the case in Chapter 9, in which Martin Ashley explores the complex issue of masculinities in the context of boys who risk the ridicule of their peers by joining a choir. Nevertheless, this is something that young boys are willing to do; understanding why this happens is at the root of encouraging more involvement in activities that are seen by others as 'uncool', and to do this theories of gender and sexuality are employed, with the focus on masculinity. It turns out that the solution is neither as simple nor as obvious as it might seem, and the realignment of feminist theories to explore masculinity is a striking feature of this case.

Madeleine Sclater's project in Chapter 10 is also concerned with young people and problems of disenfranchisement, and explores this through constructivist learning theories, particularly situated learning. Her project looked at these theories in the context of collaborative learning with young people through online art education. Sclater's application of these theories gave rise to further theories of meaning-making in art, whereby the process of making art, the practice, materials and procedure, is fundamental to the interpretative meanings that arise. The consequence of this, theoretically at least, is that the meaning of the young people's artwork is thoroughly integrated into the means of their production, hence the importance of the theory of practice. Sclater is particularly concerned with maintaining a 'bricolage' of theoretical perspectives, perhaps reflecting the complexity of adapting older constructivist theories to the evolving and dynamic context of engagement with virtual worlds.

The interest in constructivism is continued in Graham Rogers' project described in Chapter 11, which traces the history of a selection of these theories and their associated theorists, such as Vygotsky and Dewey, to explain and justify their use in his own research. A writer of great experience, Rogers draws on his enduring engagement with these ideas in his study of the acquisition of notions of professionalism in beginning teachers, where their changing values and ideals as are explored as their identities evolve. Theories of constructivism feature in the work of several writers in this book, and its popularity may be due, at least in part, to its legitimation and vindication of the collaborative processes that have been a characteristic feature of practices in the arts and humanities for generations.

McAteer and Adams, in Chapters 12 and 13 respectively, both attempt to theorize the process of research itself, and in doing so they adopt the stance of critical theorists: the very act and procedure of research in the contexts to which they refer is an intervention which has emancipatory aims. In her 'theory generative' approaches in practitioner research, Chapter 12, McAteer advocates 'action research' as a way to consider, reflect upon and analyse practice. She shows how Elliott's (1991) action research model was adopted to research the 'problem' of girls' under-representation in Physics at A-level. In action research, the research itself becomes part of the practice researched, while the practice becomes a research vehicle. McAteer suggests that this provides a powerful means by which practitioners can enhance the potential for their practice to become *praxis*, or 'practical philosophy'.

In Chapter 13, 'Art Practice as Education Research', the closing chapter of the book, Adams explores the nature of research itself and what constitutes a meaningful medium for it to occur. His chapter challenges the traditional model of data collection and analysis followed by a written thesis, and explores the use of filmmaking as a valid way of expressing educational research. Adams's approach is to consider how such research is viewed by theorists, and contrasts this with the sceptical views of those who prefer the textural modes of research presentation.

Reference

Elliott, J. (1991) *Action Research for Educational Change*, Open University Press, Milton Keynes.

9

Should I be Singing This, and if So, How High?
Theoretical Approaches to Boyhood and Masculinity

Martin Ashley

Key Theoretical Approaches in this Chapter: Raewyn Connell's Theories of Multiple Masculinity

Connell's ideas are often applied in education research to explore masculinity and boyhood. Paradoxically, the theories often appeal to male researchers who describe themselves as pro-feminist, a position that sits close to that described as critical masculinity studies. It may seem strange, but some of the most important work on boyhoods and masculinity is carried out within a feminist framework, commonly termed 'pro-feminist' when the researchers are male. Somewhat removed from these positions is the notion of recuperative masculinity, which is associated with a male backlash against perceived feminist advance and the need for boys to 'catch up'. Connell's work is used by those who are motivated by gender equality. The other important idea is that of gender as relational – that which is masculine is all that is not feminine. Multiple masculinities build on but take us beyond that position.

Applying Theory to Educational Research: An Introductory Approach with Case Studies, First Edition. Edited by J. Adams, M. Cochrane and L. Dunne.
© 2012 John Wiley & Sons, Ltd. Published 2012 by John Wiley & Sons, Ltd.

Key texts

Connell, R. (2005) *Masculinities*, Polity, Cambridge.
Kehily, M. (2007) *Understanding Youth: Perspectives, Identities and Practices*, Sage, London.
Martino, W. and Pallotta-Chiarolli, M. (2003) *So What's a Boy? Addressing Issues of Masculinity and Schooling*, Open University Press, Maidenhead.

Introduction to the Research Project

A fundamental task of the research project was to explain why boys in Western cultures, particularly those between the ages of 11 and 14, perceive choirs as 'uncool' and are so reluctant to sing. Choral, as opposed to solo singing, can also be perceived as 'uncool' by girls, but boys are presented with a particular issue because this kind of singing requires them to sing in the same high range as girls. Choral practitioners have for some time felt that this may be a problem. The research was needed to address an ongoing and pressing practical problem for musicians who are daily confronted by gender imbalance and difficulties in finding enough male voices to balance females and provide the lower vocal parts. Its applicability to schooling, however, was far wider than this for it both sat within the boys' achievement debate and confronted fundamental ontological questions of boyhood. Is there a reality that we can call 'boy' or is boyhood reducible to a series of prescriptions and proscriptions of gender appropriate behaviour?

The idea that singing is 'sissy' and not a proper activity for 'real boys' has a long history. It is not only singing that has been proscribed for real boys in this way. So also have been dance, poetry, languages and many other activities, including academic work itself. The term hegemonic masculinity is used throughout Connell's writing and refers to an idealized, normative repertoire of behaviours and attitudes. The playing of sport, physical toughness, emotional independence, competition, hierarchy and a particular form of humour ('havin' a laff') would figure regularly. Crucially for Connell, these behaviours are associated with oppression of subordinate identities that include all females, gay men and non-white ethnicities.

At one level, then, our research had to identify reasons given by boys for their reluctance to sing and fit these into an explanatory framework that made connections with similar cases, such as boys' reluctance to learn modern foreign languages (Carr and Pauwels, 2006). These connections needed to be related to an over arching theory, and the theory justified in relation to other, possibly competing, theories. This might be considered in part an epistemological problem. How do we know what we know about boys and how valid is this knowledge? However, behind every epistemological problem, there is usually an ontological one. What is the nature of boyhood? What *is* the being of a boy? Epistemology and ontology are often confused, but they are quite distinct. Epistemology is the philosophical discipline that deals with what is to count as knowledge. Ontology is the philosophical investigation of existence. So while the former asks what are the grounds for knowing, the other asks what exists. The ontological problem thus raises difficulties when it ponders whether boys actually exist as a class of human uniquely different from others. Are statements about boys to be simply empirical, that is, descriptive observations of how boys actually behave, or are they to contain a philosophic element that addresses questions of how boys ought to be? Any such element would be inevitably based on a particular pre-existing concept of what boys are.

This is what made the research so interesting and enduring. Is hegemonic masculinity a contested concept, and if so, contested by whom? What position should the research take in relation to this? The dilemma of describing boyhood as it is observed, or discussing notions of how boyhood ought to be, should not be underestimated (Mac an Ghaill and Haywood, 2006). It renders impossible the ideal of the hard sciences, through which a detached, objective position might be reached. None of the theories or methodologies that have been advanced to explain masculinity, manhood and boyhood passes such a test. This means that there are real limitations with regard to the traditional gold standard of reliability and validity and these must be acknowledged in the research. The notions of transparency and trustworthiness become important, even when the method is quantitative more than qualitative (Hollway and Jefferson, 2000; Greene and Hogan, 2005). Much of the most cited literature on boyhood comes from what is often referred to as a pro-feminist tradition, that is to say, male authors who acknowledge and draw upon the contributions of feminist scholarship. To research and write in this tradition is to be linked into certain views and values with regard to the question of how boys ought to be and what makes them the way they are (Francis, 2006).

Theories Explained and their Use Justified
in the Context of this Research Project

Notions of gender relativity, hegemonic and multiple masculinities

At the outset of the project, the theory that gender was a socially constructed, relational concept appeared attractive. In order to rehearse and assert their developing masculinity, boys needed to avoid any kind of performance associated with femininity (Paechter, 2006). Girls sang, often in large numbers. In order to assert their 'not-girlness' then, boys needed to avoid singing because that is what girls do. This attractively simple explanation was reinforced by conditions of voice. Boys below a certain age sing in a high voice that does not sound like a man's. Certain styles of singing allegedly exaggerate the potentially female qualities in boys' voices. Phillips (2003), writing in the *Choral Journal*, describes what he perceives as the shame of boys who feel they are sounding like girls, and this is illustrative of a commonly encountered theme. A significant number of writers seemed to be content with the explanation that a boy 'doesn't want to sound like a girl'. Potency is added to this by the fact that the voice is one of the most intimate and significant markers of personal identity and no more so for boys than at that difficult time of early adolescence.

Superficially at least, this 'sound like a girl' explanation was reinforced by the notion of hegemonic masculinity. Writers such as Lucy Green had made it clear that singing, which puts the body on display as a subject of the male gaze, was a feminine performance. Nowhere is such performance normalized or valorized within the prescriptive canon of hegemonic masculinity. According to Green, the gendering of music is evident in girls' display of the body and boys' self-concealment behind technology (Green, 1997). Cracks and fissures soon began to appear, however. How might the phenomenon of the Welsh male voice choir of coal miners, doubtless hegemonic in most other aspects of masculinity, be explained? Rather more importantly, how might the theory be fitted to the incoming empirical data that confirmed that boys *did* sing? Early on in the research, for example, it became clear that choirboys frequently articulated two identities: the 'weird boy' who enjoyed singing in a high voice in church on a Sunday and the 'normal boy' who kicked a football around at school during the week. The fact that boys explicitly articulated ways in which they maintained two separate identities figured prominently in early reports of the research: 'I'm a different person at school, I play football and I don't talk about singing' (12-year-old, quoted in Ashley, 2008).

In its classic formulation Connell's theory proposes that as well as hegemonic masculinities there are complicit, marginalized and authorized masculinities. Complicit masculinities do not necessarily display all the robust and classic hegemonic characteristics, but neither do they contradict them. They simply reap the 'patriarchal dividend' of association. Marginalized masculinities are those ascribed to subordinate groups and in terms of the hegemonic ideal, it is the gay male that is most frequently subordinate, although other groups can be classified as subordinate through ethnicity or class. For boys this is critically important as, according to a stream of work which originates in the writings of Adrienne Rich, young adolescent boys are obliged by 'compulsory heterosexuality' (see also Kehily, 2002) to assert publicly that they are 'not gay' – a challenge for young singers whatever their sexual orientation. The concept of 'authorized masculinity' goes some way to explaining how it is that subordinate groups, such as blacks, can be hegemonic in most other ways. The black athlete, for example, may be 'authorized' to rise in status to the degree that is permitted by the super-ordinate group of white, hegemonic males.

The Application of Theory to the Research

The theory of multiple masculinities was found to be far from neutral when applied to the research. It raised immediately the question of whether a particular type of masculinity was predominantly associated with boys who enjoyed singing. In the early stages, the assumption was made that the masculinity of singing boys must be a subordinate one. This provided a ready means of theorizing about why the word 'gay' is often used by non-singing boys as a put-down for other boys' singing (Mac an Ghaill and Haywood, 2006). However, this was a dangerous assumption that set back the progress of understanding by several years. The problem that emerged as case studies and data sets built up was that many of the boys who enjoyed singing exhibited classic traits of masculine hegemony. For example, most enjoyed sport and many were observed to engage in rough, male play. Male humour was frequently associated with singing groups, as was the tendency to misbehave or challenge the teacher. Boys who sang could draw on such resources to maintain popularity with peers while keeping their singing activities low key. This ability, to actively manage multiple identities, was itself an attribute that arguably conferred power and advantage over others.

More seriously, significant disruptions associated with other identity markers such as social class and ethnicity occurred. The majority of boys interviewed (though by no means all) were from higher social classes and membership of such classes conferred on these boys a power over less privileged peers that did not sit entirely comfortably with simplistic notions of subordination. Boys from black ethnic groups, both Caribbean and African, further disrupted simple applications of the theory partly through the strong cultural influence of Black musical traditions but also through an apparent ability of black boys en masse to draw support from their particular Adventist religious affiliation in order to resist proscriptions against singing that overwhelmed many white boys. For the white boys, the traditions of sacred music that lie behind much choral singing had become unknown or meaningless.

It was also necessary to give an account of the considerable power exercised by girls over boys. This remains one of the more challenging findings, but is also turning out to be one of the most robust as the research findings begin to impact upon school practice. Writers such as Epstein (Epstein *et al.*, 1998) have commented on the social privilege enjoyed by boys whose behaviour might be described as that of the 'loveable rogue' while similar behaviour from girls might earn them the epithet 'little bitches' (Reay, 2007). The research unearthed particularly strong evidence that this was indeed the case with regard to singing. This was mainly because of the evidence that boy singers enjoyed a particular status because of the power they wielded over both older women and girls who, in different ways, regarded them as 'cute'.

Boys' performance clearly exerted a power over the opposite sex that was not correspondingly noted for similarly aged girls, whose performance was simply regarded as commonplace. This had to be positioned against a substantial literature that discussed the sexualization of women by the music industry as well as the construction of female audiences as 'fodder' (Bennett, 2000). Connell (2005) uses the term patriarchal dividend to describe additional, hidden advantages that accrue through a patriarchal-oriented society. Some young adolescent boys at least seemed to be beneficiaries of this in the context researched. A conclusion reached was that the majority of young adolescent boys studied were beneficiaries of the patriarchal dividend as they transitioned from a state of economic innocence to a position within the music industry that opened to them the possibilities of traditional forms of male supremacy (Meier, 2008). Here, Connell's concept of complicit masculinity proved to have significant explanatory power.

However, this had to be balanced against the undoubted extreme vulnerability felt by boys in the age group studied as a result of their uncertain (changing) voices coupled with smaller average stature than similarly aged girls and the greater social confidence shown by girls in the context of the performing arts. Against such odds, there was much evidence that the majority of boys just 'crumbled'. Here it was necessary to look outside Connell's writings to a body of theory referred to by Jackson, who writes at some length about boys' fear of failure and the self-worth strategies adopted to cope in the face of feminine success (Jackson, 2003). These theories gave a good interpretation of the evidence collected from boys where triangulation was possible between those boys aged around 12 who dismissed singing as 'gay' and the slightly older boys who described the fear of girls' dominance of the performing arts space experienced by 12-year-olds.

There is a possible limitation in Connell's theorizing here. Much of the explanatory power of Connell's work is rooted in its notion of power relations and, coming from a pro-feminist perspective, gender as a factor in power relations is privileged in the theory. This has led to some criticism. Demetriou (2001) has found Connell's theories inadequate in explaining the combinations of 'sensitive' and 'tough' that are found amongst men associated with an American pro-fathering movement known as the Promise Keepers. He noted that different masculinities were brought together to defend patriarchy and invented the term 'hybrid bloc' to describe this. Such a suggestion comfortably fits the evidence gathered in the boys' singing research.

The Relevance and Effectiveness of Using Theory

In my later work, I have been increasingly interested in the role of age and generational status in power relations. Boys of around 13 or so years of age present a particularly interesting case as it can be shown that they are on the cusp of rising in power above subordinate groups which previously held power over them (mothers, for example). At the same time, great cultural power wars rage between youth and adults over musical taste (Stalhammar, 2003). It has been found that a fine balance of power exists between youth and adults that increasingly needs to be explained. This has tended to take the work in a fresh direction that looks to seminal theories on generation as a cultural marker, such as those of Mannheim. Originally published in the

1930s, Mannheim's theory (Mannheim, 1952) has been around longer than Connell's yet its relevance, and that of the subsequent literature it has spawned, was not readily apparent when the original research questions were proposed.

This raises profound questions about the selection of theories by the new researcher. An assumption was made at a relatively early stage of the research reported in this chapter that the problem – boys' reluctance to sing – must inevitably be one of gender. Experience of researching the problem over some 12 years has shown otherwise. Crucial here is the need, not to defend a chosen theory, but to use it, to test its limitations and to be open to other bodies of theory that might need to be called upon in interpreting the data. A scientific theory is only ever a theory and some familiarity with the philosophical works of Karl Popper and Thomas Khun, I would argue, has to be part of the preparation of anyone who would use theory to take the interpretation of data to any level of sophistication (Popper, 2002; Kuhn, 1996).

Undoubtedly, a great debt is owed to Connell, who remains probably the most frequently cited author with regard to masculinities, and in consequence of that, boys and boyhood. Perhaps the debt to Kuhn and Popper is even greater?

Summary Conclusions and Recommendations

The discovery of the appropriate theories

I discovered my theories through reading, in the company of like-minded researchers who might discuss theory in seminars or informally in coffee bars. This is not a flippant comment. It is part of the intellectual thrust of academe. There are, of course, many general texts on research methods and methodologies, and there are texts on doing certain kinds of research. For example, if you knew that you wanted to research boys' perspectives on their lives (as was the case in this project) you might be attracted to a title such as *Researching Young People's Lives* (Heath *et al.*, 2009). However, theories might be discovered in the journals that deal with the topic being written about and in which one might hope to publish. Any researcher will need to know the key journals for his or her field. In the present case, the journals *Gender and Education* and *Psychology in Music* were consulted. In such places I found articles that discussed similar topics to that which I was researching. It becomes evident that, in any topic area, there are key seminal writers (such as Connell); other well known writers who discuss the theories of the seminal writers and are themselves frequently cited; and finally other writers who are perhaps less well known but whose work is the closest to your own specific focus. Thus it was that Connell's theories became those upon which the current research was founded.

The ease or difficulties with understanding the theories and the difficulties of application to data and texts

Theories have to be lived and tested before they are fully understood and owned by the work to which they are being applied. This chapter has hopefully revealed something of that process. At the outset of the work, the theory was applied too simplistically. It didn't seem so at the time, but in retrospect, it clearly was. This, of course, raises the question of whether we can ever be fully confident that the theory we have chosen, and our understanding, exposition and interpretation of it, gives an adequate account of the phenomenon we have set out to describe and analyse; hence my reference to the philosophy of science. The hard sciences proceed through small refinements and, very occasionally, through great leaps of refutation which may have their origins in intuition. Similar processes are at work in the social sciences, but it is perhaps sometimes harder to disentangle the ideological dimension. The process of creating knowledge in social science is usually an iterative one that involves several drafts and redrafts of the work. It is during those times that theory develops. The process of reading too is iterative. Theory is never static.

What the application of the theories revealed

This particular account has shown the necessity of drawing on other theory, for example, psychological theories about self-worth protection. Through this, we construct our own, unique meta-theory.

For boys and singing, there is clearly a strong tension between the processes that reproduce patriarchy and other more transitory and context specific processes when boys are clearly vulnerable and, to all intents and purposes, 'the weaker sex'. The interdisciplinary study of voice and boyhood also raises unique tensions between essentialist (or at least bio-medical) and social-constructivist ways of viewing boyhood. While the social-constructivist account emerged through this work as the richer and more robust, the bio-medical dimension was undeniable and supported by measurements of 'hard' science. Only the unique meta-theory of the study itself can really piece all this together.

How the absence of these theories might have impaired understanding

Without the theories, the study would never have progressed beyond the 'boys don't want to sound like girls' stage, which is a dangerously naïve way of understanding the situation and not an adequate basis for worthwhile knowledge transfer that might follow on from the original research. However, the fact that the study has created its own, unique, meta-theory brings new problems of communication. For what preconceived 'personal theories' are brought to bear on what is written by the reader and how much space can be devoted to explaining complex new theory to the practitioner who simply wants to know 'what works'?

The limitations of the theories

Ellis (2008) has argued that Connell's pro-feminist stance and preoccupation with the concept of gender oppression results in insufficient attention to other cultural markers such as age, class and ethnicity, which all combine with gender to interact in the complex process of identity formation. It has certainly been necessary to draw on a range of cultural markers other than gender to give an adequate account of the data gathered on boys and singing.

Reflection and recommendations of the experience

Gender is undoubtedly important in addressing boys' attitudes not only to singing, but also to other activities and school subjects considered 'feminine'. Gender and social class are so heavily intertwined that it is difficult to draw boundaries between where the one influences the other. Gender is constructed differently by the working classes and the middle classes and this needs to be taken more account of in future work. Generally, more eclectic theories of identity would serve well in the future for this kind of work and these need to take account of age and generation as identity markers. In relation to gender, these have tended to have 'Cinderella status' in identity studies and this study at least has show that this may not be a tenable position.

Recommended texts for further reading

Connell, R. (2005) *Masculinities*, Polity, Cambridge.
Foucault, M. (1978) *The History of Sexuality, Vol. 1: An Introduction*, Penguin, Harmondsworth.
Martino, W. and Pallotta-Chiarolli, M. (2003) *So What's a Boy? Addressing Issues of Masculinity and Schooling*, Open University Press, Maidenhead.

Journals

Gender and Education (Taylor and Francis)
THYMOS: Journal of Boyhood Studies (Men's Studies Press)

References

Ashley, M. (2008) *Teaching Singing to Boys and Teenagers: The Young Male Voice and the Problem of Masculinity*, Edwin Mellen, Lewiston, NY.

Bennett, A. (2000) *Popular Music and Youth Culture: Music, Identity and Place*, Macmillan, Basingstoke.

Carr, M. and Pauwels, A. (2006) *Boys and Foreign Language Learning: Real Boys Don't Do Languages*, Palgrave Macmillan, Basingstoke.

Connell, R. (2005) *Masculinities*, Polity, Cambridge.

Demetriou, D. (2001) Connell's concept of hegemonic masculinity: A critique. *Theory and Society*, 30, 337–361.

Ellis, H. (2008) Boys, boyhood and the construction of masculinity. *THYMOS: Journal of Boyhood Studies*, 2 (2), 119–124.

Epstein, D., Elwood, J., Hey, V. and Maw, J. (1998) *Failing Boys?* Open University Press, Buckingham.

Foucault, M. (1978) *The History of Sexuality, Vol. 1: An Introduction*, Penguin, Harmondsworth.

Francis, B. (2006) Heroes or zeroes? The discursive positioning of 'underachieving boys' in English neo-liberal educational policy. *Journal of Educational Policy*, 21 (2), 187–200.

Green, L. (1997) *Music, Gender, Education*, Cambridge University Press, Cambridge.

Greene, S. and Hogan, D. (2005) *Researching Children's Experience: Approaches and Methods*, Sage, London.

Heath, S., Brooks, R., Cleaver, E. and Ireland, E. (2009) *Researching Young People's Lives*, Sage, London.

Hollway, W. and Jefferson, T. (2000) *Doing Qualitative Research Differently: Free Association, Narrative and the Interview Method*, Sage, London.

Jackson, C. (2003) Motives for 'laddishness' at school: fear of failure and fear of the 'feminine'. *British Educational Research Journal*, 29 (4), 583–598.

Kehily, M. (2002) *Sexuality, Gender and Schooling: Shifting Agendas in Social Learning*, Routledge Falmer, London.

Kehily, M. (2007) *Understanding Youth: Perspectives, Identities and Practices*, Sage, London.

Kuhn, T. (1996) *The Structure of Scientific Revolutions*, Chicago University Press, Chicago.

Mac an Ghaill, M. and Haywood, C. (2006) *Gender, Culture and Society: Contemporary Feminities and Masculinities*, Palgrave Mcmillan, London.

Mannheim, K. (1952) On the problem of generations, in *The Collected Works of Karl Mannheim*, Routledge, London, 111–142.

Martino, W. and Pallotta-Chiarolli, M. (2003*) So What's a Boy? Addressing Issues of Masculinity and Schooling*, Open University Press, Maidenhead.

Meier, L. (2008) In excess? Body genres, 'bad' music, and the judgement of audiences. *Journal of Popular Music Studies*, 20 (3), 240–260.

Paechter, C. (2006) Masculine feminities/feminine masculinities: power, identities and gender. *Gender and Education*, 18 (3), 253–263.

Phillips, K. (2003) Creating a safe environment for singing. *Choral Journal*, 43, 41–43.

Popper, K. (2002) *The Logic of Scientific Discovery*, Routledge, London.

Reay, D. (2007) 'Spice Girls', 'Nice Girls', 'Girlies' and Tomboys: Gender discourses, girls' cultures and femininities in the primary classroom, in *Gender Relations in Global Perspective: Essential Readings* (ed. N. Cook), Canadian Scholars Press, Toronto, pp. 213–222.

Stalhammar, B. (2003) Music teaching and young people's own musical experience. *Music Education Research*, 5 (1), 61–68.

10

Theorizing from Bricolage
Researching Collaboration in Art and Design Education

Madeleine Sclater

Key Theoretical Approaches in this Chapter

In order to acknowledge and account for the complexity of situations encountered in educational settings, an array of theoretical ideas may be required – a 'Bricolage'. For this reason, the research described here has drawn on ideas from a number of theoretical frameworks within the Computer Supported Collaborative Learning movement (CSCL) and Networked Learning (NL) to inform research associated with an Internet-based Art and Design project. These ideas can be traced to *socially* orientated theories of learning, as distinct from more psychological theories that focus on the individual. This chapter draws upon three theoretical perspectives about learning, namely constructivism (especially social constructivism), situated cognition, and socio-cultural theory, all of which are employed in NL research (McConnell, 2000). Inevitably, these frameworks are limited in scope, and may not, individually, be capable of providing a full account of, or the context for, the situations encountered in this research. However, together, they helped to

Applying Theory to Educational Research: An Introductory Approach with Case Studies, First Edition. Edited by J. Adams, M. Cochrane and L. Dunne.
© 2012 John Wiley & Sons, Ltd. Published 2012 by John Wiley & Sons, Ltd.

shape and focus the research, and provided a basis for understanding and interpreting the findings.

Key texts

Dewey, J. (1907) *The School and Society*, University of Chicago Press, Chicago.
Dewey, J. (1966) *Democracy and Education (1916)*, Free Press, New York.
Lave, J. (1988) *Cognition in Practice*, Cambridge University Press, Cambridge.
Vygotsky, L.S. (1978) *Mind in Society: The Development of Higher Psychological Processes* (trans. M.S. Cole, S. Scribner and E. Souberman), Harvard University Press, Cambridge, MA.

Introduction to the Research Project

This chapter describes a research case study entitled 'Researching Networked Collaboration in Art and Design Education'. Our project was designed to provide a creative, educational adjunct to studio-based activity, in the form of a collaborative Internet art project that employed 'Networked Learning'. The term Networked Learning (NL) refers to the use of Internet-based communication and Information Communication Technology (ICT) to foster co-operative and collaborative links between learners and their tutors, and between a learning community and its 'tools' (Banks, Goodyear and McConnell, 2003).

There has been an upsurge in designing networked learning environments to support social interaction involving co-operative and collaborative learning. More recently there has been a shift in outlook from a preoccupation with outcomes and products of collaborative work towards a concern with *examining interactions* as a way to illuminate and understand the *processes* of collaborative learning (Littleton and Hakkinen, 1999, p. 20). The research project described in this chapter involved the linkage of two institutional cohorts of printmaking students from Institution 'A' and Institution 'B'. Pairs of participants from each institution joined 'virtually' to form two groups, each of which contained four participants. Over a ten week period, we focused the research on the way in which creative visual processes were articulated, developed and sustained within an entirely asynchronous (delayed time, e.g., discussion board), text-based learning environment.

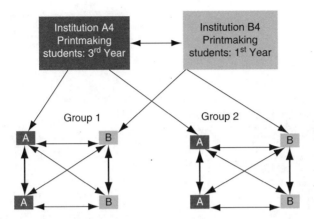

Figure 10.1 The organization of the two groups in this case study and the strength of the ties between participants in the groups (thicker arrows imply stronger ties).

Participants in this project did not know or ever physically meet their institutional collaborative counterparts. Figure 10.1 illustrates the relationship between the participants within the two institutions. The thickness of the arrows represents the strength of ties between the participants. The ties between participants located within the same institution were obviously stronger than the ties between participants across institutions. The groups were of mixed educational levels; students from Institution 'A' were in their third year of study whereas students from Institution 'B' were in their first year. Each group comprised two third-year students and two first-year students. In this chapter, I focus on the findings of Group 1.

Each group worked together through four distinct project phases with the aim of creating a small series of joint creative artefacts reflecting the theme 'Disruptions of time and space'. Figure 10.2 illustrates the project phases.

In Phase 1, participants collected two digital images twice daily for nine days. These images reflected each individual's everyday environment and/or the activity that they were engaged in at particular times. At the end of each day participants uploaded their images to the virtual learning environment and attached a short piece of writing to contextualize each image. Participants responded to their peers, images and writings through written communication laying the foundations for further dialogue and the development of a shared history. The rationale for the brainstorm phase was to create a common context in which group members, living in different environments and engaged in different activities, could become united in

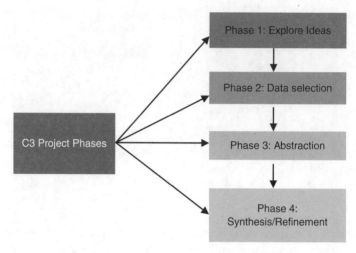

Figure 10.2   Project phases.

time rather than place. Recording snippets of daily life for over a week using a diary format was a way of enabling group members to catch a glimpse of one another's visual thinking: the way they viewed the world, what they found interesting and why.

During Phase 2, participants reviewed all the images and textual communication uploaded during Phase 1. They each singled out seven images that they favoured from the group (not their own) and justified their choices in writing. Additionally group members selected their own seven favourite images and commented on why they had made these choices. Participants then commented on one another's selection and put forward their ideas for an emerging theme. The synthesis phase (Phase 3) involved group members digitally manipulating a small selection of single images from the previous phase for further manipulation by other members of the group. Therefore, the result was not just the work of one person, but also varying levels of input by all the members of each team. During the refinement phase (Phase 4) participants amalgamated several abstracted images from Phase 3 into a collage. It was suggested that one person begin the process by amalgamating a selection of images into a single collage and then for the collage to be passed between the other members of the group for further transformation. Three to four compositions were created in this way with each member initiating one collage involving other members of the group in refining and transforming it.

The activities of each group were analysed separately. My analysis concentrated on three guiding research questions:

- *Research question 1*: How did participants communicate and negotiate their visual creative processes and products?
- *Research question 2*: What are the background factors that appear to influence participants' orientation to the creative collaboration within the networked environment?
- *Research question 3*: What are the perceived hindrances and affordances of certain factors on the development and articulation of creative visual processes and products?

Theories Explained and their Use Justified in the Context of this Research Project

Given the complexity of the relationship between creativity, learning and collaboration within networked learning environments there is a need to draw on a plurality of theoretical perspectives about learning in order to help us understand how these aspects of human activity are linked. Constructivism (especially social constructivism e.g., Salomon and Perkins, 1998) provides a focus on what people bring to learning and how they interact in order to learn. Constructivism, whose origins can be traced to Jean Piaget's work in developmental psychology, is an evolved theory (one that has been extensively referenced and developed) and one that represents an important theoretical perspective in educational research today (Koschmann, 1996, p. 11). Piaget argued that people learn most effectively when they are encouraged to engage in active exploration particularly where such engagement exposes a 'gap' between their existing knowledge representations and their experience (Dalgarno, 2001, p. 184). Constructivism, as a theoretical perspective, has also been key to the development and formulation of new ideas about learning, in particular the role and importance of peer interaction in cognitive development promulgated by the so-called neo-Piagetians (Koschmann, 1996, p. 11). Within the constructivist perspective there has, more recently, been a burgeoning curiosity in the situativity of learning processes (Koschmann, 1996, p. 11). 'Socio-constructivism' is a school of thought in educational research that emphasizes the importance of the setting or context not only for the 'purpose' of learning, but also for its 'generation' (Jones, 1998, p. 37).

Unlike other constructivist movements, social constructivism regards knowledge construction fundamentally as a social process.

In terms of thinking about constructivist and social constructivist theory and its application to the case study presented here, practitioners develop their creative ideas and realize these in some kind of material form via processes that are essentially 'constructive'. This means that creative ideas are drawn from a wide variety of sources that, over time, become assimilated and personalized. From a socio-constructivist perspective, ideas are not only 'pieced together' and derived from people's personal life experiences but also from their interactions with their peers and other significant people. Together, these act as resources for action in learners' creative, visual endeavours, but on the basis that creative ideas are co-constructed (rather than developed in isolation) through 'participation'.

Situated learning (e.g., Lave, 1988) is concerned with the contexts in which people learn and the meaning they derive from learning in these contexts. According to Koschmann, the word 'situated' within 'situated learning' or 'situated cognition' has a number of meanings within different disciplinary areas. Situated learning is a theoretical perspective that highlights the notion that much of what is learned or acquired is specific to a setting in which learning takes place (Anderson, Reder and Simon, 1996, p. 5). This theoretical perspective emphasizes that cognitive activities are always situated or embedded in the social and cultural context in which learning occurs (Brown, Collins and Duguid, 1989; Lave and Wenger, 1991). Situated learning theorists such as Lave (1988) and Rogoff (1995) view learning in terms of a process of entry into and participation within a social practice and not as a process of knowledge transmission (Cobb and Bowers, 1999, p. 5; Koschmann, 1996, p. 12). There are many terms given for the type and context of this participation. Brown, Collins and Duguid (1989) refer to 'enculturation', Rogoff (1995) to 'guided participation' and Lave and Wenger (1991) to 'legitimate peripheral participation'. Within this framework, knowledge not only is 'constructed', but humans and their identities are also 'constructed' and learning becomes a process of personal as well as social change (Lipponen, Hakkarainen and Paavola, 2004, p. 34).

Situated theories within the context of Art and Design education point to the notion that genuine experience and real life are aspects of human activity that enable practitioners/learners in Art and Design to inject meaning into their creative work. When a break-through in creative thinking occurs, a learner is able to develop further insight into a problem or issue that in turn leads to the formation of meaning for that person. However, within this perspective, individuals do not undertake such creative 'discoveries' on their own but, rather, through a process of entry into and participation within a social/cultural practice.

Practitioners/learners might be 'legitimate peripheral participants' (Lave and Wenger, 1991) in the sense that they may be located within a social practice (e.g., art and design) but are essentially on the 'edge' of that practice because they are new to the field. They become full members of their community by participating in and learning from those more experienced. The way in which this theory impacts on creative practice, is in its insistence that creative thinking processes and products (artefacts) cannot be divorced from the context out of which actions arise and are subsequently developed.

Socio-cultural theory (e.g., Vygotsky, 1962, 1978; Dewey, 1907, 1966) is concerned with the 'cultural structures' with which people interact and the 'tools' they use to learn. The socio-cultural perspective was influenced principally by the research of the Soviet psychologists, notably Lev Vygotsky, whose work is concerned with the 'cultural basis of human intellect' (Koschmann, 1996, p. 11) and the 'dynamic interaction between the collective and the individual' (O'Connor, 1998, p. 38). Broadly speaking, while the social-constructivist perspective is an approach that suggests a distinction between individual thinking processes and the environment in which the individual operates, the socio-cultural perspective views the individual as integral to that environment (De Laat and Lally, 2003, p. 14; O'Connor, 1998, p. 38). In Vygotsky's writings, individual development is considered to have its foundation in social processes (O'Malley, 1995, p. 284). It appears that while Vygotsky acknowledged the importance of process, he was more concerned with bringing the child nearer to socially defined goals. In this view, the educational process occurs from 'the outside in' (Glassman, 2001, p. 3) and is perhaps best encapsulated by Vygotsky's notion of the 'zone of proximal development' (Vygotsky, 1978) that essentially emphasizes the way in which children's competencies might be amplified and developed by the guiding presence of more skilled adults and/or competent peers (Haenen, 2001, p. 159; Kumpulainen and Mutanen, 1999).

The way in which Vygotsky's (1962, 1978) socio-cultural theory relates to creative design practice is in its articulation of the relationship between process and product in developing visual thinking and in relation to the role of the educator in that process. Vygotsky emphasized the role of the group in achieving goals, and a more proactive role for the tutor in the learning and teaching process. This raises a number of issues concerning how individual and social (group) processes might be accommodated in learning and teaching situations in order to co-develop creative thinking and knowledge.

The Application of Theory to the Research

Table 10.1 summarizes how these three theoretical areas relate to particular foci of explanation in this case study and how theory informed and directed my research. In the first column I have listed the theoretical areas and indicative researchers. In the second column I have listed the foci of explanation and research for each theoretical area. The third column outlines how these theoretical areas have been used to focus this research and highlighted the key research questions for each.

Our case study was concerned with examining what happened when co-operative and collaborative approaches were used to support the development of visual creative processes and outcomes within a networked environment. This involved looking at participants' motivations and socio-emotional orientations to group-work, their understanding of the task requirements and the strategies they adopted to develop, support and motivate the communication (research question 1). This was followed by an analysis of participants' background and, in particular, their previous educational experiences (research question 2). Lastly the analysis considered factors that participants identified as having a key role in hindering or advancing visual creativity while engaging in collaboration (research question 3). The following summary is, therefore, a systematic attempt to distil the findings presented under each research question. These questions were generated by the application of the 'bricolage' of theory to the research problem – understanding online collaboration in art and design education.

Research question 1 asked 'How did participants' negotiate and co-ordinate their visual creative processes and the target of their co-operative and collaborative endeavours?' Situated learning theory, when applied in this research, led to a focus on contexts for learning. In a group situation where collaboration is essential to the success of a group's efforts, the group itself is part of the context, for each of the group members. Therefore, situated learning theory pointed the research towards the communications and motivations of members, and their orientation towards each other, as being significant features of the learning context. Hence the following brief account of an investigation of the group's processes is framed by this theory. The findings revealed that participants' motivations to participate centred

Table 10.1 Table summarizing how the three theoretical areas relate to particular foci of explanation, and how these informed and directed my research.

'Theoretical areas' and indicative researchers	Some foci of explanation and research	How I have used these theoretical areas to focus this research
Social constructivism (e.g., Salomon and Perkins, 1998)	This is concerned with what people bring to learning and how they interact to learn.	• Exploring participants' understandings and beliefs of learning past and present. • What they say about their learning in groups. *Research Question 2: What are the background factors that appear to influence participants' orientation to the creative collaboration within the networked environment?* • Understanding the background factors influencing participants' orientation to co-operation and collaboration.
Situated learning (e.g., Lave, 1988)	This is concerned with the contexts in which people learn and the meaning they derive from learning in these contexts.	• Exploring how meaning is embedded in process. Looking at the power of the context on the development of creative practice. *Research Question 1: How did participants communicate and negotiate their visual creative processes and products?* • Negotiation of processes, influence of socio-emotional disposition and feelings. *Research Question 3: What are the perceived hindrances and affordances of certain factors on the development and articulation of creative visual processes and products?* • Issues associated with pedagogical design: participants' experiences of the process and product

(Continued)

Table 10.1   (*cont'd*)

'Theoretical areas' and indicative researchers	Some foci of explanation and research	How I have used these theoretical areas to focus this research
Socio-cultural theory (e.g., Vygotsky, 1962, 1978; Dewey, 1900, 1966)	This is concerned with the 'structures' with which people interact and the 'tools' they use to learn.	• Understanding the effects of textuality, asynchronicity, and ideas about collaboration/group work and technology on visual creative processes. *Research Question 3: What are the perceived hindrances and affordances of certain factors on the development and articulation of creative visual processes and products?* • Participants' experiences of the constraints and affordances associated with key factors, such as pedagogical design, technology, textuality, time and group work.

on the development of their technical skills rather than on their desire to learn about collaborative processes. Their socio-emotional orientations were not aligned with the kinds of behaviours that one would expect from participants engaged in fruitful collaboration. Participants made personal justifications to explain why their group failed to cohere. These justifications ranged from preferring to work alone to not having the disposition for networked collaboration. While participants, possessed similar levels of motivation (e.g., in developing their technical skills), their socio-emotional orientations reflected little understanding or experience of collaborative working practices. Participants were divided in their understanding of the task and did not share a common understanding of what it means to collaborate. They expressed a view of collaboration that was more concerned with product than process.

Participants felt, overall, that the group had not worked together successfully because their communication was impoverished. The reasons included lack of confidence in using technology and in initiating conversations, difficulty in articulating ideas in relation to creative work, uneven levels of commitment to the project, and differing expectations with respect to how much communication to send and receive. Participants had difficulty making the transition between spoken and written communication. In spite of these difficulties they appeared intuitively aware of the strategies they needed to adopt and, in their own way, took a variety of steps to support and develop the collaboration. However, because participants did not have the skills and/or the experience to help the group form, the group struggled to gel.

Research question 2 asked 'What were the background factors (personal orientations, previous educational experiences, previous experiences of group-work, previous experiences of online group-work) that appeared to influence participants' orientation to co-operation and collaboration within a networked learning environment? This research question arises from the application of social constructivist theory to the research problem. This results in a clear focus on what beliefs, understandings, and general background people bring to their learning, and how this interacts with the learning process. The findings showed that participants, while having some experience of face-to-face collaboration, had no previous experience of networked collaboration and were new to online group work; it would appear that their limited previous experience had little bearing on the way they worked in the project. They also expressed a low level of confidence in their visual work and in their skills in using computers.

Research question 3: What are the perceived hindrances and affordances of certain factors on the development and articulation of creative visual processes and products? How constrained and/or free did participants feel when working as part of a distributed group within a networked learning environment in which co-operative and collaborative working practices were central pedagogical strategies? This question arises from the application, in particular, of socio-cultural theory to the research problem. This leads to a focus on the structures in which the participants found themselves, which is distinct from what they personally 'bring' to the learning context, and, subtly, from the meaning that is created by the context. It leads, principally, to a focus on the learning design, especially the co-operative and collaborative aspects. The following selections of findings illustrate how insights into these aspects are revealed by this theoretical focus.

In spite of poor communication, participants enjoyed the exposure to one another's images and found this to be a particularly motivating feature of the creative process. Additionally, they felt excited by the process of sharing images with one another and appeared to take pleasure in the group's responses to their inputs. Participants also enjoyed the anony-mous nature of the exercise; this appeared to make the creative process more exciting.

Participants exhibited differing conceptions of the creative collaborative process. Some became highly engrossed in the process; they were excited, intrigued, inspired and motivated by the creative possibilities that the abstraction process offered while others were less enthusiastic.

The most important finding that emerged in relation to the influence of a largely text based environment on the development of visual creativity was the need for social grounding in networked collaboration. Participants acknowledged their co-ordination and management of their creative activity was poor. Participants were of the opinion that the asynchronous text based nature of the communication medium affected their capacity to co-ordinate, regulate and schedule their creative activity.

When considering the impact of asynchronicity on creative visual processes, participants within this group experienced more hindrances associated with the effect of delayed time than affordances. This group, in the first instance, did not possess the team-working skills to co-ordinate their creative activity and this was further compounded by the largely asynchronous text-based environment and the fact that they did not know or meet their collaborative counterparts.

In relation to group work, participants felt isolated and frustrated; they effectively worked as individuals rather than as a team. Two of the participants confessed to being poor time managers. Participants also struggled to ground their relationships. This difficulty can be partly attributed to the fact that the two cohorts did not know one another. This factor appeared to have an impact on the way the group communicated, the result being that they found it virtually impossible to establish a reciprocal relationship through written communication. However, despite the fact that participants did not know one another, they appeared to know what strategies to adopt in order to work together. This finding has implications for pedagogical design in networked environments and points to the value in helping individuals and groups to develop the 'social glue' necessary for further interaction and collaboration.

The Relevance and Effectiveness of Using Theory

The research in this case study focused on the use of asynchronous communication in learning and teaching and the theoretical perspectives that are employed to conduct learning in this way, including social constructivism, situated learning and socio-cultural learning. All three of these theoretical perspectives advocate the adoption of co-operative and collaborative learning approaches. The need to draw upon multiple theoretical perspectives to reach new understandings is reflective of an increasing trend among educational institutions to integrate and cross boundaries as a way of surviving, as well as to progress their individual research agendas (Johnston, 1998).

Adopting a multi-theoretical approach is both creative and problematic. In one sense it is creative because it allows a diverse range of interesting theoretical perspectives to be taken on board to help illuminate the research. It is problematic because the perspectives that researchers and educators bring tend to be partial and fragmented (De Laat *et al.*, 2006).

While the study of collaboration has a fairly short history, the field has witnessed some noticeable changes in research emphasis. For example, researchers were initially more concerned with ascertaining the extent to which collaborative learning was more effective than learning alone (Dillenbourg *et al.*, 1995). This resulted in the development of a substantial evidence base demonstrating the positive effects of social interaction in learning (Teasley and Rochelle, 1993). Researchers swiftly recognized the potential usefulness and value of computers as a context for researching social interaction (Crook, 1996).

Theorizing is an activity that humans undertake as part of any practical action. However, educators may not always be able to account for their theories explicitly, because theorizing is not always undertaken consciously or employed reflectively (to look at a practical context), reflexively (to look at one's self) or systematically (Nulden, 2001, p. 363). The first step, therefore, in educational contexts, is to take cognisance of the fact that theories probably do influence what educators/researchers do, albeit sometimes tacitly, and that, together, these theories contribute to the framework for action. In this sense practice almost always represents a theory of learning (Nulden, 2001, p. 363), as well as accumulated experience.

In many domains of research – for example the natural sciences – one theoretical 'paradigm' might be adequately authoritative to generate consensus that becomes the foundation of further research activity and practical action. However, in the much more complex domains of human activities – such as the human sciences – this is mostly not the case. There may be several relevant and applicable theoretical frameworks, given that overlapping (as well as conflicting) theories arise in similar contexts that assist with actions. These domains are 'multi-theoretical' in the sense that there is no single theory of adequate power to generate consensus: human learning is one such domain.

Summary Conclusions and Recommendations

The discovery of the appropriate theories

In order to acknowledge and account for the complexity of situations encountered in educational settings, an array of theoretical ideas may be required – a 'Bricolage'. For this reason, the research described here has drawn on ideas from three theoretical frameworks within computer supported collaborative learning movement (CSCL) and Networked Learning (NL).

The ease or difficulties of understanding the theories

Theories are rarely explained in neat summary form by their exponents. They are often developed by multiple researchers, with competing versions, over many years. It can often be difficult to find good explanations of how a researcher has used a theory, and why she/he has rejected competing theories. Theories are often embedded in the research work of the originators, and this may be in an unfamiliar field of work. Each of the theories I used was selected after discussion with experts in the field, and some trial and error application, using best judgements at the time.

The difficulties of application to data and texts

As indicated above, educational settings are often complex and care is, therefore, needed to match the 'focus' of theory to the data in order to interpret it. I used three theories to achieve this, and it was not always clear which theory was more useful, as there was overlap between them. Further, until each theory was applied to the data, it wasn't clear what this would achieve. The three theories I used were applied to the research questions I had posed, sometimes with hesitation, in the following ways:

Situated learning is concerned with the contexts in which people learn and the meaning they derive from learning in these contexts. It leads to an exploration of how meaning is embedded in learning processes. So the research is guided by an examination of the power of the context in the development of creative practice. Each participant in a group forms a significant part of the 'context' for the other participants. My research questions asked how are group learning processes negotiated, and what is the influence of socio-emotional disposition and feelings of participants upon this? What are the issues arising for pedagogical design; in particular, how participants experience the process and products of the learning activities?

Social constructivism provides a focus on what people bring to learning and how they interact in order to learn. This leads the research to focus on exploring participants' knowledge and understanding and beliefs as they enter a learning activity, and how that changes. It also focuses on learning in groups. This supports research question 2: What are the background factors that appear to influence participants' orientation to the creative collaboration within the networked environment?

Socio-cultural theory is concerned with the 'cultural structures' with which people interact and the 'tools' they use to learn. Understanding the effects of textuality, asynchronicity (bulletin board type activity), and the effect of participants' ideas about collaboration/group work and technology on visual creative processes, are all brought into focus by this theoretical framework. Arising from this, research question 3 asks: What are participants' experiences of the constraints and affordances associated with key factors (pedagogical design, technology, textuality, time and group work)?

What the application of the theories revealed

Theory can act as a lens through which to view phenomena. The 'best' theories can help to explain phenomena, illuminate events or focus on aspects of a situation that might otherwise be missed, or seem insignificant (see Halverson, 2002 for more exploration of this).

How the absence of the theories might have impaired understanding

Without theory many educational situations would appear so complex and confusing that it would become impossible to make sense of them, or know where to start investigating them.

The limitations of theory

All theories are inevitably 'reductionist': they focus on some 'significant' aspects of our world, helping us to research it, while setting other phenomena aside as not 'significant'. This is a 'double-edged sword' in research terms. It is for this reason that I adopted the 'Bricolage' approach in the research described here. By assembling a 'mosaic' of complimentary research theories, I have attempted to take into account more aspects of a complex research setting while still enabling a clear focus on what is significant for the understanding of the setting.

Reflections and recommendations of the experience

Theories, then, are 'cognitive tools' that we use to make sense of the world, in the everyday sense, as well as in research activities. It's just that in research they are more formalized, and shared among researchers, rather than personal ways of viewing the world. Shared theories can be modified by the data that are gathered in their name, so a living theory will change as a result of research (see the idea of a 'theory–praxis (meaning practical action) conversation' in De Laat *et al.*, 2006).

Recommended further reading

Brown, J.S., Collins, A. and Duguid, P. (1989) Situated cognition and the culture of learning. *Educational Researcher*, 18 (1), 32–42.

De Laat, M., Lally, V., Simons, R.-J. and Wenger, E. (2006) A selective analysis of empirical findings in networked learning research in higher education: questing for coherence. *Educational Research Review*, 1 (2), 99–111.

Wenger, E. (1998) *Communities of Practice: Learning, Meaning and Identity*, Cambridge University Press, Cambridge.

References

Anderson, J.R., Reder, L.M. and Simon, H.A. (1996) Situated learning and education. *Educational Researcher*, 25 (4), 5–11.

Banks, S., Goodyear, P. and McConnell, D. (2003) Introduction to the special issue on advances in research on networked learning. *Instructional Science*, 31 (1–2), 1–6.

Brown, J.S., Collins, A. and Duguid, P. (1989) Situated cognition and the culture of learning. *Educational Researcher*, 18 (1), 32–42.

Cobb, P. and Bowers, J. (1999) Cognitive and situated learning perspectives in theory and practice. *Educational Researcher*, 28 (2), 4–15.

Crook, C. (1996) *Computers and the Collaborative Experience of Learning*, Routledge, London.

Dalgarno, B. (2001) Interpretations of constructivism and consequences for computer assisted learning. *British Journal of Educational Technology*, 32 (2), 183–194.

De Laat, M. and Lally, V. (2003) Complexity, theory and praxis: researching collaborative learning and tutoring processes in a networked learning community. *Instructional Science* (Special Issue on Networked Learning), 31 (1–2), 7–39.

De Laat, M., Lally, V., Simons, R.-J. and Wenger, E. (2006) A selective analysis of empirical findings in networked learning research in higher education: Questing for Coherence. *Educational Research Review*, 1 (2), 99–111.

Dewey, J. (1907) *The School and Society*, University of Chicago Press, Chicago.

Dewey, J. (1966 [1916]) *Democracy and Education*, Free Press, New York.

Dillenbourg, P., Baker, M., Blaye, A. and O'Malley, C. (1995) The evolution of research on collaborative learning, in *Learning in Humans and Machines: Towards an Interdisciplinary Learning Science* (eds P. Reimann and H. Spada), Pergamon, London, pp. 189–211.

Glassman, M. (2001) Dewey and Vygotsky: society, experience, and enquiry in educational practice. *Educational Researcher*, 30 (4), 3–14.

Haenen, J. (2001) Outlining the teaching-learning process: Piotr Gal'perin's contribution. *Learning and Instruction*, 11 (2), 157–170.

Halverson, C.A. (2002) Activity theory and distributed cognition: or what does CSCW need to DO with theories? *Computer Supported Cooperative Work*, 11, 243–267.

Johnston, R. (1998) The university of the future: Boyer revisited. *Higher Education*, 36 (3), 253–272.

Jones, C. (1998) Context, content and co-operation: an ethnographic study of collaborative online learning. Unpublished PhD thesis, Manchester Metropolitan University, Manchester.

Koschmann, T. (1996) Paradigm shifts and instructional technology: an introduction. In *CSCL: Theory and Practice of an Emerging Paradigm* (ed. T. Koschmann), Lawrence Erlbaum, New Jersey, pp. 1–23.

Kumpulainen, K. and Mutanen, M. (1999) The situated dynamics of peer group interaction: an introduction to an analytic framework. *Learning and Instruction*, 9 (5), 449–473.

Lave, J. (1988) *Cognition in Practice*, Cambridge University Press, Cambridge.

Lave, J. and Wenger, E. (1991) *Situated learning: legitimate peripheral participation*, Cambridge University Press, Cambridge.

Lipponen, L., Hakkarainen, K. and Paavola, S. (2004) Practices and orientations of CSCL, in *What We Know About CSCL: And Implementing it in Higher Education* (eds J.W. Strijbos, P.A. Kirschnerand and R.L. Martens), Kluwer Academic, Boston, pp. 31–50.

Littleton, K. and Hakkinen, P. (1999) Learning together: understanding the processes of computer-based collaborative learning, in *Collaborative Learning: Cognitive and Computational Approaches* (ed. P. Dillenbourg), Amsterdam: Pergamon.

McConnell, D. (2000) *Implementing Computer Supported Cooperative Learning*, 2nd edn, Kogan Page, London.

Nulden, U. (2001) e-ducation: research and practice. *Journal of Computer Assisted Learning*, 17 (4), 363–375.

O'Connor, M.C. (1998) Can we trace the 'efficacy of social constructivism'? *Review of Research in Education*, 23, 25–71.

O'Malley, C. (1995) Designing computer support for collaborative learning, in *Computer Supported Collaborative Learning* (ed. C. O'Malley), Springer-Verlag, Berlin, pp. 283–297.

Rogoff, B. (1995) *Apprenticeship in Thinking*, Cambridge University Press, New York.

Salomon, G. and Perkins, D.N. (1998) Individual and social aspects of learning. *Review of Research in Education* 23, 1–24.

Teasley, S.D. and Rochelle, J. (1993) The construction of shared knowledge in collaborative problem solving, in *Computers as Cognitive Tools* (eds. S. Lajoiand and S.J. Derry), Lawrence Erlbaum, Hillsdale, NJ, pp. 229–258.

Vygotsky, L.S. (1962) *Thought and Language* (trans. E.H. Vakar and G. Vakar), MIT Press, Cambridge, MA.

Vygotsky, L.S. (1978) *Mind in Society: The Development of Higher Psychological Processes* (trans. V. J.-S.M. Cole, S. Scribner and E. Souberman), Harvard University Press, Cambridge, MA.

Wenger, E. (1998) *Communities of Practice: Learning, Meaning and Identity*, Cambridge University Press, Cambridge.

11

Constructivism and the Pedagogy of Teacher Education
Reflections on Practice

Graham Rogers

Key Theoretical Approaches in this Chapter:
Constructivism and Constructivist-Informed Pedagogy

Constructivism, as a theoretical model of learning, has a long history. It is rooted in the ideas of Dewey (1929) and Vygotsky (1978), both of whom gave primacy to a concern that learners should be enabled to construct their own meanings and understandings within the academic or professional field in which they are engaged.

This model holds powerful implications for a teacher-education curriculum, pedagogy and assessment insofar as the theoretical and practical perspectives of constructivism offer experiences through which student teachers can begin to shape their own visions of meaningful learning and teaching. Visions of the possible and desirable, of course, imply the adoption of a set of values in learning that reach far beyond the mere acquisition of a body of professional skills. Values also express a relationship that, for Foucault, connects knowledge, ethics and action. The case study that follows explores how far this

---

Applying Theory to Educational Research: An Introductory Approach with Case Studies,
First Edition. Edited by J. Adams, M. Cochrane and L. Dunne.
© 2012 John Wiley & Sons, Ltd. Published 2012 by John Wiley & Sons, Ltd.

relationship was nurtured through one component of a teacher-education programme that employed an overt constructivist-informed pedagogy.

Key texts

Beck, C. and Kosnik, C. (2006) *Innovations in Teacher Education: A Social Constructivist Approach*, State University of New York Press, New York.
Loughran, J. (2006) *Developing a Pedagogy of Teacher Education: Understanding Teaching and Learning About Teaching*, Routledge, London.

Introduction to the Research Project

Let me begin with a couple of highlights of a personal journey. I have spent most of the last 40 years teaching history to people whose ages ranged from seven to seventy. First and foremost I have been a practitioner and, like many teachers, I have built on experience in determining a personal style and pedagogical preferences to the ways in which I think the subject should be taught. I must confess that, for a considerable part of my career, educational 'theory' remained the province of the educational researcher. Yet, again like many practitioners interested in improving practice, I kept a log of plans, incidents and events. When I look back, two events spring to mind which had a powerful effect on not only how I construed learning but also on a personal decision to discover how theoretical perspectives might inform my understanding of what I was trying to achieve and help sharpen my teaching methods for the purpose of attaining my goals.

Some years ago I put together a local history project for a class of 11-year-olds in a local primary school. It was to do with seventeenth-century social life and home life in particular. I transcribed original documents for this purpose. I constructed a series of problem-based tasks around these sources. Children worked in groups in their efforts to solve problems of interpretation. They talked and argued relentlessly about the housing conditions in which people of the period and locality spent their lives. The language one particular child used to present her personal view of the subject left a powerful impression on me. '*Some* of the houses', she wrote, '*must* have been very cramped'. In effect she was entering the conditional discourse of the discipline in a highly sophisticated way. 'I wasn't really sure about what houses were like then', she explained, 'It's very complicated. Others in my group didn't agree but that helped in a funny way.' In hindsight this was social constructivism at work in the way in which her thinking was played out in conjunction with her peers. At the time I didn't have a label for it; but I shall return to this child's commentary later.

In the twilight of my career I was also struck by a comment made by one of my student teachers who was reaching the end of her course and who raised this tantalizing though worrying question: 'What kind of teacher am I expected to be?' she asked. She probably raised a question that has haunted many teachers about to enter the profession and to which some may never find an answer. It is also a troubling question for the teacher-educator.

This student had followed a subject-specialist course in history as part of her degree programme in primary education. The content of the course broadly reflected the requirements of the History National Curriculum for Key Stage 2. However, I had more explicit goals other than 'covering the ground'; and these were principally concerned with developing students' epistemological understanding through a pedagogical approach which would assist them in claiming knowledge for themselves. I also had more ambitious goals that included the promotion of students' self-efficacy and their personal perspectives and values in learning. The difficulty lay in ascertaining whether I had changed anything. In other words, the central question, and the basis of a research project, was whether a teacher-education course (or at least a conspicuous component part), built on constructivist principles, was capable of assisting pre-service teachers in examining their own beliefs about learning and teaching and had the potential to change their conceptions about the nature of knowledge, the complexities of teaching, and the relationship between teaching and learning.

The two incidents I have described raise very similar questions about purpose and outcome. I had the evidence that I had caused a young learner to think in a particular way. Does the evidence also exist that, over an extended period, I had modified the professional 'identity' as well as the intellectual capabilities of a group of intending teachers? It is a tall order. But research-informed evaluation is one of the most important things we do as teachers.

Theories Explained and their Use Justified
in the Context of this Research Project

Constructivism at work

The design of my subject-study modules benefited directly from the epistemological foundations of constructivism: namely, that learners can be immersed in 'meaning-making' that is authentic, personal and related to genuine problems of an intellectual and professional kind. Constructivism, of course, has become an almost universal learning and teaching paradigm across the higher education sector although, paradoxically, it is less conspicuous in the teacher-education field than might be supposed. It is not a monolithic concept. Nevertheless, there is something of a consensus around the notion that constructivism is concerned with enabling individuals to create their own understandings based on an interaction between what they already know and believe and the phenomena or ideas with which they are presented (Richardson, 1997). There are also disagreements about what it is which largely stem from theoretical differences and from translating a descriptive theory of learning into the actual practice of teaching. For instance, should the focus reside with the individual acting as a sole agent in knowledge construction or with the socio-cultural context in which the learner has his/her being? Dewey's model of cognitive constructivism portrays the learner as an autonomous agent with individual objectives and priorities. By contrast, Vygotsky's theory of knowledge acquisition, often described as social constructivism, views knowledge as a socially constructed product (Hyslop-Margison and Strobel, 2008). These differences apart, there remain the fundamental questions of whether formal knowledge matters, whether it is just a tool for classroom discourse or whether the teacher retains the primary role of disbursing formal knowledge even at the risk of defaulting into instructional teaching.

I did not choose to deploy a social constructivist approach in my teaching simply because it was more intellectually persuasive or attractive. Insofar as I was responsible for a series of history subject modules within a degree programme for intending primary teachers there were powerful reasons for infusing the design of my courses with a social constructivist dimension. First, I already had considerable experience of using a constructivist design allied to the application of learning technology in the form of a Virtual Learning Environment (VLE); and I also had the experience of researching the impact of this pedagogical tool on students' cognitive development

(Rogers, 2004). However, there were more powerful considerations behind choosing a social constructivist approach. One crucial imperative was to draw out what students already believed about learning and teaching, to explore and share their experiences and then to create conditions of cognitive challenge or dissonance which would persuade them to reconsider and possibly adjust their conceptual understanding of what it is to learn and, by association, to teach. That can only be achieved through action within a specific learning context and through social interaction; in this case the context of a cognate discipline – history – allied to the opportunities for exchanging and building alternative ideas and perspectives provided by 'online' discourse. As a pedagogic tool social constructivism translates into enabling learner-teachers to grow intellectually and professionally through their interactions not just with their tutor but also as a community of learners. Loughran (2006, p. 2) goes to the heart of the matter when he writes:

> In educational encounters, a teacher's norms and values and the extent to which they are enacted in practice, influence the manner in which students might develop their own. This personal relationship between teachers and students is crucial as identity formation and personal growth combine to shape the nature of pedagogy itself.

However, the question still remains as to whether a social constructivist approach to pre-service education is feasible and productive and that is the focus of the next sections that outline research into this question, detail the methodology employed and consider the outcomes.

The Application of Theory to the Research

My starting point was a concern that stemmed from both practice and theoretical, research-based perspectives. When asked directly to consider their own learning and their conceptions of teaching, for many student teachers this is an awkward moment. The majority construed the professional benefits of their academic course largely in terms of knowledge acquisition and transfer. What was of particular note was the virtual absence of any student recognition of the relationship between 'learning in the discipline' and how that might inform classroom practice. There is nothing new in this perception. Poulson (2001), for instance, cites research work that would indicate that even when students had sound subject knowledge they did not see it as particularly relevant to planning for pupils' learning. Where such a relationship was loosely recognized it was confined to 'enhancing personal interest which would transfer into the classroom'. However, when placed in a more reassuring though challenging environment it is more likely that alternative perspectives will emerge and reflect a personal value.

Edwards, Gilroy and Hartley (2002) draw attention to the synergetic relationship between student teachers' epistemological growth and emergent professional values. Teacher-learners, they argue, who think, question and act as academic craftsmen in their disciplinary fields are more likely to take greater pedagogic and interventionist risks in the classroom. In a similar vein Whitty (2000) refers to the linkage between teachers having expert knowledge and values and being able to make their own judgements in relation to effective professional practice. It is also a view echoed in more recent work which sees professional expertise being grounded in persistent and iterative engagement with constructing and reconstructing knowledge claims (Kelly, 2006). Others have taken a very similar stance in pointing to the relationship between epistemological beliefs and teaching and, more particularly, how teacher personal epistemology has a strong bearing on how professional practice is constructed (Kroll, 2004). Luehman (2008) identified a set of complementary dimensions to teacher learning, specifically relevant to 'new' teachers, which could assist in operationalizing the concept of professional identity development. She argues that the key to student teachers' successful transition into the profession was allied to personal visions of a preferred role anchored in deep understanding; a critical disposition and habits of thinking; conceptual tools and a readiness to share reflection on academic and professional practice with their peer community. She went on to argue that students also need the support of an 'expert voice' to contextualize or frame development in their thinking. Indeed, a social constructivist approach should not promote a relativistic outlook in the sense that any position will do (Beck and Kosnik, 2006). Teacher input has a major role.

All of this reinforced a considered application of a social constructivist model to the research in question. In practice, the model translated into a series of 'blended' online modules in which students, at strategic stages, explored resources and questions to do with the nature of historical knowledge and its construction and the development of children's historical understanding. Subsequent modules took students into the practice of history (as opposed to absorbing a body of content) and into the pedagogic field of teaching history across the primary age range. Web-based learning technology provided students with the facility to construct an archive of their thoughts, ideas, and arguments in their online correspondence within a community of fellow researchers and their tutor.

The research itself attempted to measure the impact of a pedagogically linked, social constructivist approach on student teachers' conceptions of learning and teaching. It was grounded in a rich seam of qualitative and quantitative data, involving a largely phenomenographic approach to collating and measuring shifts in learners' epistemological and metacognitive perspectives. Data were collected at strategic points in the academic programme in order to get closer to students' conceptions. An initial audit was conducted in relation to students' conceptions of knowledge and learning and, together with the archive of online commentaries and responses, provided a baseline from which to view any subsequent development. The audit was framed around central questions concerned with extracting personal meanings attached to learning and applied to the specific disciplinary context. Students returned to this questionnaire and their initial responses in the final year of their course. Recorded focus-group conversation served the purpose of extrapolating and expanding on issues that had emerged in response to the questionnaires and in more informal, spontaneous comments and observations that surfaced during scheduled teaching sessions. The implications of the research are discussed in the next section.

The Relevance and Effectiveness of Using Theory

The extracts of students' comments below are derived from a phenomeno-graphic categorization of levels of learners' conceptualization of knowledge within the academic domain of historical study. A phenomenographic approach involved coding and ordering the range and depth of students' critical engagement with knowledge construction as experienced by the group as a whole and extrapolated from a series of in-depth discussions These commentaries provide tantalizing glimpses of the connections which some students were drawing between deeper learning in the discipline and sophisticated, transferable thinking that had wider application.

Phenomenographic categorization borrowed from Baxter-Magolda's taxonomy (1996) and her interest in the emergence of the student 'voice' as knowledge constructor. She identifies four hierarchical domains of 'knowing' ranging from a 'dualist/absolutist' position which construes formal learning as a matter of the uncritical absorption of 'expert' knowledge; a 'transitional' stage where students' adopt a more critical perspective on knowledge claims; an 'independence of knowing' characterized by a stronger confidence in challenging assumptions; to an apex of 'contextual knowing' which embraces the verification of alternative perspectives mediated through evidence. 'Contextual knowing' can be viewed not only as a central tenet of historical thinking but the key to autonomous being. Clinchy (1989) offered a similar, although flatter, spectrum of development from 'subjectivism' which she associates with learners' resistance to change and 'connected knowing', associated with learners' 'openness to transformation'.

The following comment typified the dualist/absolutist position where learners prefer the 'comfort zone' of being instructed or have difficulty in breaking away from a prior experience of instructivist learning: 'As a learner I do not feel I have changed a lot. It is my choice to be here, to listen and to learn from experts' (Jane). The transitional stage identified students who were becoming more comfortable with more complex processes of learning; as questioner rather than as a passive recipient of received knowledge:

> I think I have changed as a learner especially in relation to history because I have learned there is more to the subject than the facts. Although I might not be able to write it all down correctly I am able to look at things in more depth now instead of looking for what may be the obvious answer. (Louise)

> I think that I have changed as a learner in that I am not just memorizing facts, I'm learning the skills needed to evaluate sources and interrogate evidence. (Emma)

> I am becoming aware that answers aren't always as important as I have believed them to be. Part of learning is about the questions which are asked which led to the developing of thought. (John)

The largest number of comments could be labelled as an 'independence of knowing'. They describe learners who expressed a stronger confidence in challenging assumptions, asking the searching question, reassessing knowledge and asserting their own voice. Significantly, both Anna and Jenny give us an indication of academic 'personalities' in transformation:

> Although I still write up my lesson notes to ensure that they are legible for whenever they are looked at again, they follow no set format and are done in

a way that will allow me to engage with the thoughts I and others have raised on numerous occasions. (Nathan)

I was originally expecting a similar approach to A-Level where I expected to learn a collection of facts/events in chronological order and recite these, with additional critical comments from relevant historians, to pass a set of examinations; whereas now I am forced to think for myself what I make of the facts and not just remember the opinion of others. (Anna)

I think I have changed as a learner because I now feel more confident with my own ideas, I am no longer relying on what I already know. Instead of feeling spoon-fed I feel I am thinking for myself and that I have had some input into the group. I am now more focused with my learning and I enjoy it a lot more. In learning I value being encouraged to think for myself and to give myself confidence, I value feeling good when I have learned something new. In learning it is important to know that the answer you give is not necessarily right or wrong, it is your idea or analysis; it might be improved in a lot of ways but at least you have tried and that is a good thing. (Jenny)

Finally, the three extracts below exemplify the 'contextual/relativist' stage. They are examples of students who have not only found an 'independent' critical voice but who recognize that there is an intellectual process that lends legitimacy to judgement and opinion. Moreover, Patricia demonstrates a highly sophisticated epistemological understanding that reached beyond the boundaries of a cognate discipline:

I believe that I have changed as a learner as I believe that I have changed my attitude towards reading for further understanding and knowledge. I now believe that learning is a process of discovery and relying on yourself to make some clear decisions about history, what it means to yourself and how there will always be unanswered questions to deal with. I think that is true of knowledge in general. (Patricia)

My ideas about learning have changed because I am now expected to analyse and 'read between the lines' in everything and to link one point to another. I am now encouraged to discuss ideas with others in the group to expand my own knowledge and understanding and to finish with a better idea because I have talked about it but also to go back to it in the light of new information. (Helen)

It's all about deconstructing it and piecing it back together, reaching a certain point, going off on tangents and coming back again. (Susan)

In summary, these extracts provide representative exemplars of conceptual engagement with knowledge construction among the cohort who were reaching the closing stages of their subject study course and in response to a questionnaire about their conceptualizations of knowledge and learning. Baxter-Magolda's (1996) own findings suggested that only a very small percentage of undergraduates could be expected to reach the level of contextual/relativist thinking. However, in relation to this study, there was a measure of reassurance that responses, albeit with a wide distribution range, were also located largely within the higher order categories that would indicate deeper engagement with ideas about knowledge and critical thinking. Some responses straddled the boundaries but close analysis would safely place 70 per cent of responses within the higher range of independent/relativist thinking. Further, a number of higher level responses make explicit reference to the relationship between epistemological growth grounded in the discipline and wider critical empowerment that reached beyond the confines of the discipline and suggest a self-efficacy in coming to terms with the wider world. They help to identify emerging new teachers who have come to occupy domains that Darling-Hammond and Hammerness (2005) describe as having a vision of the possible and 'preferred', and having complementary dispositions of habits of thinking and acting.

Of course, questionnaire and survey methods have inherent weaknesses, notably, respondents who are reluctant to admit doubts about what they are doing or who venture what they think the researcher wants to hear. That is especially true of focus groups that tend to comprise the more positive and enthusiastic members of a student cohort. This is also why the archived online discussion board proved so informative in that group messages (481 in total across the three-year programme), charting not only students' academic reasoning but also their metacognitive judgements, provided a corroborative source of evidence across and between the full group. Analysis showed that, whereas only about 10 per cent of responses among first-year students could be categorized as explicit and spontaneous replies to online peer-group commentary, by the final year 62 per cent of student responses would fall into that category. Their responses were laced with references to dispositions which Barnett (2009) regarded as being at the heart of 'coming to know' – a concern with authenticity, critical insight, a readiness to listen, a desire to look for new experiences, engagement with imagination, determination to press on; qualities of the good teacher in fact.

I think I'm right but I need to know. (Nathan)

It's not just about putting two and two together. History is not like that but it's not like that in most things. There are always gaps to fill. (Helen)

I'm not really bothered now if children don't come up with what's in my head. In the end they've got to do it their way. Like you I didn't used to think that way. It bothers me a little but I just feel better in myself. (Anna)

These comments add weight to an impression of students who were developing greater confidence in 'voicing' their own judgements in collaboration with their peers and who had severed an umbilical dependency on their tutor's propositional direction and instruction. Their comments also reinforce the trenchant observation of the recent *Cambridge Primary Review* (Alexander, 2009), namely that 'talk' remains the most powerful pedagogic tool in a teacher's armoury. It lies behind the child's historical thinking described in the introduction to this chapter. From a student teacher perspective, purposeful 'talk' is also the key to nurturing epistemological and metacognitive awareness. Social constructivism can be a powerful agent in that process.

Summary Conclusions and Recommendations

The discovery of the appropriate theories

The starting point was and remains reflection on practice; but theory, such as social constructivism, not only brings greater clarity to purpose and practice but also inescapably calls for research-informed judgements about the efficacy of practice.

The ease or difficulties with understanding the theories

Understanding and appreciating the legitimacy of theory only come alive when students have the self-confidence, as well as the intellectual tools, to test what they know against the increasingly available knowledge about educational change.

The difficulties of application to data and texts

Constructivism, as a theory of learning, does not necessarily lend itself to every discipline or field of study. Moreover, arguably there are distinctions to be drawn between cognitive and social constructivism each of which may have distinctive disciplinary application. Indeed, a major dilemma in constructivist teaching is the place of 'formal' knowledge and how that is imparted such that the foundations of concepts, understandings and ways of working that describe a field of cognate knowledge are established.

What the application of the theories revealed

Nevertheless, the pedagogical approach must complement the theoretical model. In this case, learning technology that encourages discourse and collaboration would seem to resonate with a social constructivist model of learning. However, the learning design to structured tasks, embedded in a VLE, risks courting the danger of promoting linear or algorithmic thinking that is at variance with an autonomous 'state of being' which a social constructivist approach is seeking to encourage and develop. Assisting students to understand what the tutor understands is not a proxy for imitation and replication.

How the absence of these theories might have impaired understanding

Promoting discourse around a range of often competing perspectives, within both an academic and professional domain and mediated by tutor interventions, was at the heart of the curriculum design of the subject study course. However, at the beginning of this chapter, reference has already been made to one student (among several) who remained in a state of confusion about her role as a teacher. The deliberate creation of conflict and dissonance does not necessarily have a positive outcome. It needs careful management.

The limitations of the theories

Constructivism is the dominant teaching and learning paradigm in higher education at both a national and international level. However, arguably it is less pervasive, influential or even feasible in teacher education for reasons that are rooted in a politically driven compliance culture, at least in the UK, and therefore in external pressures that reinforce instructional approaches towards the ways in which teacher 'training' takes place.

Reflection and recommendations of the experience

Of course, there is always a danger of reading too much into a case study which lays claim to transformative change; in this case one that was based on a small cohort of students, in one discipline and in one institution. On a more positive note, the view adopted in this chapter and predicated on a body of evidence that emerged from an underpinning case-study project is that a social constructivist informed learning environment had a discernible and measurable impact on the learning of these undergraduate student teachers that reached beyond the acquisition of a set of professional skills or specific content knowledge. In the context of this study, the knowledge students derived from the specialist, disciplinary component of their programme acquired real meaning because it deliberately promoted a shift towards more sophisticated epistemological beliefs and subsequent teaching and learning values that emanated from the learning experience itself. It directly and deliberately challenged the passive reception of knowledge from authority figures but, in varying degrees, for some it was also an unsettling experience.

Recommended further reading

Barnett (2009) provides a thought-provoking paper about the wider purposes of learning in higher education.

Kroll's (2004) work is illustrative of how student teachers, as learners, grapple with the challenges of their own learning development.

Richardson (1997) is a very accessible overview of constructivism in a wide setting.

References

Alexander, R. (2009) *Towards a New Primary Curriculum: A Report from the Cambridge Primary Review. Part 2: The Future*, University of Cambridge, Faculty of Education, Cambridge.

Barnett, R. (2009) Knowing and becoming in the higher education curriculum. *Studies in Higher Education*, 34 (4), 429–440.

Baxter-Magolda, M. (1996) Epistemological development in graduate and professional education. *Review of Higher Education*, 19 (3), 283–304.

Beck, C. and Kosnik, C. (2006) *Innovations in Teacher Education: A Social Constructivist Approach*, State University of New York Press, New York.

Clinchy, B. (1989) On critical thinking and connected knowing. *Liberal Education*, 75 (5), 14–19.

Darling-Hammond, L. and Hammerness, K. (2005) The design of teacher education programmes, in *Preparing Teachers for a Changing World: What Teachers Should Learn and be Able to Do* (eds L. Darling-Hammond and J. Bransford), Jossey-Bass, San Francisco, pp. 390–442.

Dewey, J. (1929) *Experience and Nature*, Dover, New York.

Edwards, A., Gilroy, P. and Hartley, D. (2002) *Rethinking Teacher Education: Collaborative Responses to Uncertainty*, Routledge Falmer, London.

Hyslop-Margison, E. and Strobel, J. (2008) Constructivism and education: misunderstandings and pedagogical implications. *The Teacher Educator*, 43 (1), 72–86.

Kelly, P. (2006) What is teacher learning? A socio-cultural perspective. *Oxford Review of Education*, 34 (4), 505–519.

Kroll, L. (2004) Constructing constructivism: How student teachers construct ideas of development, knowledge, learning and teaching. *Teachers and Teaching: Theory and Practice*, 10, 199–221.

Loughran, J. (2006) *Developing a Pedagogy of Teacher Education: Understanding Teaching and Learning about Teaching*, Routledge, London.

Luehman, A.L. (2008) Using blogging in support of teacher professional identity development: a case-study. *Journal of the Learning Sciences*, 17 (3), 287–337.

Poulson, L. (2001) Paradigm lost? Subject knowledge, primary teachers and education policy. *British Journal of Educational Studies*, 49 (1), 40–55.

Richardson, V. (1997) *Constructivist Teacher Education: Building a World of New Understandings*, Falmer, London.

Rogers, G. (2004) History, Learning technology and student achievement: making the difference? *Active Learning in Higher Education*, 5 (3), 232–247.

Vygotsky, L.S. (1978) *Mind in Society: The Development of Higher Psychological Processes*, Harvard University Press, Cambridge, MA.

Whitty, G. (2000) Teacher professionalism in new times. *Journal of In-Service Education*, 26 (2), 281–295.

12

Developing Professional Practice through Action Research
Theory-Generative Approaches in Practitioner Research

Mary McAteer

**Key Theoretical Approaches in this Chapter:
Action Research and Reflective Practice**

Carr (2005) discusses the practice of theorizing practice as one akin to the Aristotelian concept of practical philosophy. His discussion of the tensions between practical relevance and academic rigour reveals a pair of polar opposites, each discussion being conceived and articulated separately, and aimed at two separate audiences, which, he claims, gives an impression of the pair having irreconcilable aims and purposes. In reflecting on his own professional life and practice, he highlights the need for context-dependant practical concerns in theorizing. Bridges (2003) discusses the centrality not only of philosophy, but also of *philosophizing* in action research, and recounts the extent to which Elliott's (1991) model of action research requires an exploration of personal philosophy, and also enquiry into the consequences of practice. He reminds us that it is easy to both see

---

Applying Theory to Educational Research: An Introductory Approach with Case Studies,
First Edition. Edited by J. Adams, M. Cochrane and L. Dunne.
© 2012 John Wiley & Sons, Ltd. Published 2012 by John Wiley & Sons, Ltd.

and represent action research contrasting with, or oppositional to philosophical approaches to practice, and directs us back to such a philosophizing and theorizing articulation.

Action research is, therefore, considered in this chapter as the process that serves to consider, reflect on and analyse practice. Carr (2005) suggests that it is the most appropriate way to understand the role of educational theory in the professional development of teachers in that it simultaneously changes and theorizes the changes in practice.

Key texts

Bridges, D. (2003) A philosopher in the classroom. *Educational Action Research*, 11 (2), 181–196.

Carr, W. and Kemmis, S. (1986) *Becoming Critical: Education, Knowledge and Action Research*, Falmer, London.

Elliott, J. (1991) *Action Research for Educational Change*, Open University Press, Milton Keynes.

Introduction to the Research Project

There has historically been difficulty in getting girls to engage in the study of A-level Physics. Research I completed in 2000 (McAteer, 2000) indicated a decline over a 10-year period, in the percentage of those students qualified (by virtue of their GCSE grades) to take the subject at A-level. The project started by setting the scene and mapping out the extent of this trend through a curvilinear regression analysis, calculating the gradient, or rate of decline of uptake, for both boys and girls in the province of Northern Ireland. While there was a noted decline in the uptake trend in the previous 10 years for both girls and boys, the rate of decline was greater for girls (7.28 per cent per year) than for boys (4.84 per cent per year).

The project sought to understand some of the reasons for this province-wide trend through both historical analysis and contemporary exploration. Following this, I attempted to address these concerns on a small scale through a classroom-based action research project in my own classroom.

During an initial (reconnaissance) period, interviews were carried out in a sample of three secondary schools to gain a wide perspective on perceptions and experiences of, and attitudes to, physics and physics education. Ten teachers and 16 students were interviewed through audio-recorded semi-structured interviews. In addition, a range of classroom observations was undertaken, data on student perceptions of and attitudes to (physical) science education were collected via the Weinreich-Haste (1981) sentence completion test, and the Mead and Metraux (1957) 'Draw a Scientist' test (DAST), student focus groups were convened, and school-based documentation and other legislative documents examined. The sentence completion test required children to complete sentences in relation to their perceptions of scientists, reasons they would or would not like to be a scientist, and reasons they would or would not like to marry a scientist, while the DAST asks that children to draw freely an image of a scientist. Finally, a reflective diary was kept throughout the study as a means to produce a running commentary on the project, to record observations, and crucially, in a theory-building approach, as a space in which to become initially analytic, spot emergent themes and theoretical insights, and hence continuously review and refine the research approach.

Alongside this 'field' research, analysis of the curriculum documentation, and historical evidence on the evolution of science as a professional and educational activity revealed that the post-1988 reform curriculum drew heavily on a model of science rooted in the nineteenth century, where mathematical (rather than biological) sciences were of prime importance, and were indeed, its public 'face'. The role of women in the practice of science and science education was limited, partly because of women's limited access to the school system, but also because of social mores and norms which suggested that elements of science were inappropriate for them in terms of intellectual challenge (women being considered at the time intellectually inferior to men), social and moral challenge (in that women's participation would challenge the 'normal' domestic function of women, and disrupt social structures) and challenges of moral decency (where meetings of natural history groups might discuss reproduction or other intimate matters deemed inappropriate for women). The British Association for the Advancement of Science (BAAS) at the start of the nineteenth century was governed by men, and rules regarding admission made by these men. Women, therefore, were granted limited access, but had no voting rights through which to change the limitations placed on their membership (Phillips, 1990). Thus, an historical analysis was suggestive of a model of science based on logic of certainty and rules, an epistemology that was considered 'difficult' and structures that were exclusive of women.

Students in the interviews, described physics to me as difficult, rule-bound, overly mathematicized, and irrelevant to their lives. Classroom observations, followed by student focus groups, revealed a pedagogy of 'direction' where investigative science (a central strand of science curricula) was taught in a formulaic way, with students being (often subtly, and unrecognized by teachers) encouraged to get 'right' answers. Many very able students found the experience of physics education lacked creativity and bore little relation to the things in life that interested them. Despite children in the study having female science and physics teachers, there was a clear stereotyping of scientists as male, devoid of emotion, and obsessed with their work. (There seemed to be a separation of the role of scientist and science teacher, which is something the study at that stage did not pursue further.)

As a physics teacher at the time, I was concerned that students found physics education such a negative experience, and wanted to ameliorate this. Action research, described by Elliott (1991) as an approach whose fundamental aim is to improve practice, seemed a way in which I could search for both understanding, and practical solutions. Winter (1987, p. 21) summarizes this succinctly:

> Although the possibility of change is grounded in the distinction between action and research, it requires equally an intimate and principled linkage between the two, in order that the 'findings' of research can be translatable back into the world of action.

Action research as a theory-generative approach to this concern seemed an appropriate way not only to generate deep understanding about the nature of 'problem' itself, but also to help me to make informed judgements about possible actions I could take to address it.

Theories Explained and their Use Justified in the Context of this Research Project

In discussing the role of theory in this action research project, it is pertinent to provide an initial introduction into the conceptual and methodological bases employed. My premise was that theoretical constructs would not be identified at the start, but would emerge through iterative data analysis processes during the progressive cycles of action research. Much of that data would be generated from my practice.

> It [action research] has a very specific purpose, enabling professionals to understand their practice better, and use that enhanced understanding in order to effect changes in practice. (McAteer and Dewhurst, 2010, p. 34)

Rather than produce data to test particular, pre-chosen hypotheses or theoretical frameworks, I intended my study to yield data that would generate testable hypotheses and theory. This inductive approach to research is well documented in educational and other fields of study (Mintzberg, 1979; Van Maanen, 1988; Carr, 1980, 1986). Building on the concept of 'grounded theory', as defined by Glaser and Strauss (1967), it advocates an iterative approach to data analysis, allowing emergent themes to feed into the development of data-derived theory. Its starting point is the 'clean slate'. In practice, this involves the articulation and suspension of preconceived notions about relationships and outcomes at the outset.

There is also a question in relation to the definition of 'theory' and the extent to which a theory is generalizable. Within the confines and purposes of my study my working definitions derived from an adaptation of Pfeffer's (1982) definition that a good theory is parsimonious, logically coherent, and testable, and as Eisenhardt (2002) suggests, results in new insights. Thus, my study should yield elegantly simple insights, be grounded in the data, providing for myself and others, insights into elements of practice, and a means by which to address concerns.

The fundamental aim of the study was to understand and improve a situation within my own practice and its broader context. Many practitioners find themselves similarly faced with such real-life problems. Following the work of Stenhouse in the 1970s, the concept of classroom-based research was developed as a means of teachers' professional development. He suggested that the work of the teacher be researched by teachers themselves. Modern usage of action research owes much to this heritage. He felt, however, that this research should be supported and guided by professional researchers who would also identify the focus for the research (Stenhouse, 1975). Action research, unlike other forms of research, was designed to address specific and particular practice-based problems, developing specific and particular understanding, action hypotheses and actions steps in response to these practical problems, generating theories of practice.

Elliott developed the model, suggesting that teachers should themselves identify the focus of the research, in an effort to understand 'the social situation in which the participant finds himself' (Elliott, 1978, p. 355). Identifying a reciprocal relationship between theory and practice, he suggested that 'theories are not validated independently and then applied to practice. They are validated through practice' (Elliott, 1981: 1).

The model I chose to use in my study was Elliott's (1991), in which an initial concern is identified and considered through a fact finding or reconnaissance period. Initial analysis allows for the development of 'action hypotheses', which inform the plan of 'action steps', which are then 'implemented, monitored and evaluated'. Initial findings are then used to inform revision of the general plan and development of the next action steps. This self-reflective and evaluative process can proceed through a number of cycles, each having the potential to further review and refine the initial concern or question (or indeed, as is sometimes the case, reformulate it based on new understandings) with the subsequent action steps tending asymptotically to resolution of the issue. In the project described here, this process was undertaken through three such cycles, each comprising contemporaneous analysis and theorizing of practice that informed professional learning the planning of action hypotheses and the development of future action steps.

In order to maintain the reciprocation between research and action, between theory and practice, action research is operationally cyclical, the findings of each cycle informing the planning and carrying out of the next. Various representations of cycle are used, many of which derive from models of Kemmis and McTaggart (1981) or Elliott (1981, 1991).

In action research, the research itself becomes part of the practice researched, while the practice becomes a research practice. Given the dynamic nature of my concerns, and my desire to both develop my understanding and my practice in relation to them, action research provided a suitable framework. Action research, therefore, has the ability to transform both the nature and the possibilities of both action and research, providing a powerful means by which practitioners can enhance the potential for their practice to become praxis, or 'practical philosophy'. The action researcher, is in the words of Bridges (2003, p. 42), 'a philosopher in the classroom'.

The Application of Theory to the Research

Within an action research paradigm, conceptualized as 'an embodiment of democratic principles in research' (Carr and Kemmis, 1986, p. 164), the notion of 'applying' theory can be problematic in that there is a hierarchical assumption that theory is the academic understanding that is applied to, and hence subordinates, the lesser practice. This section deals, therefore, with the relationship between theory and practice in the project. As Winter (1987, p. 21) says:

> However, although the possibility of change is grounded in the distinction between action and research, it requires equally an intimate and principled linkage between the two, in order that the 'findings' of research can be translatable back into the world of action.

The first round of student interviews in the project yielded insights into their experiences and perceptions of science. One student gave a damning indictment of both the curriculum and the pedagogy of physics, saying: 'you copy things off the board and you learn them, and you're tested and there's not much creativity in it. ... In a set of results in an experiment, there's basically one conclusion you can draw that's right or wrong.'

Another, discussing the role of investigative work in the curriculum suggested that: 'in reality, it was not at all investigative ... it's like you were discovering things that there was a set rule to, there was nothing really to ... explore.'

This had resonances with the GCSE reports of physics investigations that I had been marking at the time, which included such conclusions as: 'this proves that my hypothesis was true and that my experiment was a success' and 'in general I am satisfied with my investigation. My predictions were proved correct.'

Initial findings like these informed reflection during the reconnaissance phase of action research. Models like those of Ghaye and Ghaye (1998) and Moon (2006) support a critically reflective analysis of findings, leading to the subsequent theorizing of practice in order to develop contextualized understanding of specific problems or concerns.

A challenge, however, for practitioners is to accept and act on the implications of findings that test our normality. 'Paradigmatic assumptions, are ... the hardest for us to challenge, as they represent the way in which we have learned to see and understand the world. Most of us are highly resistant to such challenges' (McAteer *et al.*, 2010).

The particular challenge of this 'practical philosophizing' is its inherent imperative to change practice. Day in his 1993 paper discusses the 'confrontation' of our professional learning in a way that links the outcomes to future, informed action. Analysis of my research data allowed the development of theoretical descriptors of the current situation in science education, and the proposal of alternatives, which were used to generate a more holistic model and practice of science education for students.

The Relevance and Effectiveness of Using Theory

Using a theory-generative, or theory-building approach to researching the 'problem' of girls in physics opened up for me an unexpected and unknown world. While the initial question had been about girls in physics, successive iterations of data analysis allowed me to understand that there were questions about boys in physics also. The production of initial statistical data precipitated a series of 'why?' questions, leading me to pursue a qualitative investigation that might help me understand, and do something about the situation.

As Mintzberg (1979, p. 587) puts it: 'Theory building seems to require rich description ... we uncover all kinds of relationships in our hard data, but it is only through the use of this soft data that we are able to explain them'.

Interviews with the young people opened to me their experiences of science and physics education from an entirely different perspective. Their articulations of science education experiences, alongside their cultural perceptions of science and scientists, drew me to question just where this model of the science curriculum had arisen. In the late twentieth century when science had experienced a significant shift from its underpinning of certainty and predictability located in a Boolean logic, to a binary, and later a fuzzy logic, the culture and practice of school science owed much of its structures and associated pedagogies to a model of science developed and professionalized by the BAAS in the nineteenth century. Giving hierarchical superiority to the mathematicized sciences, and promoting a male dominated social, cultural and epistemological practice of science, the BAAS model of science was still exerting its logically inconsistent influence at the cusp of the twenty-first century.

Action research in its cyclic approach to data collection, analysis, and hypotheses testing allows the initial question to shift, and new sources of data or methods of data collection to be explored. Eisenhardt (2002) suggests that this is not only legitimate, but also necessary in theory-building research approaches, talking of the 'controlled optimism in which researchers take advantage of the uniqueness of a specific case and the emergence of new themes to improve resultant theory' (Eisenhardt, 2002, pp. 16–17).

In addition, as is a central tenet of action research, the production of contextualized understandings and insights provided the supporting evidence for the subsequent production of contextualized plans of action. For the practitioner researcher, this process emulates and reinforces Stenhouse's (1975) concept of the curriculum as a process, 'procedures, concepts and criteria, which cannot adequately be translated into the performance levels of objectives' and its issues are the subject of 'speculation' rather than 'mastery' (Stenhouse, 1975, p. 85).

Summary Conclusions and Recommendations

The discovery of the appropriate theories

The approach I have taken could in some respects be seen as a rather eclectic mix of philosophical and philosophizing approaches. Given the broad reach of the study, this was felt to be appropriate in that it allowed for a data-driven approach to analysis. Thus, when issues of gender arose, for example, it was considered appropriate to explore feminist perspectives, and standpoint theory as a means of understanding the phenomena revealed through the data. Similarly, when issues relating to the nature of science were raised, analysis involved an exploration of the history and philosophy of science. This degree of match between the data themselves, and the analytic tools echoes what Green (1999, p. 106) has called, concerns with 'the particular'.

The ease or difficulties with understanding the theories

For many researchers new to data-driven, theory-generative approaches, a particular stumbling point can be, paradoxically, a tendency to ignore the data. Practitioners in policy led practice can find it difficult to listen to the data, responding instead to contemporary policy or 'flavour of the month' approaches. In addition, the new, and often insecure researcher may find the 'voice of authority' of texts initially more seductive and persuasive, and thus accord those views more credibility than their own data. This can result in a tendency to make the data 'fit' a pre-chosen theoretical framework, rather than let the data suggest the arrival at, or indeed derivation of theory.

The difficulties of application to data and texts

A particular difficulty of data driven approaches is lack of predictability in the research process. The iterative nature of an action research, or grounded approach has been well documented as a source of some concern to practitioners, and can lead to a loss of confidence in the process (and the ability to engage in it). The range of literature to be consulted cannot be pre-specified, and this may heighten feelings of insecurity in new researchers.

What the application of the theories revealed

In-depth investigations of a particular and contextualized concern are of significant value to practitioners concerned with developing deeper understanding, and formulating possibilities for improving that situation. This contextualization and specificity allows practitioners working in complex and dynamic environments to formulate possible problem-solving approaches specifically matched to the context. In the context of this research, pursuing a data-driven approach allowed a much fuller understanding of the cultural and historical derivation of contemporary concepts of science and science education to be reached than might otherwise have been done. This in turn, helped explain some of the disjuncture between student and teachers expectations of science, and their experiences of it.

How the absence of these theories might have impaired understanding

In many practice-based contexts, policy concerns dominate, and practitioners can become overly dependent on 'off the shelf' solutions to perceived problems. Without the deep exploration of the reconnaissance phase of, for example, an action research approach, it is possible that the manifestation of a particular problem or issue may be misconstrued in terms of it originary causes, and hence responded to inappropriately. Given the initial concern in the project about the decline in the uptake of physics at A-level, particularly by girls, it is almost certain that without the deep exploratory phase of this project, the possible explanation for the phenomenon might simply have related to theories of gendered choices, rather than the historical and philosophical theories of science and science education, and indeed their relationship with gender issues.

The limitations of the theories

Despite the potency of such a grounded approach to analysis and professional learning, it is important that practitioners do not over-claim the significance of their findings. Another important potential limitation of this type of work is the privileging of the author's voice. The use of participant, validation group feedback can help ameliorate this.

Reflection and recommendations of the experience

Those practitioners engaging in such an open-ended exploration of practice would benefit from reading the work of Cook (1998) and Mellor (1998), both of whom describe and discuss not only the 'messiness' of action research, but also its necessity in the process. Many metaphors exist to describe the process and the affective experiences of undertaking it, with Schön's 'swampy lowlands' and 'lily pads' probably being the best known (Schön, 1983). Having steered a course through such a process, however, I can testify to the rewards, both in terms of professional practice and also academic development. Sharing that experience enriches it further, and enables a more confident journey through it.

Recommended further reading

Carr and Kemmis (1986) Described by some as 'a hard read', the book has also been described by Carr himself as having been 'a hard write'. This text is considered by many a seminal and influential book, providing a critical theory insight into the nature, function and purposes of action research, and an ongoing discussion of the theory/practice relationship. It is worth reading this text, even in part, for its richness and depth of meaning.

Pine (2009) Combining a sound philosophical and epistemological analysis of the conceptual bases of action research, this text also addresses pragmatic and practical matters in a way that is accessible to practitioner researchers. Beginning action researchers will find it both supportive, but with appropriate intellectual challenge. The structure of the book, in making 'Practicing Action Research" the third section (rather than the first, as is the case in many such texts), following discussions of the conceptual underpinning and the validity of action research, provides a refreshing and useful backdrop to the practice-based issues involved in doing this type of research.

References

Bridges, D. (2003) A philosopher in the classroom. *Educational Action Research*, 11 (2), 181–196.

Carr, W. (1980) The gap between theory and practice. *The Journal of Further and Higher Education*, 4 (1), 60–69.

Carr, W. (1986) Theories of theory and practice. *The Journal of the Philosophy of Education*, 20 (2), 177–186.

Carr, W. (2005) The role of theory in the professional development of an educational theorist. *Pedagogy, Culture and Society*, 13 (3), 333–345.

Carr, W. and Kemmis, S. (1986) *Becoming Critical: Education, Knowledge and Action Research*, Falmer, London.

Cook, T. (1998) The importance of mess in action research. *Educational Action Research*, 6 (1), 93–109.

Day, C. (1993) Reflection: a necessary but not sufficient condition for professional development. *British Educational Research Journal*, 19 (1), 83–94.

Eisenhardt, K. (2002) Building theories from case study research, in *The Qualitative Researcher's Companion: Classic and Contemporary Readings* (eds A.M. Huberman and M.B. Miles), London, Sage, pp. 5–36.

Elliott, J. (1978) What is action research in schools? *The Journal of Curriculum Studies*, 10 (4), 355–337.

Elliott, J. (1981) *A Framework for Self Evaluation in Schools*, Cambridge University Press, Cambridge.

Elliott, J. (1991) *Action Research for Educational Change*, Open University Press, Milton Keynes.

Ghaye, A. and Ghaye, K. (1998) *Teaching And Learning Through Critical Reflective Practice*, David Fulton, London.

Glaser, B. and Strauss, A. (1967) *The Discovery of Grounded Theory: Strategies of Qualitative Research*, Wiedenfeld and Nicholson, London.

Green, K. (1999) Defining the field of literature in action research: a personal approach. *Educational Action Research*, 7 (1), 105–124.

Kemmis, S. and McTaggart, R. (1981) *The Action Research Planner*, Deakin University Press, Victoria.

McAteer, M. (2000) Contemporary science education: some historical and philosophical roots. DPhil thesis. University of Ulster, Belfast.

McAteer, M. and Dewhurst, J. (2010) 'Just thinking about stuff': reflective learning: Jane's story. *Reflective Practice: International and Multidisciplinary Perspectives*, 11 (1), 33–43.

McAteer, M., with Hallett, F., Murtagh, L. and Turnbull, G. (2010) *Achieving your Masters in Teaching and Learning*, Learning Matters, Exeter.

Mead, M. and Metraux, R. (1957) The image of the scientist amongst high-school students, in *The Sociology of Science* (eds B. Barber, and W. Hirsch), Free Press of Glencoe, New York, pp. 384–390.

Mellor, N. (1998) Notes from a method. *Educational Action Research*, 6 (3), 453–470.

Mintzberg, H. (1979) An emerging strategy of 'direct' research. *Administrative Science Quarterly*, 24, 580–589.

Moon, J. (2006) *A Handbook of Reflective and Experiential Learning: Theory and Practice*, Routledge Falmer, London.

Pfeffer, J. (1982) *Organizations and Organization Theory*, Pitman, Marshfield, MA.

Phillips, P. (1990) *The Scientific Lady: A Social History of Woman's Scientific Interests 1520–1918*, Weidennfield and Nicholson, London.

Pine, G. (2009) *Teacher Action Research: Building Knowledge Democracies*, Sage, London.

Schön, D.A. (1983) *The Reflective Practitioner: How Professionals Think in Action*, Avebury, Aldershot.

Stenhouse, L. (1975) *An Introduction to Curriculum Research and Development*, Heinemann, London.

Van Maanen, J. (1988) *Tales of the Field: On Writing Ethnography*, University of Chicago Press, Chicago.

Weinreich-Haste. H. (1981) The image of science, in *The Missing Half: Girls and Science Education* (ed. A. Kelly), Manchester University Press, Manchester, pp. 216–232.

Winter, R. (1987) *Action Research and the Nature of Social Inquiry: Professional Innovation and Educational Work*, Avebury, Aldershot.

13

Art Practice as Education Research

Jeff Adams

Key Theoretical Approaches Used in this Chapter: Practice as Research

The key theoretical perspectives used in this chapter are theories of research through practice, particularly in the case of the visual arts, and a theory of identity applied to an art teacher who is also a filmmaker. Graeme Sullivan's *Art Practice as Research* (2005) is a seminal text in this field. This work draws together a wide range of theories on the relation of arts practice and research, discussing the history and context of the contesting ideas behind this relationship. Judith Butler's *Gender Trouble* (1990) has informed much of my thinking about identity theory, and given me a framework to think about identity as a social performance rather than a fundamental 'essence' of subjectivity. Chris Park's article 'New variant PhD' (2005) is about postgraduate research and gives an account of the expansion and diversity of doctoral education, discussing emerging trends such as the professional doctorate; it's less of a theoretical stance, more of a reflective survey that provided me with a contextual framework for the preceding theoretical exercises.

Applying Theory to Educational Research: An Introductory Approach with Case Studies,
First Edition. Edited by J. Adams, M. Cochrane and L. Dunne.
© 2012 John Wiley & Sons, Ltd. Published 2012 by John Wiley & Sons, Ltd.

Key texts

Butler, J. (1990) *Gender Trouble: Feminism and the Subversion of Identity*, Routledge, London.
Park, C. (2005) New variant PhD: the changing nature of the doctorate in the UK. *Journal of Higher Education Policy and Management*, 27 (2), 189–207.
Sullivan, G. (2005) *Art Practice as Research*, Sage, London.

Introduction to the Research Project

This chapter discusses the theoretical and practical dilemmas that postgraduate students face when carrying out research projects through their art practice within the field of education. Many Masters and doctoral programmes in the arts have incorporated practice-based research and the corresponding theoretical frameworks have been successfully used to legitimize and establish art practice as a means of investigation. Buckley (2009, p. 83), for instance, outlines the history of the idea of the creation of the artwork *as* research and notes that many philosophers like Bachelard have carried out philosophical investigation through art. On the other side of the equation, there has been a pronounced shift in the ethos of art schools in their recognition that the role of the artist is changing (Pearson, 2009, p. 174) and that 'intellectual tools are more important than material techniques in the education of artists today'. These shifts and changes at the level of the ethos are important not least because, as Lakoff and Johnson (1980) have indicated, they are part of the networks of metaphors that define identities and ultimately define how practice is experienced and lived.

Exhibitions, performances and events have all been utilized as both methodological procedures and instruments of assessment within these programmes, alongside the more traditional text-based thesis or dissertation. This chapter explores these models and, using a case study example of a film from a postgraduate research student's art practice, considers the features and modifications necessary to establish and embed them within the field of education research. Art practice like this, which purports to be research, prompts a rethinking of orthodox methodologies and assessments in education, that they might more readily accommodate these relatively foreign modes and methodologies of creativity drawn from the visual and conceptual fields of art practice.

A postgraduate research student in the arts, Hazel, who was also an art teacher, made a film called 'Kalinka' about her identities as a teacher and as an artist, and in it she further explored what her genealogy meant to these practical and professional roles. The research into her ancestry made transformations in her identity that affected her subjectivity as a teacher, and also as filmmaker, as she invented and then acted out the roles of her alter ego, Kalinka; the challenge for her supervisors was to assert and legitimize this practice as educational research.

Theories Explained and their Use Justified in the Context of this Research Project

The vexed problem of practice as research has its roots in the nature of knowledge itself and the way that it is often conceived in academic institutions like schools and universities, as if it were an entity that could be discovered – usually indicated by the 'pioneering' metaphors frequently associated with more traditional, positivist academic practice, such as the 'voyage of discovery'. Many theorists have found this notion deeply problematic (e.g., de Beauvoir, 1989), and critical movements such as poststructuralism and feminism have revealed that it cannot be assumed that knowledge, particularly social knowledge, is neutral, or that it is external to the researcher's worldview and values, or that it can be found simply by diligent and methodical enquiry. This epistemological questioning has largely been to the advantage of arts-based practice's claim to be a legitimate form of research: the poststructural critiques of social tradition, political dogma and established conceptions of research have created conditions favourable to the growth and legitimization of the critical methods and forms of art practice. These methods, however, have had to engage and exist, sometimes uneasily, within institutional bureaucracies, university assessment and validation panels.

Graeme Sullivan's work in *Art Practice as Research* (2005) is one of the most important of the texts that guided thinking in justifying the apparently overtly subjective practices of art students researching in an education department. An important component of Sullivan's theory of practice as research is epistemology: his concept that knowledge is polymorphic and strange, and is not necessarily amenable to the 'iterative or accumulative model that characterises the development of knowledge in the human sciences' (Sullivan, 2005, pp. 173–174). These unknown or emerging forms which the artist seeks to reveal are bound up for Sullivan in the complexity of the cross-disciplinary fields in which the artist is compelled to practice for most, if not all of the time. The intention is important here, as this affects and determines the findings – or the type of knowledge – that is discovered: 'The aim of research in the visual arts, as in other similar forms of exploratory inquiry, is to provoke, challenge, and illuminate rather than confirm and consolidate' (Sullivan, 2005, p. 174).

Practice, as Sullivan explains it in relation to the arts, comprises imaginative and intellectual quests rooted in the experiential (Sullivan, 2005, p. 94), and these are the key components of his theory. For Sullivan (2005, p. 173) the art object, such as a visual image, can be thought of as 'raw' data, which can be transformed by interpretation – a prerequisite for all reception and recognition – into 'evidence'. This transformation from data to evidence is for Sullivan an analogy for the research process itself.

This theory of practice is complemented by Sullivan's theory of the practitioner. Here Sullivan argues that an arts practitioner is at once both theorist and practitioner, and that theory and practice are fundamentally integrated in the process of producing art (Sullivan, 2005, p. 150). He groups the different types of practice into categories, or 'sites' as he puts it, such as 'making in systems', 'making in communities' and 'making in cultures' (Sullivan, 2005, p. 150). In each case the artist is the theoretical architect, with the conception of the work a major component of the studio practice.

Chris Park's work is especially helpful in understanding the nature of academic scholarship and its relationship to the academy and government policy. His focus in the 'New variant' paper (Park, 2005) is on doctoral study, and he explores the development of new forms that have emerged in recent years, especially the professional doctorate. This has a specific resonance with my project to legitimate practice as research, since he explores the philosophical and theoretical basis upon which research degrees are founded, and in doing so reveals the problematic relationship of theory to practice. This is clearly the case in his discussion of the nature of the generation of new knowledge, which is by and large an agreed cornerstone of the principle of doctoral research in the academy. Park asks what are the salient epistemological features of 'new' knowledge or the 'contribution' to knowledge, as they are most commonly expressed in institutional regulations. In his discussion of this (Park, 2005, p. 198) he identifies two problematic areas: 'It is generally agreed that a doctorate should involve extending knowledge, but the two most difficult criteria to legislate for, and to benchmark in any meaningful way, are originality and contribution to knowledge'. Park goes on to discuss the features of these problems, such as whether a reinterpretation of an existing theory can be considered to be original, or why the *generation* of new knowledge is usually regarded as superior to its application.

Another dimension to these epistemological hierarchy problems is the ongoing tension between practice and text in the production of research, and this signifies loudly in the 'art practice as research' debate. The orthodox role that text plays is a dominant one, and exegesis is a formal part of the research interpretation that has a long and powerful history in the academy. Is there an equivalent conceptual site that the practice of the visual, sound or performance can occupy? Buckley (2009) examines the role of text in the production of arts research and ponders these questions, giving as his preference the integration of the text with practice, in what he describes as an 'elaboration on the research question, to be inter-textual to the studio or creative work' (Buckley, 2009, p. 82). Despite this, the absence of text in arts research persists as a negative factor, and militates against arts practice being acknowledged as research.

The foundational characteristics of research are usually thought to be investigation, exploration, experiment and conjecture. Theorists like Barber (2009) have made explicit the unstable nature of this position, and argue that all of these features are necessarily located in the terrain of the unknown, and that in this domain failure and error must inevitably occur. This may be ascribed to a structural attribute of the research process: the discovery or creation of that which does not work or conform to expectations; to put it another way, that which succeeds is locked into a binary relationship with that which fails, and by these recognitions and identifications a methical investigation can take place.

Research through arts practice may foreground this binary aspect of investigation in discomfiting ways. A famous example, to which Barber refers, is Marcel Duchamp's 'Large Glass' (created 1915–23, first exhibited in 1926) which accumulated dust as it lay discarded for a year in his studio (an event which was recorded photographically by his collaborator Man Ray in 'Dust Breeding', 1920), after which Duchamp fixed sections of the dust to the artwork. Later the work was accidentally smashed and then repaired, and at each juncture Duchamp's investigation of these failures were incorporated into the work. However, as Barber (2009) points out, the apprehension at the acknowledgment of failure creates an ambivalence from which it is hard to escape, and which creates many problems for the academic standardization and assessment of arts subjects. Failure can be much less well received when attempts are made to formalize this notion in academic orthodoxies, where a more pejorative idea of the concept prevails. Barber advocates a more positive approach towards failure, as a necessary prerequisite for learning and creative activity in the art studio:

> It is wise to reflect on the status of failure in the fomenting of progressive critical art practice. If research is necessarily the (perhaps blind) pursuit of the interrogative, it may be wise to reflect on the presence of failure ... as a powerful stimulant and determinant in the production of innovative art. (Barber, 2009, p. 59)

Judith Butler's seminal work on gender identities in *Gender Trouble* (1990) significantly informed the filmmaking discussed in this chapter. Although Butler's work is primarily located in gender theory, it is her theorizing of identity per se that influenced the readings of the filmmaking as research into subjectivity – that is, an investigation into the ways that identity is socially constructed. Butler establishes the idea of identity, and of gender identity in particular, as a culturally specific performance rather than a natural condition. This encouraged a reading of the film Kalinka as an exercise in explicit inter-subjective exploration, adapting Butler's theory to Hazel's analysis of the determinants of her identities in her various roles, or subject-positions.

Butler (1990) insists on distinguishing between gender as anatomy, and gender as performed. Such distinctions are, however, not easily made in the social sphere of operation, and she does not see them as acts of choice, but rather as regulated performances. Butler warns of the violence of gender policing, which is manifest in widespread misogyny and corporate oppression. This can also apply to any identity that strays from its orthodox position, and in Hazel's case these are the professional teacher, the ethnic subject, and the filmmaker; all subject positions that are weighted with characteristics that are often attributed to the 'natural' realm, which can disguise their social and conventional origins.

Butler not only established gender as performance, but also introduces the concept of performance in other domains of subjectivity, such as the performance of identity in all its realms. In doing so Butler's influence has been wide ranging, despite the lack of application to practice, and the absence of empirical data in her research; in particular her device of troubling received notions of what is natural or normal (1990) has endured as a powerful political strategy as well as a popular academic trope.

Figure 13.1 Kalinka. Reproduced with permission of the artist, Hazel Lopatkin.

The Application of Theory to the Research

The film practice that illustrates many of these ambiguities was produced by Hazel when an educational studies postgraduate student. She was an art teacher engaged on a project that investigated her identity in a variety of forms: as a teacher, an artist, a filmmaker, and as a subject transformed by the changes brought about by genealogical research into her ethnicity. As a response to all of these she created an alter ego, Kalinka, who was both the subject and producer of the film. The identity of the alter ego reflected her grandparents' origins as East European/Russian Jews, and her discovery of her ancestry through archive and personal history research. The decision to create a film as a means of the expression of these discoveries was in part due to Hazel's exposure to the medium as part of her course, and so Kalinka was developed (initially from photographs, Figure 13.1). Film had the attraction of novelty for her, and this offset her inexperience with the medium. Her increasing facility with the medium and her exploitation of its effects, became for her the means of investigation itself in visual and narrative terms, once her ancestral archive had been established.

In the film Kalinka carries out rituals that Hazel had researched as authentically as she was able given the limitations of her data, which comprised interviews with elderly and distant relatives, each of whom Hazel

Figure 13.2 Photographs for the film Kalinka by Hazel Lopatkin. Reproduced with permission of the artist.

discovered could help recreate the lives, customs and characters of her hitherto unknown and unfamiliar ancestry (Figure 13.2). With these data collection came the realization that she had unwittingly observed or participated in the vestiges of some of these rituals in her childhood, without ever recognizing them as such. In her earlier life, with anti-Semitism and xenophobia more prevalent, it was not necessarily in her family's interest to disclose too much of their origins, and so much had remained concealed.

The key decision in this visual auto-anthropology was the acknowledgement of the artifice of Kalinka's creation. Her inexperience as an actor or as a technician of film production resulted in many failures in the conventional sense of acting and editing. As with Duchamp, Hazel worked with these failures and incorporated them into the film as signifiers of the instability of identity. Kalinka was always obviously an alter ego, and is portrayed by Hazel with humour and melodrama as she responds to her newly discovered ethnic condition. Hazel's experience as a teacher and her understanding of pedagogy, particularly her performance as a classroom manager, came to the fore in her production of the work. Kalinka is manifestly an assumed role, emphasizing identity itself as an assumption of a role. For theorists like Butler (1990) this is the entirety of identity, in the sense that there can never be anything fundamental or essential about it; it is a social construction that can, therefore, only ever be acquired – or rather imposed – through social acting, as performance, no matter how nuanced.

Hazel recognized the parallels of the acting of Kalinka with her performance as a teacher, and acknowledged that the ethnographic research affected both of these subject positions. With this acknowledgement she recognized the impossibility of subordinating her other subjectivities in her professional role, and the necessity of accommodating the inter-subjectivities that resulted from the interface of genealogical rituals with professional rituals. Since the Kalinka identity was transformative for Hazel, its mythology became profound and prescriptive for her identity as a social being in her contemporary life. Once released from the lamp, the Kalinka genie exerted fundamental effects on the identity of Hazel that could not be reversed.

The Relevance and Effectiveness of Using Theory

Sullivan's (2005) theories enabled me as a programme director and assessor to articulate the case for the admission of these filmmaking practices to the institutional assessment procedures of educational research. The practice of filmmaking itself had long since been legitimized by the arts faculties, but inscribing it within educational research was a different matter, and Sullivan's (2005) comprehensive analysis provided the ground from which this could be considered and developed as a research practice in the field of education. Park's (2005) detailed survey of the diversity of postgraduate forms of research supported this, and provided evidence of other hitherto alien practices brought within the realm of academic research. Sullivan's theories enabled the film itself to be considered as both practice and theoretical investigation, even in the absence of any supporting text.

In a way it is disingenuous to present all Sullivan's work as a set of theories, as this is a position from which he is, at times, at pains to distance himself. In his guide to a framework of visual arts research, for instance, he argues: 'the quest for theory as it is currently understood in research can restrict rather than release the potential for carrying out inquiry' (Sullivan, 2005, p. 94). He argues that the concepts that he introduces at this point are a heuristic set of ideas rather than theories. It is interesting that he sees certain paradigms as outside of, or beyond theory, as this raises the question of the nature of theory itself, and its pluralistic and polymorphic forms. In Sullivan's arguments certain formations are not theories, while others are, and he resists developing a comprehensive taxonomy which would admit all forms of conceptual reckoning to theory of one type or another; all of this serves to illustrate the slippery nature of theory and theorizing.

Butler's conception of identity fitted well to Hazel's literal acting out of her multiple identities. Hazel's knowing use of acting and filmmaking techniques, to declare rather than conceal the artifice of these identity creations further exemplified Butler's theories of the temporality and impermanence of identity: the inessential nature of subjectivity.

To some extent Butler's *Gender Trouble* (1990) is a product of the academic style of its era, and as such the opacity of language presents some difficulties on first reading. These are exacerbated by the use of obscure or invented words and phrases, and the apparently meandering nature of the text. However, this may be attributed to the idea of language as a 'haunted' medium, in this case by its patriarchal origins, which is readily exposed by etymological analysis. This makes the very discussion of gender tricky, and may account for Butler's seeming obfuscation. Irigaray, Cixous and Derrida are all philosophers to whom Butler refers who have addressed the gendered character of language directly. In the work of all these theorists writing itself becomes a challenge, raising awareness of the habituated and 'natural' use of language, which may inscribe particular modes of thinking about the world. Butler's text may be deliberately tricky, therefore making us examine the inadequacies of language usage. There is always the solution of secondary texts, where other writers explain Butler's work (such as Salih, 2004). This offers its own dangers, however, in that bypassing the original work may result in missing the linguistic manoeuvres that may be fundamental to the meaning of the text.

The theorizing of art practice *as* research is at once an attractive and yet problematic idea. It is attractive because it allows for pragmatism in the appeasement of managers of institutional systems, who demand conformity, and it also legitimizes art activity by conferring an authoritative paradigm upon the discipline; that art practice is research is also, arguably, self evident, since it is difficult to imagine making a convincing case that the phenomenological exploration of the social, intellectual and sense environments, of which many artworks comprise, could *not* constitute research. However, the problematic status of art as research occurs when attempts are made to conform to institutional standardized regulations.

The designation of practice as research is not without its opponents within the art community. Welsh (2009) for example, writing about visual arts, argues that defining art practice as research does not automatically benefit the discipline, but on the contrary, can diminish it if introduced inappropriately. Welsh (2009, p. 211) particularly objects to the expedient of attempting to assess practice as research in order to subordinate art to bureaucratic and audit control for material gain, as in research assessment procedures.

Buckley (2009, p. 83) also comments on the different meanings of the term research, comparing the North American experience, where the designation 'research' may be rejected by artists as something alien to their practice. He argues that for many artists the designation is superfluous, since the generation of new knowledge through arts practice is a given. Buckley goes on to trace the introduction of the idea of art as research, and its subsequent dominance, back to British art schools' incorporation into universities and the standardization effects of the periodic research assessment exercises (2009). However, he laments this conformity because of the problems that it causes, particularly the attempts to assess creative work by the means normally used to assess sociological or scientific research.

One of the difficulties that is specific to practice-based research in education is the ambivalent standing of education itself as a discrete discipline. Dunne and MacIntyre (2002), for instance, have pointed out that teaching and pedagogy are 'means' rather than disciplines, and that education contributes to all disciplines but is not one itself:

> Any conception of a philosophy of education as a distinct area of philosophical enquiry is a mistake. Enquiries into education are an important part of enquiries in the nature and goods of those activities into which we need to be initiated by education. (Dunne and MacIntyre, 2002, pp. 8–9)

Dunne and MacIntyre's (2002) theory may be indicative of a deeply ingrained view within the academy, that education is peripheral to the specific subject disciplines, and is more of a framework for apprenticeship prior to the 'real' work of the disciplines. Disciplinary specialists within specific spheres such as science or art often recognize their ambivalent status as 'experts' when they are working in the field of education (Adams, 2003), and suffer the pejorative connotations that are sometimes associated with their role, particularly the role of the teacher. Research into education that is focused on, for example, sociological issues pertaining to schools, or the effects of a government's policy, may well have a distinctive identity; researching education from or through a specific and discrete discipline like art is, however, a different matter, and one that is much less well established.

Summary Conclusions and Recommendations

The discovery of the appropriate theories

Sullivan's theories are popular and readily available in the art world, and were my first port of call when encountering the problem of legitimizing practice as research. Butler is very prominent in the philosophy and gender study spheres, making her work a logical choice, despite the tricky character of the text.

The ease or difficulties with understanding the theories

Although slightly evasive and repetitive, Sullivan's work is on the whole straightforward and accessible, following logical sequences of thought and underpinned by a historical framework. Butler is much more difficult to assimilate, and this depends to some extent on an understanding of the work of other theorists on whose works she builds, Foucault and de Beauvoir in particular. On the other hand, the work is so significant that there is a large body of criticism and explication, meaning there is there is always support available.

The difficulties of application to data and texts

Sullivan's work seemed readily applicable to my research, and there were no obvious drawbacks or difficulties, apart from the absence of an explicit theory of education practice. Butler's work was difficult because I found myself constantly questioning my own understanding of the text, often referring back to it, and to others' readings and criticisms of it.

What the application of the theories revealed

Despite the difficulties with Butler's work it ultimately led to a richer source of potential meanings being elicited from the Kalinka film, and enabled the student to be more liberal in her generation of multiple identity roles. The emphasis on the discursive nature of identity, manifest through social performance, was a cornerstone of the Kalinka project. Sullivan's work was essential in establishing practice in the arts as a legitimate form of research, and Park's contextual information ensured a firm grounding for these interpretations.

How the absence of these theories might have impaired understanding

Art practice can be readily dismissed as research on the grounds of its overt subjectivity. Both Butler and Sullivan provide evidence of the impossibility of escaping subjectivity in all research, and so provide the basis for an analysis of its basic social construction, and the implicit values inscribed therein.

The limitations of the theories

The theoretical analysis was impaired by the unfamiliar territory of education research – my project was outside of the gender and arts fields where many of these debates have occurred. Different theories are prevalent in education research, and it would be necessary to trawl these for more specific support from within the field of education itself.

Reflection and recommendations of the experience

The use of these theories transformed the ideas generated by the project for both students and tutors. As always, theoretical application to new projects and contexts is fraught, but worth pursing for the new knowledge and awareness that it generates.

Recommended further reading

I have used several articles from Buckley and Conomos' (eds) (2009) *Rethinking the Contemporary Art School*, which proved to be a very helpful collection in thinking through the place of art practice in the academy. Similarly with *Blood Sweat and Theory* edited by John Freeman (2010), which enhanced my understanding of theories of performance.

References

Adams, J. (2003) The artist-teacher scheme as postgraduate professional development in higher education. *International Journal of Art and Design Education*, 22 (2), 183–194.

Barber, B. (2009) The question (of failure) in art research, in *Rethinking the Contemporary Art School: The Artist, the PhD and the Academy* (eds B. Buckley and J. Conomos), The Press of the Nova Scotia College of Art and Design, Halifax, NS, pp. 45–63.

Buckley, B. (2009) What is with the ceiling! The artist, higher degrees, and research in the university art school, in *Rethinking the Contemporary Art School:*

The Artist, the PhD and the Academy (eds B. Buckley and J. Conomos), The Press of the Nova Scotia College of Art and Design, Halifax, NS, pp. 76–86.

Buckley, B. and Conomos, J. (eds) (2009) *Rethinking the Contemporary Art School: The Artist, the PhD and the Academy*, The Press of the Nova Scotia College of Art and Design, Halifax, NS.

Butler, J. (1990) *Gender Trouble: Feminism and the Subversion of Identity*, Routledge, London.

de Beauvoir, S. (1989) *The Second Sex* (trans. H.M. Parshley), Vintage Books, New York.

Dunne, J. and MacIntyre, A. (2002) Alasdair MacIntyre on education: in dialogue with Joseph Dunne. *Journal of Philosophy of Education*, 36 (1), 1–19.

Freeman, J. (ed.) (2010) *Blood Sweat and Theory: Research Through Practice in Performance*, Libri, London.

Lakoff, G. and Johnson, M. (1980) *Metaphors We Live By*, University of Chicago Press, Chicago.

Park, C. (2005) New variant PhD: the changing nature of the doctorate in the UK. *Journal of Higher Education Policy and Management*, 27 (2), 189–207.

Pearson, G. (2009) The outskirts of town: a peripheral centre for agency and academia, in *Rethinking the Contemporary Art School: The Artist, the PhD and the Academy* (eds B. Buckley and J. Conomos), The Press of the Nova Scotia College of Art and Design, Halifax, NS, pp. 164–181.

Salih, S. (2004) *The Judith Butler Reader*, Blackwell, Malden, MA.

Sullivan, G. (2005) *Art Practice as Research*, Sage, London.

Welsh, J. (2009) Transitions, dialogues, interruptions, pregnant pauses, and leaps into the void: recent experiences in Norwegian higher education, in *Rethinking the Contemporary Art School: The Artist, the PhD and the Academy* (eds B. Buckley and J. Conomos), The Press of the Nova Scotia College of Art and Design, Halifax, NS, pp. 206–214.

Postscript

Jeff Adams, Matt Cochrane
and Linda Dunne

In this book we have tried to show, through case study examples of researcher experiences, how theory has been applied to education research. Compiling the book has been an exciting and sometimes fraught experience, rather like the research process itself. The contributors were very keen to share their experience of applying theory to education research and to learn from one another.

Research can sometimes seem like a lonely endeavour. As each person's research projects are different researchers are invariably working alone, especially if they are doing a Masters dissertation or a doctorate. As some of the contributors to this book have shown, working collaboratively on research projects can ease the challenge inherent in understanding and applying theory: exchanging ideas, articulating frustrations and sharing experiences on joint research projects. For our lone researchers, attendance at research seminars, interest groups and workshops eased the sense of isolation and provided opportunities for sharing ideas. This was sometimes a difficult thing to do for those who were so fully immersed in their research that they were inclined to see it as an extension of themselves. The prospect of 'revealing' or 'exposing' research ideas to others, especially when in the midst of grappling with difficult ideas, seemed a little daunting. However, once they had bitten the bullet and their research was 'out there', sometimes simply by talking around the ideas to colleagues and receiving critical feedback, they could 'see' it more clearly. Having a research mentor, a critical friend or someone who was prepared to be a sounding board for ideas, was also of assistance, especially to our new researchers.

Applying Theory to Educational Research: An Introductory Approach with Case Studies, First Edition. Edited by J. Adams, M. Cochrane and L. Dunne.
© 2012 John Wiley & Sons, Ltd. Published 2012 by John Wiley & Sons, Ltd.

At the time of writing this book the UK policy climate appears to be putting further constraints on educational research by continuing to favour and fund research that is 'evidence based' or more positivist in nature. Novice researchers are increasingly pressured to become research active (Sikes, 2006) and established researchers are under pressure to 'publish or be damned' in preparation for periodic research assessments. If research has an ethical and a moral foundation, then it is becoming more urgent that researchers question their own position and their motivation for doing research, and not be coerced into doing research that complies with or sanctifies an audit culture. Theory and theorizing should make us think and question. Applying theory to a research project in many respects questions and refutes the 'evidence-based' research agenda; it opens up, rather than closes down, thinking and possibilities.

Thinking through ideas, and taking a critical and questioning stance, needs time, which must be staked out and claimed; without time, theory may be the first casualty of our research. It may help us to remember that taking our time and theorizing can be a political act, or, as Badiou (2006) puts it:

> Our world, you know, is marked by its speed: the speed of historical change, the speed of technical change, the speed of communications, of transmissions, and even the speed with which human beings establish connections with one another. This speed exposes us to the danger of a very great incoherency. It is because things, images and relations circulate very quickly that we do not even have the time to measure to what extent all that is incoherent. Speed is the mask of inconsistency. Philosophy must propose a slowing down process. It must construct a time for thought, which in face of the injunction to speed, which is the mask of inconsistency, will constitute a time of its own, and only this time will slow down. I would consider this as a singularity of philosophy, that its thinking is leisurely, because today revolt requires leisureliness and not speed. (Badiou, 2006)

References

Badiou, A. (2006) The Desire for Philosophy and the Contemporary World, http://www.lacan.com/badesire.html (accessed 27 May 2010).

Sikes (2006) Working in a 'new' university: in the shadow of the Research Assessment Exercise? *Studies in Higher Education*, 31 (5), 555–568.

Index

Applying Theory to Educational Research: An Introductory Approach with Case Studies,
First Edition. Edited by J. Adams, M. Cochrane and L. Dunne.
© 2012 John Wiley & Sons, Ltd. Published 2012 by John Wiley & Sons, Ltd.